Note: Commands preceded by an apostrophe (') are transparent.

For every kind of computer user, there is a SYBEX book.

All computer users learn in their own way. Some need straightforward and methodical explanations. Others are just too busy for this approach. But no matter what camp you fall into, SYBEX has a book that can help you get the most out of your computer and computer software while learning at your own pace.

Beginners generally want to start at the beginning. The **ABC's** series, with its step-by-step lessons in plain language, helps you build basic skills quickly. Or you might try our **Quick & Easy** series, the friendly, full-color guide.

The **Mastering** and **Understanding** series will tell you everything you need to know about a subject. They're perfect for intermediate and advanced computer users, yet they don't make the mistake of leaving beginners behind.

If you're a busy person and are already comfortable with computers, you can choose from two SYBEX series—**Up & Running** and **Running Start**. The **Up & Running** series gets you started in just 20 lessons. Or you can get two books in one, a step-by-step tutorial and an alphabetical reference, with our **Running Start** series.

Everyone who uses computer software can also use a computer software reference. SYBEX offers the gamut—from portable **Instant References** to comprehensive **Encyclopedias, Desktop References,** and **Bibles**.

SYBEX even offers special titles on subjects that don't neatly fit a category—like **Tips & Tricks**, the **Shareware Treasure Chests,** and a wide range of books for Macintosh computers and software.

SYBEX books are written by authors who are expert in their subjects. In fact, many make their living as professionals, consultants or teachers in the field of computer software. And their manuscripts are thoroughly reviewed by our technical and editorial staff for accuracy and ease-of-use.

So when you want answers about computers or any popular software package, just help yourself to SYBEX.

For a complete catalog of our publications, please write:

SYBEX Inc.
2021 Challenger Drive
Alameda, CA 94501
Tel: (510) 523-8233/(800) 227-2346 Telex: 336311
Fax: (510) 523-2373

SYBEX is committed to using natural resources wisely to preserve and improve our environment. As a leader in the computer book publishing industry, we are aware that over 40% of America's solid waste is paper. This is why we have been printing the text of books like this one on recycled paper since 1982.

This year our use of recycled paper will result in the saving of more than 15,300 trees. We will lower air pollution effluents by 54,000 pounds, save 6,300,000 gallons of water, and reduce landfill by 2,700 cubic yards.

In choosing a SYBEX book you are not only making a choice for the best in skills and information, you are also choosing to enhance the quality of life for all of us.

AutoCAD
for the Mac
Visual Guide

AutoCAD®
for the Mac®
Visual Guide

Genevieve Katz

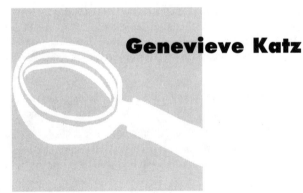

San Francisco
Paris
Düsseldorf
Soest

SYBEX®

Acquisitions Editor: Rudolph S. Langer
Developmental Editor: Richard Mills
Editor: David Krassner
Technical Editor: Steve Lukrofka
Book Designer: Ingrid Owen
Technical Art: John Corrigan and Aldo Bermudez
Page Layout and Typesetting: Len Gilbert
Proofreader/Production Assistant: Sarah Lemas
Indexer: Matthew Spence
Cover Designer: Archer Design
Cover Photographer: David Bishop

SYBEX is a registered trademark of SYBEX Inc.

TRADEMARKS: SYBEX has attempted throughout this book to distinguish proprietary trademarks from descriptive terms by following the capitalization style used by the manufacturer.

SYBEX is not affiliated with any manufacturer.

Every effort has been made to supply complete and accurate information. However, SYBEX assumes no responsibility for its use, nor for any infringement of the intellectual property rights of third parties which would result from such use.

Autodesk makes no endorsement of *AutoCAD for the Mac Visual Guide* or user manuals accompanying Edutech's AutoCAD for Students Release 12 for the Macintosh®, nor does Autodesk guarantee the performance of the software. Autodesk assumes no responsibility for the performance of the software or for errors in this manual. This product is not upgradeable to new releases of AutoCAD.

AutoCAD Technical Support   The Autodesk Helpline staff answers all types of questions about AutoCAD, from how to get it running for the first time to advanced questions about customizing AutoCAD.

The Autodesk Helpline, 1-900-228-6375, is available from 8:30 to 5:00 EST, and costs $3/minute; the average call is 6 minutes. There is a free gift for first-time callers, and a money-back satisfaction guarantee for all calls. For additional information, please call 1-800-356-1429.

Library of Congress Card Number: 93-87707
ISBN: 0-7821-1516-0

Manufactured in the United States of America
10 9 8 7 6 5 4 3 2 1

To my husband Lou who has given new meaning to the phrase "Could not have done it without you" and to my son Steven whose phrase "Yes you can" echoes in my mind.

Acknowledgments

My thanks to the people at SYBEX:

To Rudolph Langer who enthusiastically supported "something new and different."

To Richard Mills, for his continuing involvement and guidance.

To David Krassner for his clear editorial hand.

To Guy Hart-Davis and his marvelous Sybex Author Template.

To John Corrigan for wrestling with all the graphics.

To the many others at SYBEX who helped create what you hold in your hands: Ingrid Owen, book designer; Len Gilbert, typesetter; and Sarah Lemas, proofreader/production assistant.

To Steve Lukrofka, my technical editor, for his knowledgeable and helpful suggestions.

To Rose and Carol for Chapter 11 and Thanksgiving.

And to the people at Autodesk:

To Neele Johnston, the perpetual writers' friend, who knows where to find everything.

To Meryl Dean for her faith in the Mac platform.

To Rodger Payne for his academic support and encouragement.

To Anthony Catsimatides and Anoosh Mostowfipour and the unnamed heroes of tech support who provided answers beyond the manual.

And to my students at California College of Arts and Crafts who, by their learning, taught the teacher.

Contents
at a
Glance

Table of Contents

Introduction

This book is written for those who, when words aren't enough, pick up a pencil to draw; for those who still work out designs on the backs of envelopes and napkins; for those who still find the feel of pencil on paper sensuous; and for those who see the world in pictures, explain things with a sketch, find a drawing infinitely superior to pages of text, and who take mouse in hand to venture into CAD.

How to Use This Book

This book grew out of a frustration of having to use a book written for the PC while teaching on the Mac—even when that book was mine. The concept for my books started out when I tried to understand why my students didn't read manuals. It became clear to me that the people learning CAD are those who are engaged in the drawing process—and for those people, a picture conveys the concept much more effectively than words. And so the focus of this book is to explain AutoCAD through drawings.

AutoCAD for the Mac Visual Guide can be used as a beginning guide or as a quick pictorial reference to help you remember how the AutoCAD commands work. Because one of the difficulties beginners often experience is not knowing where to find commands, icon palettes and menus appear at the beginning of each chapter, showing at a glance where the command can be found.

Originally I would get students up and drawing as quickly as possible. While that is certainly more fun, you are drawing for a reason: designing a building or creating a product. There are basic procedures that will make your work more productive, and it is important to know them before you start drawing. These basics are covered in the first five chapters; you need to know how to handle the information that is presented on the screen, how to tell AutoCAD what you want it to do, and how to move about the screen.

You will need to understand some file management techniques and, finally, to be able to set up your drawing. The book then steps you through all the commands necessary to complete the layout design and rendering of an office space, which you will work on throughout the course of the book.

Because this is a basic book, some advanced commands and the more complex and less-used options of some commands are not covered. Two applications, AME (the Advanced Modeling Extension—a solid and region modeling program) and SQL (Standard Query Language—this writes out files from AutoCAD to a database such as FileMaker Pro), are advanced topics and are not within the scope of this book.

AutoCAD for the Mac Visual Guide uses architectural examples for the tutorials, because I have found that they are more easily understood by people in a wide variety of professions.

The book is organized into chapters that cluster related groups of Auto-CAD commands. Each chapter is divided into two parts: the first contains individual descriptions of AutoCAD commands, while the second contains a tutorial that makes use of the commands introduced in the first part.

Each chapter includes:

- Icon and menu illustrations showing where the commands are located
- A list of command options (if applicable)
- A "Using the Command" section, which uses actual AutoCAD drawings and screen captures, accompanied by text, to show you how to use the command
- Helpful notes and tips
- A tutorial based on the commands covered in the chapter

While the "Using" sections can be used as a quick reference, the tutorials have been designed to be followed sequentially. As you progress through the tutorials and become more familiar with AutoCAD commands, you will create an office space, place windows and doors, design and lay out furniture, dimension the plan, label it, produce 3-D views of it, insert a title block, and plot the plan (if you have access to a plotter or printer).

Instructions are very specific at the beginning. As the book progresses, they become less specific, since you should be getting accustomed to the rhythm and feel of the program. My attempt is to actually wean you away from the book so that, by the end, you are comfortable working on your own. If you need more help than is provided in this book, AutoCAD's Help command accesses what amounts to a condensed version of the AutoCAD manual.

Conventions Used in the Book

I have employed some conventions in the book to help you use it. In the tutorials, instructions to the user are explained by the use of text, drawings, and special program lines that combine AutoCAD prompts and user responses.

- **Line ➤ Segments** means to pick the Segments command from the Line menu.
- AutoCAD prompts are in program font.
- User keyboard actions are in **boldface**.
- Other actions that the user is required to carry out, usually with the mouse (such as picking a point), are in *italic*.
- Additional information on what a prompt or instruction means is in parentheses.
- For consistency, because not all the editing commands work with the Noun-Verb (pick first) action, the instructions are given with the commands listed first. However, pick first actions can be easily substituted. AutoCAD will prompt you for an additional selection pick if the command must be chosen first. I tend to mix and match them indiscriminately. Commands that do work by picking the objects first (Noun-Verb) are indicated with a *[pf]* in the command lists in the chapters where they occur.

Simplifying AutoCAD's Prompts

When you pick a command from an icon or a menu, AutoCAD responds by repeating the command with the options. Since you have already made your choice, this line is redundant and confusing and I have eliminated it from the instructions. For example:

You have selected Zoom window from the icon palette. AutoCAD prompts with:

```
Command: '_zoom
All/Center/Dynamic/Extents/Left/Previous/Vmax/Win-
dow/<Scale(X/P)>:_window
First corner:
Other corner:
```

In the book, this command appears as:

Command: ZOOM ➤ Window
First corner: Other corner: *Window the lower left quadrant*

Options such as:

```
All/Center/Dynamic/Extents/Left/Previous/Vmax/Win-
dow/<Scale(X/P)>:
```

will be included only when you have to make a choice.

AutoCAD also confirms the number of entities you have chosen when you have made a selection. For example:

34 found.

This number can be confusing if you pick slightly differently than I do. The prompt is useful when you think you have picked something and it prompts "0 found," or when you think that you have picked one item and the prompt is "53 found." The exact number is not important, rather the feedback of some, none, or many is what you want to know.

1

Getting
Started

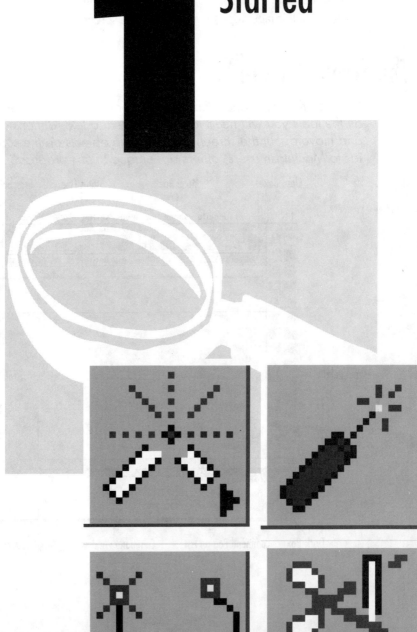

Before you start creating drawings, I would like to give you a mini tour of AutoCAD. By now you should have AutoCAD installed (if you haven't done so already, refer to Appendix A for instructions) and be seated at your computer. Double-click on the AutoCAD icon and, after the nautilus shell image appears, you will see a screen ringed about with icons.

● The Screen Layout

Between the icons and menus (on the bar at the top of the screen) you have all the tools you will need to draw, edit, add text, dimension, add symbols, and move about the screen. Many of the objects on the screen will be familiar to Macintosh users, others are unique to this program.

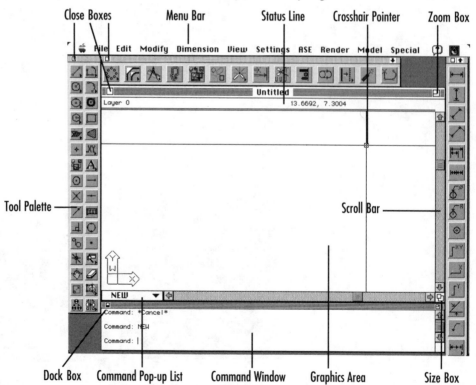

Close Boxes Menu Bar Status Line Crosshair Pointer Zoom Box

Tool Palette Scroll Bar

Dock Box Command Pop-up List Command Window Graphics Area Size Box

Icons

The most noticeable set of icons is the double column on the left of your screen. This is a composite set of commands that Autodesk, along with their users, has found to be those most frequently used. This set is referred to as the *tool palette*. It contains all the drawing commands, plus commands for editing and zooming, as well as tools to help you with your drawing.

   Icon tool bars can be removed from the screen. It is a good idea to keep this one on, though, because the only other way to give drawing commands is to type them in. If you do close this palette, it can be reopened with the Modify ➤ Show Tools.

Tool palette

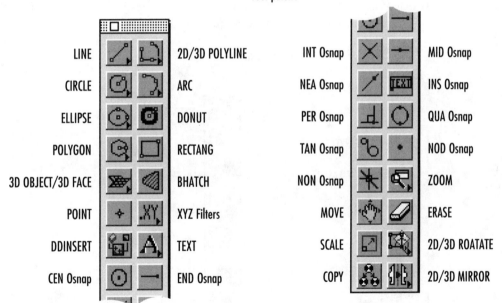

N O T E

The ➤ icon means that you must choose an option from the indicated menu (in this case, the Show Tools option from the Modify menu).

In this book, I will use icons as the preferred method for selecting commands. Icons have other values besides looking sexy—they take up less space on your screen than text and they execute commands immediately when you click on them. To become familiar with icons, I suggest copying the graphic images in this book that show the icons with their names and keeping the copies close to your computer. Once you get used to icons, you will find that they speed up your work.

The top row of icons, called the *Modify tear-off palette* (or menu), are for additional editing commands not contained in the tool palette. This is the same menu you get when you click on Modify in the menu bar.

Modify tear-off palette

ARRAY

CHAMFER/FILLET

DIVIDE/MEASURE

OFFSET

BLOCK

DDMODIFY

BREAK

EXTEND

TRIM

ALIGN

STRETCH

CHANGE

EXPLODE

PEDIT

The right-most palette, called the *Dimension tear-off palette* (or menu), contains the various dimension types and, like the Modify palette, is duplicated under Dimension in the menu bar.

Dim tear-off palette

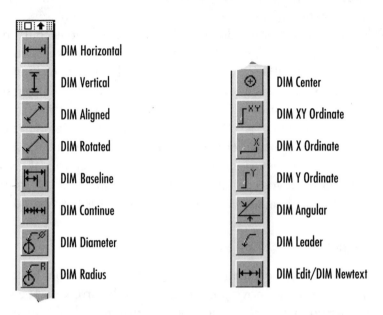

Each of these palettes has its own close box (the white square in the upper-left corner). Clicking on the close box will close the palette. These palettes also have arrows, which, when clicked, will change the orientation of the palette on the screen from vertical to horizontal (or vice versa).

Mouse Moves

When you move your mouse, the *cursor* moves around on the screen. The cursor is made up of cross hairs that extend to the edges of the drawing area. When you move the mouse into the menu or icon area, the cursor assumes the shape of an arrow.

Before we go further, a brief explanation of clicking is in order. To *click* means to press on the mouse button once. This will be your main action with the mouse. You click when your cursor is on the close box to put away or *close* an item such as a palette, menu, or drawing. You click to activate commands from an icon palette and you click to select objects from the screen or to place points when you draw.

Double-clicking means pressing down and releasing the mouse button rapidly, twice in succession. You might have to try it a few times to get the tempo correctly. You double-click to start AutoCAD and other programs. However, the double-click is not used once you get inside the program.

Press and drag means to press and hold down the mouse button while moving the mouse. When you reach the place you want, you release the mouse button. This is how you make your selections from the menu bar.

In AutoCAD you will be using a *click-drag-click* sequence to make selections on screen. You click, move the mouse (which drags the diagonal point of the selection box), and click again when the selection box is the size you want.

Pull-Down Menus

The *pull-down menus*, listed on the menu bar, contain all the commands you will need. To access them, move your mouse until the arrow on the screen is over the heading you want, press the mouse button to *highlight* (reverse the background/foreground colors on) the title, drag down the mouse until the command you want is highlighted and then release the button.

All the menus (excepting the Apple, File and Edit menus) can be "torn off" so as to remain open on your screen, but only the Modify, Dimension, and Edit menus have icons. You can change the options on these two menus from icons to text (or vice versa) by choosing Settings ➤ Menu Style. To tear off a menu, place your cursor in the menu area (below the title on the menu bar), then press and drag the menu into the drawing area. Tear-off menus can be changed from horizontal to vertical or back by clicking on the arrow in the title bar. Although the number of selections on the menu bar may seem daunting, the first three—Apple, File, and Edit—are familiar Macintosh menus; you have already seen the icons for the Modify and Dimension menus and the only others we will use with any regularity will be View and Settings.

Sometimes these menus will contain arrowheads that lead to another menu, which *cascades* from the original one.

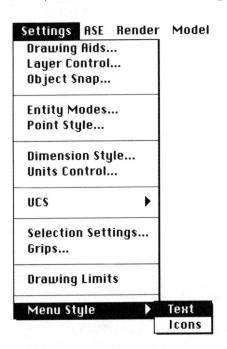

You will also find ellipses on the menus—those three dots (…), which indicate that a dialog box is to come. A *dialog box* is an on-screen form that you fill out when AutoCAD needs more information. We will cover dialog boxes in Chapter 2.

The Graphics Window

The graphics window takes up most of your screen, and it should, because it is where you do most of your work. Your cursor appears in this area as crosshairs extending to both borders. The name of your drawing appears on the title bar.

The Command Pop-Up List

This is a list box in the lower-left corner of your graphics window. The last command you used appears in the box. You can access any one of the last ten commands you used by clicking on the down arrow and selecting the command. This is particularly useful when repeating a sequence of commands.

The Status Line

On the top of your graphic screen is the status line. This line gives you information about the current status of your drawing, including:

- What layer you are on
- Whether you have activated the Snap or Ortho modes
- The coordinates of your cursor

The Command Window

At the bottom of the screen is the command window, where you will see three or four lines of text. AutoCAD is verbose; it always seems to be talking to you. Beginners freeze up because they don't know how to tell AutoCAD what they want it to do. To use AutoCAD, you have to learn to "Autospeak." Here are some helpful tips:

- Don't let all the text on the bottom of the screen confuse you; read and respond to the *last* line.
- When you see the

  Command:

  prompt, AutoCAD is waiting for you to issue a command. Select Line, Copy, or any of the 160 or so other commands. AutoCAD will laze around until you do.

- If nothing happens, and you have responded to the Command prompt, press ⏎. Each time you type something in the prompt area, a command or a response to a command, you must enter ⏎ after each line. When you start, it is easy to forget to press this key; after a while you won't even remember doing it.

- An "Invalid" response from AutoCAD means that you did not give it the answer it wanted. It could be a simple thing, such as omitting a comma or entering feet as the unit of measurement when only decimals are allowed. Reread the prompt and try again.

The command window has the standard Macintosh window functions, with the addition of the *docking box*. This black-and-white box in the upper-left part of the command window attaches and detaches the command window from the graphics window. I suggest keeping it attached unless you are working with two monitors, one for text and one for graphics.

The screen contains the standard Macintosh functions. A brief overview follows, but for a more detailed description, refer to your *Macintosh User's Guide*.

Close Box	`Ends your drawing session, prompts you to save or discard changes and then starts a new drawing.
Zoom Box	Expands the window to fill the screen. Clicking on it again returns the window to its previous size. Not used much for the graphic window which is generally kept as large as possible, but is useful to expand the text window when you want to refer to previous commands you have used.
Size Box	Change the size of a window by pressing and dragging the size box. This will always cause AutoCAD to regenerate the drawing.
Scroll Bars	Used for moving up and down lists and scrolling back in your text window to check on your command history. They are not great for manipulating the graphic screen— the AutoCAD Pan command works better.

● Minimum Basic Essentials

There are a few commands that are particularly useful to beginners, and they involve getting help, getting out of trouble, moving about the screen and getting in and out of a drawing. These commands can get you out of some tight spots, even if you aren't all that comfortable with AutoCAD.

Getting Help

The Help command provides information on a specific command or provides a list of commands from which you can make a choice. Help is in the Special pull-down menu. Help can be used *transparently*. That is, you can access help without interrupting the current command. It is also *contextual*, in that it gives you information specific to the command or option you are working with. If you select it while in a command, it will give you information specific to that command.

```
┌─────────────────────────────────────────────────────────────┐  ⬆
│                                                                │
│   Type the name of the command or system variable for         │
│   which you want help and press RETURN.                        │
│                                                                │
│               - OR -                                           │
│                                                                │
│   Pick the Index button, select an item from the list         │
│   box, and pick OK.                                            │
│                                                                │
│                                                                │
│                                                                │
│   Done     Exits the HELP dialogue box.                        │
│   Top      Displays these instructions.                        │
│   Previous  Displays help for the previous item in the index.  │
│   Next     Displays help for the next item in the index.       │  ⬇
└─────────────────────────────────────────────────────────────┘
   Help Item: [                                    ]   [ Index... ]
              ( Top )  ( Previous )  ( Next )  ( Done )
```

You can use Help in the following ways:

- You can type a question-mark (?) to access the command from the keyboard.
- If you use the apostrophe (') before typing **Help** or ?, the command can be used transparently.
- Help can be used as a on-line reference manual. It is a condensed, simplified version of the AutoCAD manual.
- Unfortunately, balloon help has *not* been implemented for AutoCAD.

Changing Your Mind—Cancel, Undo, and Redo

You don't have to worry about trying out things if you know that you can undo, get out of, or cancel your actions. There are many ways to cancel. While there is no icon for this command, the function key F2 will cancel a command. Function keys will be covered in the next chapter.

- ⌘+Z will cancel a command midstream or undo the effect of the last command executed, depending upon when it is issued.
- ⌘+. (period) will cancel a command after it has been selected.
- ⌘+. (period) will deselect highlighted items when you have picked them before selecting a command.
- To cancel a dialog box pick the Cancel button.
- To get out of Help, pick Done.
- To get out of a pull-down menu without selecting something, move cursor back up to the menu bar.
- To get out of a drawing without saving the results of the drawing session, click on "Discard Changes" in the prompt, "The current drawing has been changed".
- Selecting Undo from the Edit menu will undo the effect of the last command, but will not cancel a command once it has been started. Each time you enter this command, it steps back and undoes the previous command.
- Redo reverses the effect of the last Undo.

A Little Lite Zoom

The icon on the tool palette with the magnifying glass represents the Zoom command. It will be covered more completely in Chapter 4 but for now, there are three options that are very useful:

Window	Click on a point and drag the window until it encompasses the area you want to fill the screen and click again. This always enlarges an area on the screen.
Previous	Zooms back to the view you had previously.
All	Zooms so that you can see the entire drawing.

TUTORIAL

● Opening and Ending a Drawing

The book will go into detail on the commands and the steps for creating a drawing. The following instructions are meant as a brief introduction should you want to experiment on your own. Working with an actual drawing is more helpful than working on an empty one, but, since you have not created one yet, I suggest using one of AutoCAD's drawings until you create one of your own.

1. If you have already opened a drawing, choose File ➤ Open. Save or Discard the changes to your existing drawing and open the drawing, PSGLOBE.DWG. It is the one pictured in the tutorial in Chapter 2. You will find it in the Sample folder inside the AutoCAD folder.

File   Edit   View   Label   Special   8:49 PM

AutoCAD Release 12

39 items	259.5 MB in disk	23.8 MB available

acadps   asifmp2   goop3.dwg   Sample
acad_ads.xmx   asiora   geomcal   Source
acad_ase.xmx   auto.sv$ IGESFont   Support
ADS   ave.cfg   PLAN.dwg   Tutorial
adslib   averendr   readme.ave   Fonts
ase   averendr.xmx   readme.doc   Plot Files
ASI   base.dcl   region
asidb3   appload.dfs   region.txt   new12.dwg

Sample

66 items	259.5 MB in disk	23.8 MB available

dlgtest.lsp   edge.lsp   engine.dwg   ep.lsp   es.shp
fact.lsp   fcopy.lsp   fplot.lsp   fprint.lsp   gp.lsp
housepln.dwg   julian.lsp   mface.lsp   nozzle3d.dwg   pc.shp
pentagon.dwg   planprof.dwg   project.lsp   psfilpat.dwg   psglobe.dwg
pumpsol.dwg   pvt_hgr.dwg   regdemo.dwg   rpoly.lsp   sextant.dwg
site-3d.dwg   solmaint.lsp   solview   spiral.lsp   sqr.lsp
st.shx   stlsup.lsp   tables.lsp   tablet.dwg   tabletac.dwg
tabletrm.dwg   troll.dwg   wblksol.lsp   xdata.lsp   xplode.lsp

Studios

AutoCAD alias

Trash

If you have not started AutoCAD, you can start it with the PSGLOBE drawing by locating the drawing, and dragging and dropping it onto the AutoCAD icon.

2. Zoom to get a closer view of parts of the drawings. Use any commands that catch your eye. Experiment with Undo. If you have questions, go to Help. Don't worry about destroying the drawing. If you are getting blue squares all over your drawing, you can turn them off by going to the Settings menu, clicking on Grips..., and deselecting the Enable Grips check box. Grips are useful for editing and they are covered in Chapter 8, but right now, they can get in the way.

3. When you are finished, choose File ➤ Exit AutoCAD, and when you get the prompt, "The current drawing has been changed," click the Discard Changes button. The drawing will remain as it was, before you opened it.

If you wanted to continue working in AutoCAD, you could have selected File ➤ New or File ➤ Open instead of Exit AutoCAD.

2

Communicating with AutoCAD

You can communicate with AutoCAD in many ways: clicking on icons, selecting from menus, typing commands, using a digitizer—though the latter is not used frequently with the Macintosh. You will find that most commands allow for both screen and keyboard entry. For example, you can show AutoCAD a distance or length by pointing on the screen or typing the value with the keyboard. It is important to try the different techniques and come up with one of your own that feels right for you.

Dialog Boxes

When AutoCAD needs more information to perform a function, it provides you with a form to fill out, called a *dialog box*. Dialog boxes contain check boxes for on-and-off options, lists of choices, and text boxes where you can type in information. Once you know what to expect, they are easy to fill out. If you get stuck, many dialog boxes have a Help button—very useful for beginners.

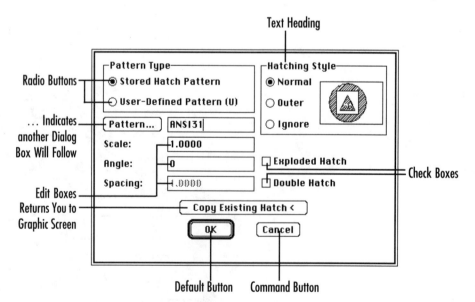

Dialog boxes may contain one or more of the following:

Radio Button These are the simplest—only one choice is allowed. Clicking on the item highlights your choice.

Check Boxes These are used to turn many items on or off. The choice is selected when an X appears in the box. They really should be called X boxes. You can select one, several, or none.

Command Buttons These are rectangular buttons with rounded corners and labels. Clicking on them will execute the action indicated on the label. The most familiar ones are the OK, Cancel, and Help buttons, which appear at the bottom of dialog boxes.

Some command buttons have graphics to indicate modifications to the actions on their labels:

Ellipses The three dots (...) that you have already encountered on the pull-down menus indicate that another dialog box will appear.

Heavy Borders These surround the button that is the default. Defaults are actions that will be performed if you press the ⏎ key. You will find default values elsewhere in AutoCAD. They are enclosed in angle brackets (< >) when presented to you.

A Single < Sometimes referred to as "less than," means that you will be temporarily returned to the graphic screen to perform some action, such as picking a point or object.

Dimmed Items Options that are not available are dimmed.

List Boxes

These present you with a list of items to choose from. When all the items are visible, the scroll bars are dimmed. When the list contains more items than can appear in the box, scroll bars can be used to move up and down the list. The most familiar of these boxes are the lists for files and layers.

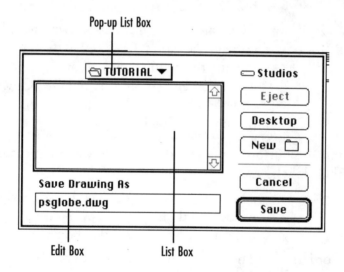

Edit Box   List Box

Pop-up List
Boxes

Boxes where all options except one are hidden. They have a downward arrow on the right side of the current option on the list. To access the whole list, click on the down arrow.

Edit Boxes	These require the most input from you—you have to type something in the space. Sometimes these boxes already contain a value. You can either accept it or type in a new value. A blinking text cursor appears at the insertion point of text. You can change the location of the text cursor by moving your arrow pointer to a new location and clicking. If an edit box is highlighted (filled in with a color), typing anything will erase the existing text and the new text will take its place. This action often surprises new Macintosh users when they want to do a minor edit such as changing a single character and find that once they start typing, the original name is gone.
Text	Labels and headings that appear outside of boxes are not changeable. On the more complicated dialog boxes, lined borders with titles defining the various functions help users navigate through the dialog box.

Keyboard vs. Mouse

For those who are more comfortable with the keyboard than the mouse, commands can always be typed in directly. There are numerous shortcuts to cut down on the amount of typing. When responding to a AutoCAD prompt, you can abbreviate many of the options. AutoCAD indicates this by capitalization—for example, Window can be specified by *W* and Remove by R. Text can be entered either in upper- or lowercase. All keyboard input must be followed by ⏎ .

For technical reasons, when you select from a menu or icon, AutoCAD reprints the command preceded with an underbar on the command line. This is done to make it efficient to produce a foreign language version. You do not have to type in commands with an underbar.

In addition, there are one- and two-letter abbreviations that you can enter instead of the whole command for some of the more frequently used commands. Here is a list:

Alias	Command
A	Arc
C	Circle
CP	Copy
DV	Dynamic View
E	Erase
L	Line
LA	Layer
M	Move
MS	Model Space
P	Pan
PS	Paper Space
PL	Poly Line
R	Redraw
Z	Zoom

Command Key Equivalents

Commands under the File and Edit menus are listed with their command key equivalents and follow the familiar Macintosh assignments. Object snaps,

which aid in placing points on certain geometric locations, also have command key equivalents. Object snaps or Osnaps are covered fully in Chapter 7. In the meanwhile, here is a list of common commands:

Key Equivalent	Osnap
⌘+1	Endpoint
⌘+2	Insertion point
⌘+3	Intersection
⌘+4	Midpoint
⌘+5	Near
⌘+6	Node
⌘+7	Perpendicular
⌘+8	Quadrant
⌘+9	Tangent
⌘+0	Center

Function Keys

The keys on the top of your keyboard, with the numbers F1 through F15 are called function keys. Some commands and features are used so frequently in AutoCAD that function keys have been assigned to them. These allow you to turn the commands on and off easily by pressing just one key. Here is a complete list:

F1 acts as the ⏎ key. As a return, it will return the last command, terminate a line sequence, and can be used instead of the ⏎ after each typed command.

F2 is cancel. It will cancel a command in progress and works the same as ⌘+. (period).

F3 toggles Snap on and off. When Snap is on, it constrains line and cursor placement to the snap increments that have been previously set. If the grid spacing is the same as the snap increment, then you can draw only from point to point on the grid. Setting Snap to Off removes this constraint.

F4 turns Ortho on, which constrains lines and cursor placement to horizontal and vertical directions. Setting Ortho to Off enables you to draw lines at any angle.

F5 turns the grid to visible (on) or invisible (off).

F6 cycles through three different coordinate display settings:

> **Off**   X and Y coordinate display is updated only when you pick a point.
>
> **On - Absolute**   X and Y coordinates are continuously updated.
>
> **On - Relative**   Displays distance and angle from *last point* picked.

This last setting provides dynamic feedback on the length of line you are drawing, the distance you are moving an object or the angle you are rotating about. I keep it on all the time.

F7 toggles between the three planes in an isoplane drawing: left, top, and right.

F8 turns the tablet mode on or off.

T I P

Sometimes your cursor seems to "bounce" away from the point or entity that you are trying to pick. This happens because you have Snap on and the point you want is not on the snap increment. Toggle Snap off (F3), pick your point, and toggle Snap back on. It makes for a more accurate drawing if you keep Snap on, and turn it off only when you need to.

Transparent Commands

Some commands can work within other commands. These are called *transparent* commands and allow you to do things like zooming in close to get a better view when in the middle of drawing a line from one point to another. Help, Pan, Redraw, View, Zoom (but not Zoom All or Zoom Extents) and Osnap are some of the more useful transparent commands that can be picked from the icons. In dialog boxes, Layer Control, Drawing Tools, and Osnaps (which are accessed from the Settings pull-down menu) can also be used transparently.

If you use these commands from the keyboard while working in another command, you must precede the command with an apostrophe for it to be used transparently, such as 'Z, but it's much easier to select them from the screen menus and icons.

NOTE

Sometimes commands selected from the icons and pull-down menus will differ from the command when typed. Generally speaking, the newer options, and those using Lisp functions, will occur in the icons and pull-down menus. The original form of the command is more likely to appear as the typed-in version.

Entity Selection Sets

How do you show AutoCAD what objects or entities you want it to work on? (The terms *entities* and *objects* are used interchangeably in this book; they refer to single items, such as a line segment, not to a series of lines, a circle, or a line of text.) AutoCAD provides many ways to make this selection; the group you select is called a *selection set.*

The default selection settings are Noun-Verb and Implied Windowing, and we will use this setting throughout the book. It means that you can either pick an entity from the screen and then tell AutoCAD the action you want performed (Noun-Verb) or choose an action to be performed and then select the entities for the action (Verb-Noun). Macintosh users are more familiar with the first procedure, old time users of AutoCAD with the latter.

Not all commands will work with the Noun-Verb action. Those commands that do are: Erase, Move, Copy, Mirror, Rotate, Change Property, Array, Stretch, Scale Explode, and List.

Pick First (Noun-Verb) with Implied Windowing

If your pick box (the small square that replaces your cursor) is on an object, you will get only that object. If your pick box is on a blank portion of the screen, and you drag the cursor to the right, the *window* selection mode takes effect; if you drag it to the left, the *crossing* selection mode takes effect. You can tell that you have a crossing window because it is shown dotted; the standard window is shown with a continuous line.

In the window mode, only objects that are completely within the window are selected. In the crossing mode, objects that are (entirely) within the window or are crossed by the window are selected.

Should you wish to deselect items you have chosen with the pick first format, you can use ☐ +. or [Ctrl]+C. The [F2] function key works only when a command is active; with the pick first style, the command has not yet been selected.

Action First (Verb-Noun) with Implied Windowing

The action is the same as for Pick First except that there are additional options for the old time users. These commands provide a way to make a more complex selection set.

Command	Function
Add (Type **A**)	Allows the addition of objects to the set.
Remove (Type **R**)	Allows the removal of objects from the set.
Last (Type **L**)	Selects the last *visible* object drawn.
Previous (Type **P**)	Recalls the last selection set made.
Undo (Type **U**)	Will undo the last selection you made but not the entire selection set.
Fence (Type **F**)	For the fence mode, draw a continuous series of line segments through whatever you want to select.
Window Polygon (Type **WP**)	A free-form window that you shape by dragging the rubberband line and entering points. As with window selection, only objects completely within its boundary are selected.
Crossing Polygon (Type **CP**)	A polygon that acts as a crossing window.
All (Type **All**)	Remember the saying, "Be careful of what you ask for, you may get it"? Well, users have asked for an option that would select everything in the drawing. This one will select everything except entities on layers that are frozen (locked layers are corrected but cannot be edited). I recommend care when using this option.

NOTE

When using this form of selection, you must indicate that you have completed your selection by pressing ⏎. Most new users forget this and sit for long periods of time looking at the prompt *Select objects:* AutoCAD always waits for you tell it that you have finished with your selection by waiting for ⏎.

TIP

You can always tell when entities are selected—they are highlighted. Highlighting can refer to different effects, depending on where it is used. In the graphic screen, high-lighted entities appear dotted. On the menu bar and on pull-down menus the color is reversed, and on some list boxes, such as the file, layer, and edit boxes, an assigned color appears.

Entering Coordinates

Many times you will place points and draw lines simply by looking at the screen and using your pointing device. But more often you will want to draw a line with an exact length or move something a specific distance; you do this by entering coordinates from the keyboard. There are several methods, which can all be used interchangeably.

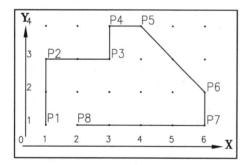

Absolute Coordinates	
P1	1, 1
P2	1, 3
P3	3, 3
P4	3, 4
P5	4, 4
P6	6, 2
P7	6, 1
P8	2, 1

Absolute Coordinates

The *absolute coordinates* for points on the screen are the x-coordinate, the y-coordinate, and if you are working in 3-D, the z-coordinate. Assuming that 0,0 is the lower-left point on your screen, the x-axis runs along the bottom of the screen in a positive direction from 0,0 toward the right, and the y-axis goes in a positive direction toward the top of the screen. The positive direction for the z-axis is from 0,0 straight out at you.

For the most part, in this book, we will be using only the x and y coordinates. The convention for entering coordinates is to enter x first, a comma, then y, such as 3,4. This indicates a point located 3 inches in the x direction and 4 inches in the y direction. When entering inches, it is not necessary to affix the inch symbol, ". However, you must indicate feet with an apostrophe, '. Negative x is to the left of 0,0 and negative y is below 0,0. Specifying absolute coordinates is similar to giving a street location, such as 14th Street and Third Avenue.

Relative Coordinates

More generally, it is not the absolute coordinates that are useful to know so much as distances from existing points, which are described by *relative coordinates*. These are distances or directions from the last point that AutoCAD has stored in its memory. This last point can be accessed by the @ (at) symbol. (You would need to use relative coordinates if you were moving a desk 5 feet from a wall or placing a door 4 inches from the corner of a room.) There are two common ways to enter relative coordinates.

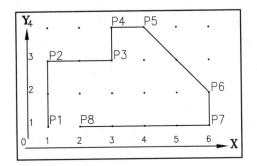

Relative Cartesian Coordinates	
P1	1,1
P2	@0,2
P3	@2,0
P4	@0,1
P5	@1,0
P6	@2,-2
P7	@0,-1
P8	@-4,0

One way is to use the regular Cartesian coordinates, which are the x and y values, such as @2,3.

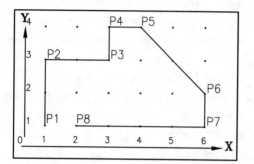

Relative Polar Coordinates	
P1	@1,1
P2	@2<90
P3	@2<0
P4	@1<90
P5	@1<0
P6	@2.8<315
P7	@1<270
P8	@4<180

Another way is to use polar coordinates, which require a distance and an angle in the x-y plane.

The symbol for the angle is the less-than sign, <. A point 2 inches to the left of a previous point would be entered as @2<180.

The value of this last point, which is accessed by using @, can be controlled by using the ID command and picking a point. This becomes the last point and relative coordinates work off the point you specified with the ID command.

And now for some practice on selection sets using the PSGLOBE drawing.

TUTORIAL
● Destroying the Globe

In this lesson you will use various ways of selecting objects to erase parts of the PSGLOBE drawing.

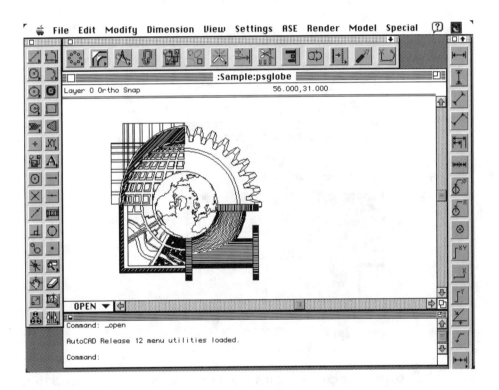

Selection sets are used when you are editing—using such commands as move, erase, copy, and change. In other words, whenever you are selecting something which has already been drawn. You could use any of the editing commands for the tutorial, but erase clearly shows the effect of your selection. The first three of these options will work whether you pick the entities first or use the command first.

1. This time, start AutoCAD by double clicking on the PSGLOBE drawing in the Sample folder in the AutoCAD folder.

2. Click on the Zoom icon and window the lower-right quadrant of the drawing.

Command: **ZOOM ➤ Window**
First corner: Other corner: *Window the area*

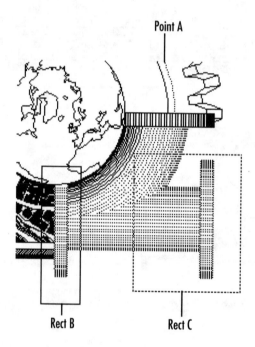

3. If your cursor seems jumpy, you may want to use ⌨F3 to turn off Snap.

4. Start erasing the drawing with the simplest type of selection, a single pick. Refer to point A.

Command: **ERASE**
Select objects: *Pick the outer circle* (Point A—AutoCAD confirms the number of entities found)
Select objects: ⏎ *To end the selection* (The circle is erased)

5. Now use the window option to make your selection. Refer to rectangle B.

Command: **ERASE**
Select objects: *Start a window moving from left to right* (Rect B)
Other corner: *Click on the right corner* (AutoCAD confirms the number of entities found)
Select objects : ⏎ *To end the selection* (The entities completely inside the window will be erased)

6. Continue erasing and make a window like the one marked C but this time move from right to left. This is a crossing window and will erase everything it crosses and encloses.

Command: **ERASE**
Select objects: *Start a window moving from right to left* (Rect C)
Other corner: *Click on the left corner* (AutoCAD confirms the number of entities found)
Select objects : ⏎ *To end the selection* (All entities crossed by and completely inside the window will be erased)

7. The following are additional selection options that work only when you pick the command first. Zoom to the upper-left quadrant of the drawing.

Command: **ZOOM ➤ Previous** (This returns to the previous view so you can select the upper-left quadrant)
Command: **ZOOM ➤ Window**
First corner: Other corner: *Window the upper left quadrant*

Fence E

Polygon D

8. Erase the square coffers in the dome by clicking on Erase and then using the crossing polygon option. Refer to the polygon marked D.

Command: **ERASE**
Select objects: **CP** *For crossing polygon*
First polygon point: *The first point starts the polygon*
Undo/<Endpoint of line>: *Continue to pick points for the polygon*
Undo/<Endpoint of line>: ⏎ *To indicate you are finished drawing the polygon* (AutoCAD confirms the number of entities found).
Select objects: ⏎ *To end the selection* (If you did not enter a ⏎ you could continue building your selection set).

9. Erase the horizontal and vertical lines with the fence option as shown with fence line E.

Command: **ERASE**
Select objects: **F** (For Fence)
First fence point: *Start the line*
Undo/<Endpoint of line>: *Continue the line*
Undo/<Endpoint of line>: ⏎ *To indicate you are finished drawing the line* (AutoCAD confirms the number of entities found).
Select objects: ⏎ *To end the selection*

10. As you continue erasing, you may notice that some entities are erased as a group. Blocks, hatches, and plines behave this way. The globe is a block and the gears are drawn with a pline.

In this tutorial, you were asked to respond with a ⏎ to the prompt, "Select object" at the end of each type of selection set. This was done to provide a clear example of the different types of selection options. You could have continued selecting, using all the options, until you were finished and then press ⏎ at the "Select object" prompt to erase all your selections at one time.

When you have finished, exit AutoCAD and discard the changes to the drawing. You will be using it again to practice zooming in the next chapter.

Command: **FILE ➤ Quit AutoCAD**
The current drawing has been changed.
Select Discard changes

3

Display
Commands

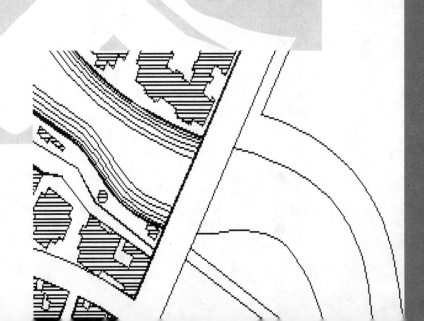

Because you no longer have to work on drafting-table–size sheets of paper, you can use AutoCAD's many commands to get about your small screen-size drawing area. These commands manipulate the screen images only—they do not change your drawing size. Beginners often work with too small an image. Save your eyes—work large enough for comfort!

- Zoom
- Pan
- Redraw and Redrawall
- Regen and Regenall
- Regenauto
- View

● Zoom

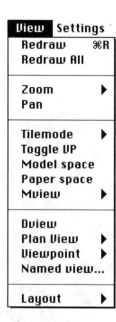

Manipulates the screen display of your image; you can zoom in to show more detail and zoom out for a "bird's-eye view." Zoom changes only the screen view; it does not change the scale or size of your drawing.

Zoom Options

- All
- Extents
- Window
- Vmax
- Previous
- Scale (X/XP)
- Dynamic

Using the Zoom Command

Clicking on the Zoom icon gives access to the most common options of zoom. To enter the command from the keyboard, type **Z**, ⏎, and then the first letter of the option you want.

Most zooms can be done transparently, which means that you can call them up while in another command. The All and Extents options cannot be used transparently because they require a *regen*. (When the screen is regenerated, AutoCAD recalculates the coordinates for all the entities in the drawing. With Release 12, zoom speeds and regens have been sped up, so there is no need to be so concerned about them.) Zooms entered from the keyboard are not transparent unless preceded by an apostrophe (').

The following pictures illustrate the uses of the Zoom options. Use the PSGLOBE drawing to try these Zoom options:

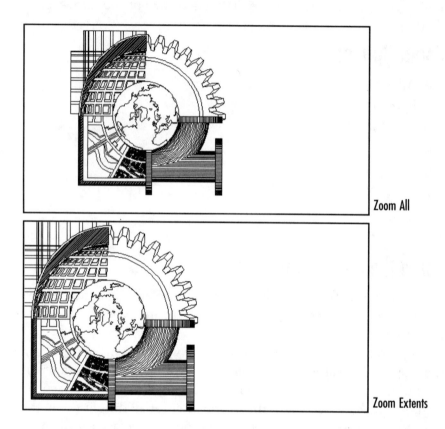

Zoom All

Zoom Extents

The All (A) option displays your drawing up to the drawing limits specified in the Limits command or up to a border if you have placed one there. If you have drawn objects outside of the limits, they will also be included in the screen view. The Extents option (see the previous page) fills your screen with all the entities in your drawing and disregards limits unless they are defined with a border.

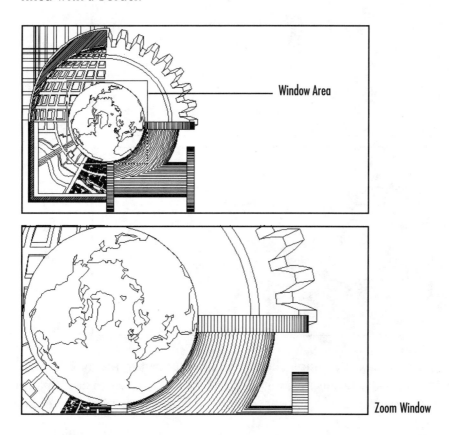

Window Area

Zoom Window

The Window (W) option fills the screen with the area you have specified within your window box.

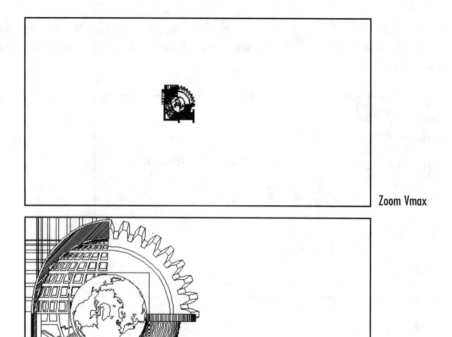

Zoom Vmax

Zoom Previous

The Vmax (V) option allows you to zoom out to the maximum extents allowed, without causing a regen. Sometimes it is faster to use Vmax and then a window zoom in place of a Zoom All, which requires a regeneration.

The Previous option restores the previous view and can stack up to ten views. In addition to the views available with the Zoom command, views created with the Pan, Plan, Vpoint, Dview, and View commands are also included in the stack.

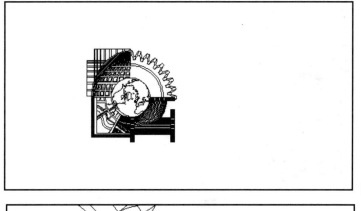

Zoom .5x

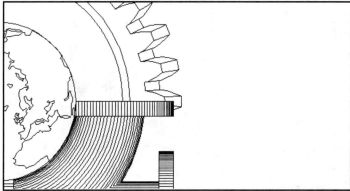

Zoom 2x

There are two options when specifying Scale in model space (model space is the space you draw in, as opposed to paper space, which is a drawing, sheet-layout space). Placing an X after the value indicates that the scale will operate on the existing screen display. Specifying a value without the X uses the limits of the drawing as the base for change. Scale changes are indicated numerically; .5 reduces the view by half and 2 enlarges it two times. To use the Scale option just type Zoom and then the numerical value you want. The XP option is used when working in paper space to scale the image inside the viewports to a specific scale for plotting (you will use this option in Chapter 19).

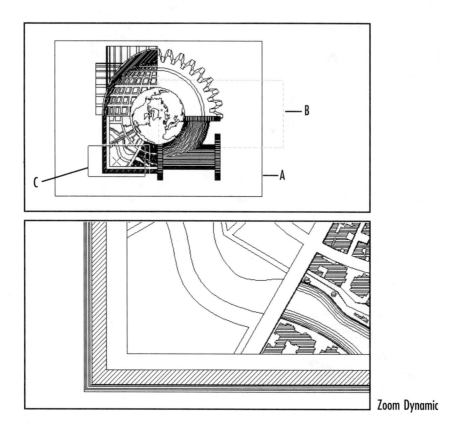

Zoom Dynamic

The Dynamic (D) option generates an image of your drawing that you can zoom and pan about by moving and resizing a view box. It eliminates a step because you don't have to use Zoom previous to relocate the Zoom area. After you select the option, you see a special screen showing the following:

A: View of drawing at last regen enclosed in a white border if your screen color is black or a black border if your screen color is white.

B: Last zoomed view enclosed in a dotted green border.

C: View box that moves and changes size as you move your mouse. Clicking the mouse alternately activates the sizing and panning actions. When the arrow icon is visible, the box can be resized by moving your mouse. When the X appears in the middle of the box, the box can be moved about the drawing with the mouse. The new view is activated when ⏎ is pressed.

N O T E

With the new 1000 to 1 zoom capability in Release 12, you may never see the red corners and the hour glass, but if you are working in earlier versions, the red corners define the area you can zoom to without causing a regen, and the hour glass icon appears in the lower-left corner, indicating that the limits of the virtual screen have been exceeded and a regen is required.

Zoom Notes

- Use the All option after you have changed your limits to display your new drawing limits.

- The Extents option is useful in locating objects that may have "disappeared" during the Move command when your base point was not placed on or near the object you were moving.

- The Scale option is useful when you can't window your drawing because your image fills the screen from corner to corner. Zoom .9X makes your drawing just a shade smaller so you can window it. It is also easier to use this option than some of the others when you want to make your drawing just a little larger.

- If you have trouble finding the view box when using Zoom Dynamic, try clicking and moving your mouse. The view box may be as large as the whole screen, so you won't see its border until you make it smaller.

● Pan

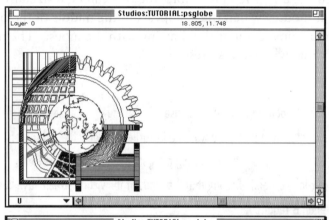

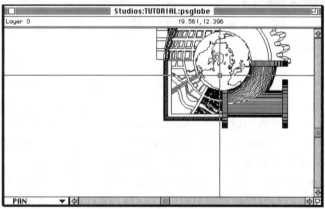

Moves the screen image from one place to another.

Using the Pan Command

To pan your drawing, you indicate the displacement by first picking the *from point* and then the *to point*. Pan is one of the transparent commands, so it can be used while in another command. You can also use the scroll bars to pan your drawing in the standard Macintosh way, but with the AutoCAD pan, you can move in both the X and Y directions at the same time.

● Redraw and Redrawall

Redraw cleans up your screen.

Using the Redraw Command

These commands redraw entire entities that appear broken (but actually are not); they restore missing grid points and clear blip marks from the screen. *Blip marks* are the little crosses that mark the points you have picked on the screen. When using more than one viewport, (the screen can be divided into separate sections, or *ports*, to show different views of your drawing) Redrawall will redraw all of them. Both commands are transparent, so they can be used while in another command.

T I P

Occasionally you may have lines continuing from one of your viewports onto another. Redraw will clean them up. Turning off Grid or Layer causes an automatic redraw.

● Regen and Regenall

These commands recalculate the drawing display and redraw the screen based upon the drawing database.

Using the Regen Command

The Regen command is necessary to show the changes made to drawings when you use certain command options, such as turning Fill on or off, changing linetypes, and redefining Style or Blocks. Generally, the regen is done automatically, unless you have set Regenauto to Off (see "Regenauto," next).

● Regenauto

Certain options available with some commands and certain operations regenerate the screen automatically: Fill and Layer; making changes in linetypes and text style; and updating or redefining blocks. Regenauto allows you to control whether the regeneration is automatic or queued.

Regenauto Options

- On
- Off

Using the Regenauto Command

The On option (the default setting) updates your screen automatically to reflect the changes you have made to your drawing. If you select Off, AutoCAD asks your permission before it regenerates the drawing.

T I P

If you are a beginner, you should keep Regenauto turned on; otherwise, you may be confused by the effect of some commands if the screen is not regenerated to show the result of a change you have made. As your drawings get larger, you may want to turn Regenauto off so you can choose when to regenerate your drawing.

● View

Saves screen views that you have defined so that you can recall them by using the View command. Both plan and 3-D views can be saved this way.

View Options

- New accesses the dialog box that lets you name your view
- Delete (D) removes the views you no longer want
- Restore (R) recalls the view you request
- Save (S) saves the current screen view with the name you supply (can be up to 30 characters long)
- Window (W) allows you to define only part of the screen to be saved as a view
- ? shows you a list of views saved when typing in the command

Using the View Command

The dialog box named Views lists the views that have been saved.

```
                          Views
  *CURRENT*                                    ⇧
  ALL                              MSPACE
  LR                               MSPACE
  UR                               MSPACE




                                               ⇩
  Restore View: *CURRENT*
  [ Restore ]  [ New... ]  [ Delete ]  [ Description... ]
      [[ OK ]]      [ Cancel ]      [ Help... ]
```

Each view needs to have a name. Click the New button when you want to save a new view. If you want to save a portion of the screen instead of the entire screen, click the Window button and window the area you want saved.

T I P

Saving 3D views is particularly useful. It takes a fair amount of effort to get the view you want when doing perspectives. Saving a view guarantees that you can get it back. You can avoid the regeneration that is automatic with Zoom simply by saving that screen view as a View. In these tutorials, regeneration is not much of a concern, but once you get up to speed, you will find that regeneration breaks your stride.

4

Managing
Your
Files

Page Setup...

Plot...   ⌘P

Print Window...   ⌘D

    File Info...   ⌘I

    AutoCAD File Exchange...

File Utilities   ▶

Configure

      Quit AutoCAD   ⌘

The commands in this chapter enable you to manage your files. (You may think of your drawings as drawings; AutoCAD thinks of them as files.) Many of the commands under the File menu will be familiar to Macintosh users who have already managed other programs and documents.

With these commands, you will open existing drawings, start new ones, save additional copies, and get information about them; and because there are other platforms out there, this chapter will cover translating drawings to and from the Macintosh.

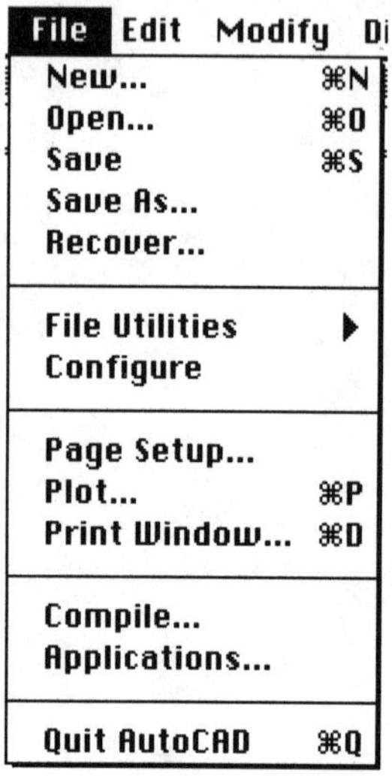

File Edit Modify Di	
New...	⌘N
Open...	⌘O
Save	⌘S
Save As...	
Recover...	
File Utilities	▶
Configure	
Page Setup...	
Plot...	⌘P
Print Window...	⌘D
Compile...	
Applications...	
Quit AutoCAD	⌘Q

- ● New
- ● Open
- ● Save
- ● Save As
- ● Recover

- File Utilities
- Quit AutoCAD
- Rename
- Purge
- Apple File Exchange

Managing Files

Managing drawing files does not get to be critical until you are into actual production drawings. First off, it is not good practice to work in the Auto-CAD folder. In the beginning this will take a conscious effort on your part, because AutoCAD starts up in the AutoCAD folder and defaults to saving your files into the AutoCAD folder. Make folders for your work, with client names, projects, or whatever makes sense. For the book, we have a folder named Tutorial where you will keep the drawings. Keeping your drawings out of the AutoCAD folder makes it easier to update AutoCAD when the time comes, and keeping folders for your projects makes it easier to locate drawings when they become numerous.

Naming Conventions

- File names should be kept under 20 characters in length. If you will be moving files between PC's and the Macintosh, keep your file names to eight characters.
- No two files in the same folder can have the same name. If you try to save a file into a folder that contains a file of the same name, the new one will overwrite the older one.
- File names should not have spaces in them.
- AutoCAD makes a backup copy of your drawing file each time you edit a drawing. This file has the same name, but the extension is .BAK instead of .DWG. If something happens to the drawing, you can use the backup file, but you first have to rename it and give a .DWG extension.

- Release 12 will open drawings produced by earlier versions of Auto-CAD. AutoCAD 11 will open files produced by Release 12 and earlier versions. Release 10 will not open drawings produced on later versions. This is referred to as the drawings being *upwardly compatible*. Generally, versions of AutoCAD open drawings made by that or earlier versions.

Storing Drawings on Floppy Disks

- The $3\frac{1}{2}$" floppy disks come in two sizes: 800K (800,000 bytes—"double density") and 1.4 Mb (1,400,000 bytes—"high density"). Drawings are quite large in comparison with text files. Text files are around 10K to 20K bytes, the PSGOLBE drawing is about 160K bytes, and the plan drawing that you will be creating in this book is about 70K bytes. Depending on the size of your drawings, you can store between seven and fifteen drawings on a 1.4 Mb disk.

- If you plan to work from the floppy disk, you must leave enough empty space on the floppy disk for AutoCAD to make a working copy of your drawing. When you open a drawing, you are working on this copy. This allows AutoCAD to restore the original drawing should you decide to discard the changes you made during the editing session.

● New

Starts a new drawing file.

Using the New Command

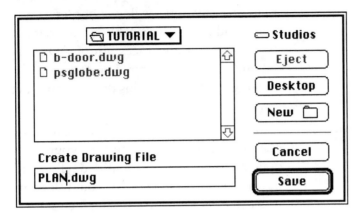

The New dialog box provides the following choices:

Prototype	This is an existing drawing that establishes the settings for your new drawings. Items set up in this way, such as limits, borders, text styles, and layers can establish a standard drawing format for offices. AutoCAD starts out with *acad* as the simple prototype drawing. You can edit this drawing and save it with different settings.
No Prototype	Starts the drawing with the system default values.
Retain as Default	Sets the named drawing as a prototype drawing.

Prototype	This is an existing drawing that establishes the settings for your new drawings. Items set up in this way, such as limits, borders, text styles, and layers can establish a standard drawing format for offices. AutoCAD starts out with *acad* as the simple prototype drawing. You can edit this drawing and save it with different settings.
New Drawing Name	Names your new drawing. If you leave the edit box blank and click on OK, your new drawing will be named "Untitled". To avoid having to know the name of your folder in order to type it in, click on the New Drawing Name command box (remember the ellipses means that you will get another dialog box). It will provide a file dialog box where you use the arrow in the pop up list box to pick the folder for your drawing. This dialog box also provides easy access to the desktop and floppy disks and will create a new folder for your drawing file.

● Open

Opens an existing drawing file.

Using the Open Command

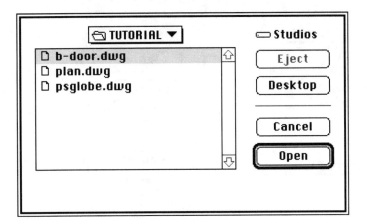

With the Open dialog box you can access folders containing your drawing files. Clicking the close box on the drawing will have the same effect as selecting the Open option.

● Save

This is a quick save option. It saves the drawing with its current name to the current folder.

Using the Save Command

This command is best used as an ongoing save after you have already named and saved your drawing to your file folder. There is no dialog box associated with this command and you will not be prompted for a drawing name or file. It is essentially a command for intermediate saves while you are in the drawing session. Saving your work as you continue with your drawing is called *updating* your drawing.

● Save As

```
┌─────────────────────────────────────────────────────┐
│   ┌──────────────────────────┐    ⊏⊐ Studios         │
│   │ 🗁 TUTORIAL ▼ │                                    │
│   ┌────────────────────────┬──┐  ┌─────────────┐     │
│   │ 🗋 b-door.dwg          │⬆️│  │    Eject    │     │
│   │ 🗋 plan.dwg            │  │  └─────────────┘     │
│   │ 🗋 psglobe.dwg         │  │  ┌─────────────┐     │
│   │                        │  │  │   Desktop   │     │
│   │                        │  │  └─────────────┘     │
│   │                        │  │  ┌─────────────┐     │
│   │                        │⬇️│  │   New  🗂   │     │
│   └────────────────────────┴──┘  └─────────────┘     │
│   Save Drawing As                 ┌─────────────┐     │
│   ┌────────────────────────┐      │   Cancel    │     │
│   │ PLAN-2.dwg             │      └─────────────┘     │
│   └────────────────────────┘      ┌─────────────┐     │
│                                   │    Save     │     │
│                                   └─────────────┘     │
└─────────────────────────────────────────────────────┘
```

Allows you to save the drawing with a new name or to a different folder.

Using the Save As Command

The Save As dialog box shows all the drawing files in your current folder so you can avoid naming the drawing with the name of an existing one. The name of your current drawing file appears in the edit box. When you save the drawing with a new name, the drawing with the new name becomes the current one. If you use this command to save a drawing using the same name, you will be asked if you want to replace the existing drawing. Answer yes when you are simply updating it. Using the Save command is better for updating drawings. Drawings can be saved directly to a floppy disk by selecting Save As, clicking on the Desktop button, double-clicking the name of the disk, and then clicking on Save.

T I P

AutoCAD automatically saves your drawing at the timed intervals that you specify in the Preference file (see Chapter 8). However it is still good practice to save when you have completed part of a drawing and find yourself sitting back to take a breath. Also, it is wise to save before you plot.

● Recover

Recovers a damaged drawing.

Using the Recover Command

Generally AutoCAD will automatically perform a recovery when it detects a damaged drawing upon opening the file. If you need to recover a damaged drawing in other instances, find and select the drawing using the Open file dialog box. AutoCAD reports on the status of the recovery process as it proceeds to repair the drawing.

● File Utilities

There are two options under this heading.

The **File Info** option provides information on drawings and other types of files. It functions similarly to File Info in the Finder. Select the file from the File dialog box. Click on the Open button to get information about the file.

The **AutoCAD File Exchange** option marks files that have been created on different platforms as being created by AutoCAD and assigns them the AutoCAD/Macintosh icon, but in doing so it removes the file extension .DWG. While these drawings can now be opened by double-clicking and dragging and dropping, they cannot be brought into an existing drawing as blocks. In transferring files between the Macintosh and DOS platforms it is better to use Apple File Exchange.

Using the AutoCAD File Exchange

While this procedure will mark files brought in from a DOS platform with an AutoCAD icon, it will remove the .DWG file extension from the file. You need the .DWG extension on files you want to bring in as blocks. It is better to simply open files that you have transferred by using the File Open dialog box inside of AutoCAD. Once opened and saved, these files will automatically have the AutoCAD icon. You must first use Apple File Exchange to bring the drawings into the Macintosh.

● Quit AutoCAD

Exits AutoCAD and closes your drawing, giving you the option to save or discard changes to your drawing.

● Rename

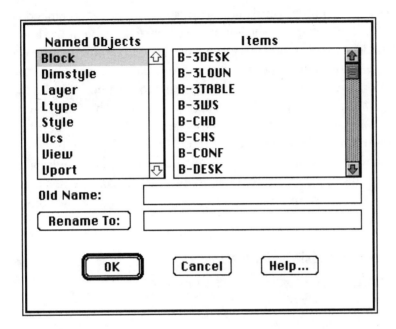

Changes the names of various items used in your drawings.

Rename Options

- ● Block
- ● Dimstyle
- ● LAyer
- ● LType
- ● Style
- ● UCS
- ● VIew
- ● VPort

Using the Rename Command

To use this command type **ddrename**. The *dd* in front of the command name indicates that it is the dialog box version of the command. Some of the lesser-used but nevertheless useful commands are not on the icon or pull-down menus and must be entered from the keyboard, unless you are using the side menu.

When you select the type of item you want to rename from the Named Object list, a list of the related items appears to the right. Click on the item you want to rename and type in the new name in the rename edit box.

As you do more complex drawings, you will find this command quite useful. For example, you can use the option for renaming layers when, as the drawing progresses, you find that some of the layer names you originally chose need more descriptive names or that you have made a spelling mistake.

N O T E

You cannot rename files with the Rename command; use the Finder to rename your files. The Layer dialog box has its own option for renaming layers.

● Purge

Removes certain unused items from a drawing. This reduces the size of the drawing, which enables AutoCAD to load it faster.

Purge Options

- Blocks
- Dimstyles
- LAyers
- LTypes
- SHapes
- STyles
- All

Using the Purge Command

Purge is another one of the few commands that you must enter from the keyboard. The Purge command works only at the beginning of a drawing session, before you have made any changes to the entities. However, you can use commands that do not change the entities, such as inquiry commands, and display commands, such as List and Zoom, and still purge your drawing.

After you have selected the option specifying the types of items to be purged, AutoCAD steps through a list of the selected items and asks you whether you want to purge each one. Press Y to purge the item. If you accept the default value (N) by pressing ⏎, the item will not be purged.

● Apple File Exchange

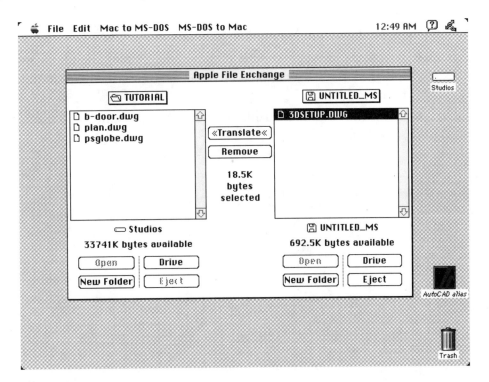

This is an Apple utility program that will translate files between the Mac and DOS platforms.

Using Apple File Exchange

Locate and click on the Apple File Exchange Icon. To move files from DOS to Mac:

- Insert a 3$\frac{1}{2}$" floppy disk formatted on a DOS machine that has drawings you want to move to the Mac.
- Select the folder where you want to place the file, then select the files on the floppy disk that you want to transfer and click on the translate button.
- To use these files, you have to use the Open dialog box inside of AutoCAD. Once opened and saved in AutoCAD, you can open them in the standard Macintosh way.

To move files from Mac to DOS:

- Follow the same procedure as above, except pick the files from the folder on the hard disk and click on the translate direction to the floppy.
- These files will be readable by the DOS and Windows version of AutoCAD.

5

Setting
Up
the
Drawing
Environment

When you set up your drawing space, you establish certain parameters, such as the units of measurement for your work (feet and inches, decimal, or metric), a grid for your drawing area, an increment for your cursor movement, and the size of the drawing space. Auto-CAD calls this *model space* to distinguish it from *paper space*, which is the space you manipulate when plotting drawings.

In this chapter you'll learn about some basic setup commands. There are additional commands for controlling your drawing environment that will be useful as you get further into your drawing (see Chapter 7).

- Units
- Snap
- Grid
- Blips
- Ortho
- Limits
- Layer

● Units Control

Lets you select the system of measurement, units, and the degree of precision appropriate to the type of drawing you are working on.

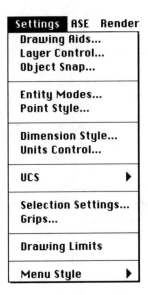

Units Options

- Units and Precision
- Angles and Precision
- Direction

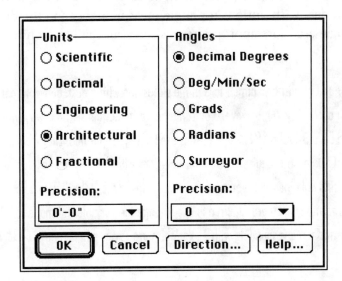

Using the Units Command

In setting up your drawing space, you start by defining the type of units you will be working with. Your choices are

- Scientific
- Decimal
- Engineering
- Architectural
- Fractional

The examples in this book use architectural units, which comprise feet and inches. Fractions of inches are displayed as fractions. However, architectural units allow both fractional and decimal input.

After you have made your selection of the type of units, set the precision from the pop-up list. Use your judgment in setting this. For example, if you are drawing a floor plan, you certainly don't want units shown to $1/64$ of an inch. On the other hand, if you are detailing something, you will want to work in smaller parts of inches. The number you select controls only the *display* of units; AutoCAD keeps track of your drawing with much greater accuracy than you specify.

Leave the default angle measurement at decimal degrees. The Angles options, which deal with options for angle measurements and the direction for 0 degree angle are more appropriate to surveying than to architecture.

N O T E

For clarity, AutoCAD displays dimensions in the status line with a dash between feet and inches (such as *1'-3 1/2"*); however, you cannot enter the dimension this way. The valid entry would be *1'3-1/2* or *1'3.5*. The dash is used only to separate inches from parts of inches. AutoCAD doesn't require you to indicate inches with the *"* symbol or to specify 0 feet when using only inches. If you wish the dimensions in the status line to be displayed in the same form that you are required to use, change the variable Unitmode to 1 by typing **unitmode** and responding with 1. Variables are covered in Chapter 16.

When checking on the size of objects or text, remember that the precision that you specified in the Units command controls only how the numbers are displayed, not the actual dimensions. For example, if you have selected 1 as the smallest fraction to display, you will only get whole inches in response to any inquiry, even if the object's dimension is ¹/₂″.

TIP

If you get the error message "Invalid 2D point," you are probably in the wrong system of units. Check to see that the coordinates you are specifying are in the same system of units that you selected with the Units command. For example, if you are in AutoCAD's default unit system, Decimal, you will get an error message if you specify 44 feet as *44′*.

● Drawing Aids

The Drawing Aids dialog box under Settings offers an easy way to set Snap, as well as other settings for your drawing environment.

```
┌───────────────────────────────────────────────────────────┐
│ ┌─Modes──┐ ┌─Snap────────────┐ ┌─Grid─────────────┐       │
│ │ ⊠ Ortho │ │ ⊠ On            │ │ ⊠ On             │       │
│ │         │ │                 │ │                  │       │
│ │ ⊠ Solid Fill │ X Spacing [1'0"] │ X Spacing [2'0"]│    │
│ │         │ │ Y Spacing [1'0"]│ │ Y Spacing [2'0"] │       │
│ │ ☐ Quick Text │ Snap Angle [0] │ ┌─Isometric Snap/Grid─┐│
│ │         │ │ X Base [0'0"]   │ │ ☐ On               │    │
│ │ ☐ Blips │ │ Y Base [0'0"]   │ │ ⦿ Left ○ Top ○ Right│   │
│ │ ⊠ Highlight │                │ └────────────────────┘  │
│ └─────────┘ [ OK ]  [ Cancel ]  [ Help... ]               │
└───────────────────────────────────────────────────────────┘
```

Snap

Sets the cursor movement to a fixed increment.

- On/Off
- Snap spacing X and Y
- Snap Angle (rotated)—covered in Chapter 16
- Base X and Y—covered in Chapter 16

Using the Snap Command

Set the snap spacing to the smallest usable increment. This increment will depend upon what you are drawing. For working on details, $1/8''$ works well, but if you are working on a site plan, $1'$ is more appropriate. The default is $1''$.

When you specify a snap increment, the Snap function must be set to ON to function. If you don't want your cursor to move in specific increments, you can turn off Snap by de-selecting the On box, or more conveniently, by toggling F9. Remember that a function key acts as a switch, alternating between turning a function on or off. Function keys also work while you are in the middle of using another command. (See Chapter 2 for a discussion of function keys.)

AutoCAD accepts the value you indicate for X and the default value for Y, however, X and Y spacing can be set with different values.

Grid

Places a grid of dots on your computer screen.

- On/Off
- Grid spacing X and Y

Using the Grid Command

Grid is set the same way that snap is, except that if you enter 0, the grid spacing will be the same as the snap spacing. Generally in architectural practices, the grid is set much larger than the snap—often to the dimension of the building module.

You can turn the grid on and off by checking the On box in the Drawing Aids dialog box, but as with the snap command, it is easier to use its function key—in this case, [F5]. Remember that function keys will work while you are in the middle of using another command. The grid, like blips and the cursor, does not plot or print, even though it appears on the screen.

The Snap option automatically sets the grid spacing to match the snap spacing and is indicated by the 0 setting in the grid edit box.

Grid Notes

If you get the message, "Grid too dense to display," either zoom in or increase your grid size. If the grid doesn't appear at all, you may have zoomed in too close. Using the Zoom command with the All option should fix this.

Sometimes the grid will not cover the entire area displayed on the monitor. This is because the grid covers only the area defined by the limits of your drawing. If you want to extend the grid, increase your limits (see "Limits," later in this chapter).

After drawing and editing, some of the grid dots will disappear. To restore your grid type **R** for Redraw or press [F5] twice.

Modes

These settings also effect your drawing environment.

Ortho

Setting this to on will constrain all lines and cursor movement to the horizontal and vertical directions only. Ortho can be turned on and off by pressing [F4] or can be set in the Drawing Aids dialog box.

Blips

Displays tiny crosses, called *blips,* that appear on your screen as you select a point. They remain on the screen after some editing commands are used. You control the display of blips by clicking in the On box. Seeing the location of your last action can be helpful, but with a lot of editing the crosses get in the way.

Solid Fill

Draws solid entities filled or with outlines (See Chapter 9). Generally left on.

Quick Text

Draws bounding boxes for text instead of the actual characters. A time saver when a drawing has a lot of text (See Chapter 14). Generally left off.

Highlight

Keep it on. Only expert users who are working on large drawings and know exactly what entities they have selected might turn it off.

● Drawing Limits

Establishes the size of your drawing space.

Using the Limits Command

Unlike a manual drafting sheet, the AutoCAD drawing space is sized to match the actual size of the object you are drawing. For example, if your building plan is 60'×20', your drawing space would represent that size, plus an allowance for notes and dimensions. You would enter the coordinates for your limits as Lower-left 0,0 and Upper-right 70',30' to accommodate the 60'×20' building plan.

The input format for specifying limits requires a comma and no spaces between the coordinates. Remember that dashes are allowed only between the inch settings and fractions of inches (3$^1/_2$). You will get an error message if you put a dash in the wrong place.

Always use the All option under the Zoom command after changing limits. AutoCAD doesn't resize the screen after you change limits; the All option will display the new limits.

● Layer Control

Using layers is similar to doing overlays in drafting. By placing different items on different layers, you can produce many different kinds of plans by selecting which layers you want to see.

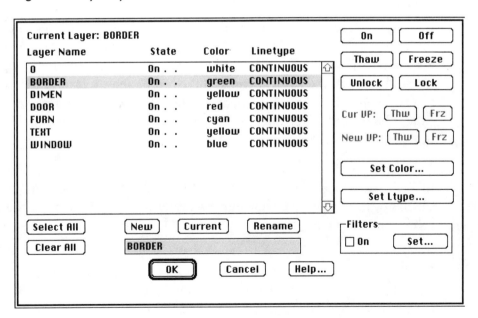

Layer Options

- New
- Current
- Rename
- Set Color
- Set Ltype
- On/Off
- Thaw/Freeze
- Unlock/Lock

Using the Layer Command

Although you can access the layer options by typing LA, it is much easier to set options in the Layer Control dialog box. The list box displays twelve layers at a time. To see more than twelve layers, use the arrows on the right side to scroll through the list. Clicking on the layer names selects and deselects layers. There are buttons for Select All and Clear All. Layer 0 is a given and cannot be purged or renamed. It has special properties for blocks. The options are described below.

New To add new layers, type in the layer name in the edit box, above the OK button and press the New button. If you want to create more than one layer, keep on typing the names, separated with commas.

Current There can be only one current layer. To make a layer current, highlight the layer in the list box and then press the Current button. That layer is then listed as current at the top of the dialog box.

On/Off Use the On and Off buttons to turn the layers on and off. A layer is already turned on if On is listed next to the layer, if On doesn't appear, the layer is off.

Thaw/Freeze Layers that are frozen are not visible. When a layer is frozen, AutoCAD does not reference or search it, which helps speed up some drawing processes such as hide and regeneration. Highlight the layer and press the Thaw or Freeze button. A layer is frozen if F appears next to its name and thawed if there is no F.

T I P

Objects on layers that are frozen will not be selected when the All selection is specified. Objects on layers that are locked cannot be edited.

Unlock/Lock Layers that are locked are visible; you can draw on them, snap to entities, and perform queries, but the layer cannot be edited. Extremely useful when you are working on multilayers and want to keep one static. Highlight the layer and press the Lock or Unlock buttons. These layers are selected with the All selection option.

Cur VP (Current Viewport) Refers to the Vplayer command; selectively freezes and thaws layers in different viewports. It is used to control paper-space views when preparing a drawing for plotting.

New VP (Current Viewport) Used in paper space. Creates new layers that are frozen in all viewports. The thaw option allows you to thaw the layer in your chosen viewport.

Set Color Any layer color, other than white, is selected by highlighting the layer and then picking the Set Color button. The Select Color dialog box opens, showing the colors available. Click on the color; the color name or number appears in the box marked color. Click OK to leave the dialog box.

Ltype To change a linetype to something other than continuous, highlight layer and pick the Set Ltype button. A second dialog box opens, showing what linetypes are available. Use the arrow to highlight the box next to the linetype you want to set for that layer. Click OK to leave the dialog box. For a linetype to be available, you must first load it by using the Linetype command.(See Linetype in Chapter 16).

N O T E

In this book you will deal with only a few layers, however some office practices can lead to drawings with 40 or 50 layers. In cases like these, being able to select layers by their color, name, frozen state, or locked state can be a great help. You can use filters to specify what layers to select.

TUTORIAL

● Setting Up a Drawing Environment

In this exercise you will set up the drawing environment and draw a border for the Plan drawing.

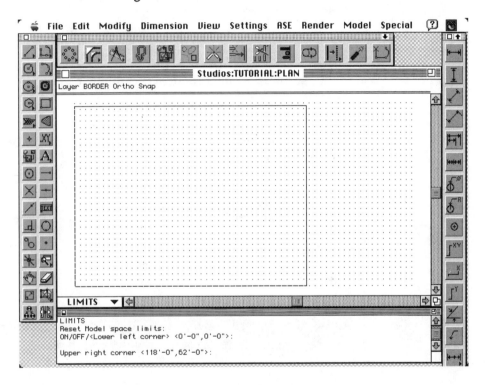

1. Before you start AutoCAD, use the Finder to make a folder named TUTORIAL on your hard disk but not in the AutoCAD folder. All your drawings will be saved to that folder.

2. Start AutoCAD by double-clicking on the AutoCAD icon. The graphic screen opens with Untitled. While you can name and save the drawing at the end of your drawing session, the procedure used in this book is to name the drawing at the beginning of the session; this way, saves during the drawing session are quick and to the right folder.

Command: **File ➤ New**

3. Click on New Drawing Name, select the folder (**Tutorial**) and name the drawing **PLAN**, then click on Save.

Command: **Settings ➤ Units Control** (Set the following)
Units: **Architectural**
Precision: 0'-0" ⏎

4. Accept the default precision of 0'-0" because you will not be using fractions in this drawing.

Command: **Settings ➤ Drawing Aids** (Set the following)
Snap: X and Y: **1"** *and* **On**
Grid: X and Y: **2'** *and* **On**
Ortho: **On**
Solid Fill: **On**
Quick Text: **Off**
Blips: **Off**
Highlight: **On**

5. The AutoCAD standard drawing space is 12"×9". Architectural drawings require much more room, so you need to reset the limits.

Command: **Settings ➤ Drawing Limits** (Set the following)
ON/OFF/<Lower left corner> <0'-0",0'-0">: ⏎
Upper right corner <1'-0",0'-9">: **118',62'**

6. When changing limits, you must select **Zoom ➤ All** for the screen to show the extent of the new setting. The grid appears within the limits you specified.

7. Turn off the UCS icon. You will turn it back on when you work in 3D.

Command: **Settings ➤ UCS ➤ Icon Off**

8. You will find that keeping your coordinate readout active will give you a better sense of orientation. If the coordinate readout doesn't change when you move your mouse, press the F6 function key.

9. The PLAN drawing will have layers. In the edit box, type in the new layer names separated by a comma (no spaces). Once they appear in the list box assign the indicated colors to them. Keep layer 0 white. Select BORDER and make it the current layer.

Command: **Settings ➤ Layer Control** (Set the following)
BORDER: **green**
DIMEN: **yellow**
DOOR: **red**
FURN: **cyan**
TEXT: **yellow**
WINDOW: **blue**

10. Use the Rectangle command to make a border for your drawing. It will be green because you have made the BORDER layer current. The border is sized to plot at $1/8'' = 1'$ on an $8\,1/2'' \times 11''$ sheet of paper. The aspect ratio of drawing sheets and of your computer screen are different, which is why there is empty space to the right of the screen. This space can be used as temporary scratch space.

Select the icon for rectangle. You can refer to the next chapter for more information on the Rectangle command.

Command: **RECTANGLE**
First point: **0,0** (Enter the coordinates from the keyboard)
Second point: **81',61'**

11. To see the entire border you will have to zoom out a bit. Enter the following from the keyboard:

Command: **zoom** (Type it)
All/Center/Dynamic/Left/Previous/Vmax/Window/<Scale(X/XP)>: **.9x**
⏎ (Notice the decimal point)

12. This is a good view to return to, so save it with the View command. Whenever you want to return to it select the Restore option.

Command: **View ➤ Named View ➤ New**
New Name: **All**

You have set up the drawing environment for the PLAN drawing. In Chapter 7 you will start drawing the office. For now, end your drawing session.

Command: **File ➤ Quit AutoCAD** *click on Save Changes*

6

Drawing Commands

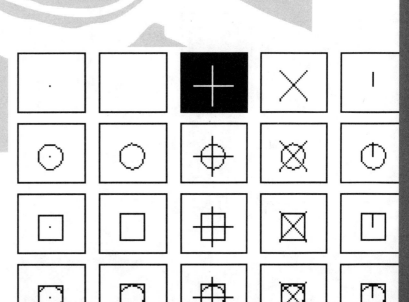

The graphic primitives available in AutoCAD to "lay down line" (that is, the drawing commands used to create lines, arcs, and circles) are not very different from the ones you have been accustomed to using in manual drafting. You will find, however, that drawing lines, circles, and polygons controlling line weights is much easier with a CAD system. Not only can you access "templates" for all these objects, but you can also get information on the entities you have used in your drawing by using the inquiry command List.

In spite of the help CAD systems give you for drafting, you will find that laying down line still takes time. The real speed of these systems lies in their powerful editing commands. The goal to aim for is to draw as little as possible, to edit as much as possible, and to avoid throwing away any lines that you can use somewhere else.

When AutoCAD prompts you for a point, distance, radius, length, or height, you have the option of typing in the number or showing it on the screen. When you know the dimension you want, such as a radius or a length, type it in. When you want to design on the screen, use your cursor to place the points and check the readout on the status line for feedback.

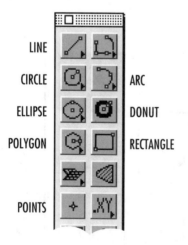

LINE

CIRCLE   ARC

ELLIPSE   DONUT

POLYGON   RECTANGLE

POINTS

- Line
- Circle
- Ellipse
- Arc
- Donut
- Polygon
- Point
- Rectangle

● Line

There are four different types of lines listed under the Line Icon.

Segments

This is the workhorse of the line command. It will draw line segments with each click of the mouse, ending only after you terminate it by pressing F1, F2, ⏎, or the spacebar. If you hold your mouse very still, you can double-click to terminate the Line command. Find out which one suits you best.

Using the Line ➤ Segments Command

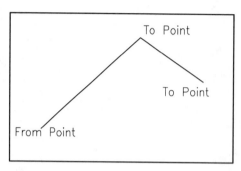
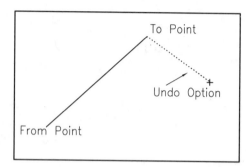

To start a line, move the cursor to the point where you want the line to begin and click. Then move the cursor to the next point desired and click again.

As you move the cursor from the first point to the endpoint, a rubber-banding line tracks your movement. Additional line segments are drawn by moving the mouse and clicking until the command is terminated by one of the methods already mentioned. While using the Line command, the Undo option will erase the previous line segment. You can undo all the lines you have drawn with the current Line command.

Line Notes

- Other line types, such as hidden and dashed, are also drawn with the Line command, except that the lines are drawn on a layer to which that special linetype has been assigned (see the Linetype command in Chapter 16).

- The Ortho setting constrains lines to orthogonal directions, and Snap allows a line to begin and end only at snap locations.

- If you press ⏎ after re-entering the Line command, the new line will continue from where you left off. With this handy option, you can interrupt your drawing with other commands (except Pline and Arc).

- If you type **C** for Close, a line will be drawn automatically from the last point to the first point.

1 Segment

This draws a single line segment that is automatically terminated. It can be efficient because you don't have to press ⮐ to terminate the command.

Double Lines

Double wall lines are drawn using a Lisp program that is automatically loaded when you select Double Lines from the Line Icon. When you first select the command, you are presented with a number of options:

Double Line/Dline Options

Width   Sets the width between the two lines. You can change width in the middle of the program and continue drawing lines.

Break/On/Off   breaks existing wall lines found at the start and end of newly created walls. Breaking will not work unless the Snap option in this command is turned on.

Snap/Size/On/Off   On will connect new walls when cursor is within the search range specified. Off requires manual placement. Size sets snap size (1–10 pixels is the range; 3 is the default). Since a pixel is the smallest graphic unit, 10 is fine for architectural drawings.

Offset   Permits offset from the first known point.

Dragline   Set dragline position to: Left/Center/Right. The *dragline* is the line that is attached to your cursor.

Caps   specifies how the double line will be finished. The Auto option is the most useful. The options are

- Both end caps
- Ending end cap only
- None

- Start end cap only
- Auto—Cap any end not on a line or arc (default)

After you have started drawing double lines you are offered two additional options:

CLose   Automatically closes the polygon you have drawn.
Arc   Draws double lined arcs.

Using Double Lines

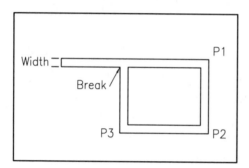
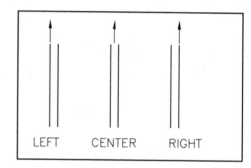

The Double Line command, or Dline draws double wall lines and will automatically break the walls it intersects. You specify the wall width and set the dragline to be left, right, or center. You can imagine the orientation of the dragline as though it were pointing upwards or North.

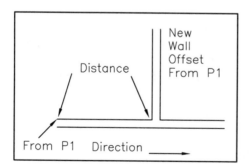
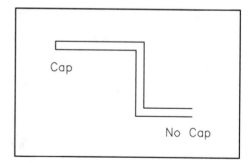

Caps, ending on walls, are best set to Auto. When you first start the command, you are given the option of offsetting the wall from a point. This is much easier to use than specifying @ and then a relative point. Just follow the prompts.

> Offset from: *Enter a point*
> Offset toward: *Point to a direction*
> Enter offset distance: *Enter a distance*

● Sketch

Allows freehand drawing with the mouse.

Sketch Options

> **Pen/Up/Down**   Typing **P** sequentially starts and stops the pen.
>
> **eXit**   Terminates the command and saves the lines.
>
> **Quit**   Quits the commands without saving the lines.
>
> **Record**   Saves the lines while in the command.
>
> **Erase**   Erases lines before they have been recorded.
>
> **. (period)**   Draws a line from the last point to a point indicated when you type a period. The pen must be in an up state to use the period option.
>
> **Connect**   Continues a line nearest to the end point you pick.

Using Sketch

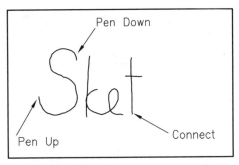

This is an awkward command to use with a mouse but it does get you the effect of freehand drawing. Pen Up and Pen Down are only figurative statements, your mouse is always on the mouse pad.

You are first asked to record the length of the incremental line segments. The incremental line size is what controls the smoothness or jaggedness of your line. Start with .1" and work down from there.

Before the lines are recorded or the Sketch command is exited, the lines are temporary and are drawn in a different color from the layer color. When they are finally recorded, they are redrawn in the color set by the layer.

Sketch can dramatically increase the size of your drawings. A simple word like *Sketch* will have close to 200 lines. (200 lines can draw a lot of building.)

If you set the variable *Skpoly* to 1, you will get a joined polyline instead of many line segments. It makes it easier to move and manipulate the lines.

Turn Snap and Ortho off before you use Sketch.

● Circle

Draws a circle after you specify its radius or diameter. AutoCAD provides five ways to draw a circle.

Circle Options

These are five circle drawing options, two are covered here:

- Center Radius
- 2 Point

You may also want to investigate these options:

3 Point   prompts you for three points on a circle.

TTR   draws a circle based on two tangent points and a radius.

Center Diameter   works like the Center Radius option, except that you specify a diameter instead of a radius.

Using the Circle Command

In this section we'll look at two methods for drawing circles: Center Radius and 2 Point.

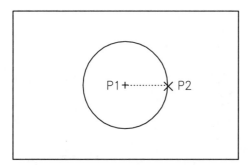
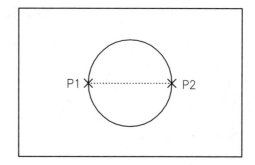

With Center Radius you pick the first point (P1) as the center of the circle; the second point (P2) indicates the radius length. With the 2 Point option, you specify the two points at the ends of the diameter.

● Ellipse

Draws ellipses from major and minor axes. You specify the axes by indicating their endpoints.

Ellipse Options

AutoCAD provides two ways to draw ellipses.

Axis, Eccentricity   Pick the endpoints of one axis and specify the mid-distance for the second axis.

Center, Axis, Axis   Specify the center of the ellipse to pick the endpoints of the two axes.

Using the Ellipse Command

You can draw an ellipse using two different methods.

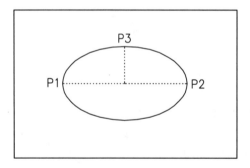 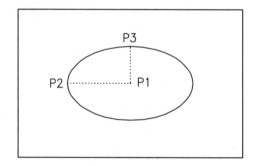

With the first method, after specifying the endpoints of the first axis, a rubber-banding line from the axis's center appears. You use the cursor to indicate the distance between that center point and one endpoint on the second axis. With the second method, you first specify the ellipse's center point. You then indicate the first axis's endpoint with a rubber-banding line from the center point. Finally, you indicate the distance for the other axis with another rubber-banding line from the center point.

● Arc

Draws a segment of a circle. You specify three items: a starting point, an ending or a center point, and one other option, which can be an angle, a radius chord, a direction, or a second point.

Arc Options

The Arc menu has many options for drawing arcs. The points should be entered in the order they are presented in the option.

Here are four frequently used Arc options:

- 3 Point (the default option)
- Start, Center, End
- Start, End, Angle
- Start, End, Dir

Other Arc options use radius and the length of a chord.

Using the Arc Command

An arc requires a starting point, an ending or center point, and an angle, a radius, a chord, a direction, or a second point. An arc is not drawn on the screen until after you place the second point. As you place the third point, the image is dragged along with the cursor, showing the arc as it is being formed. In this section you'll learn about four frequently used methods of drawing arcs.

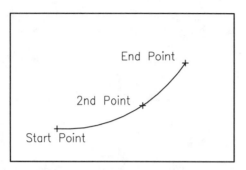 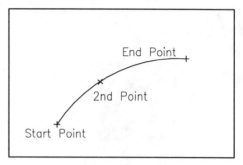

The 3 point arc is the default arc. This arc can be drawn in any direction, depending on the points chosen.

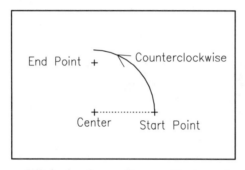 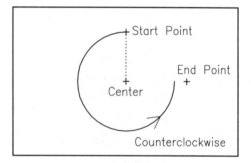

With the Start, Center, End method, the arc is always drawn counterclockwise around the center from the start point toward the endpoint. Because the radius for the arc is determined by the distance from the starting point to the center, it may not always pass through the endpoint specified.

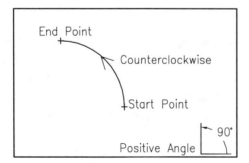 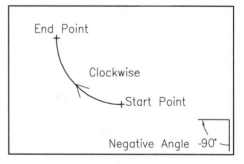

The Start, End, Angle method is also direction-sensitive. Specifying a positive angle draws the arc in a counterclockwise direction; specifying a negative angle draws the arc in a clockwise direction.

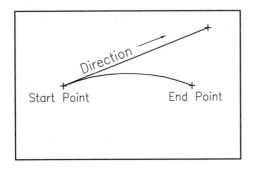
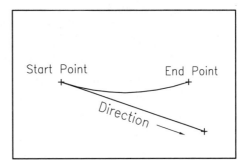

The Start, End, Dir method draws an arc in any direction. The direction is determined by the location of the cursor and is tangent to the rubber-banding line from the starting point of the arc to the cursor.

Arc Notes

- Make sure that Ortho mode is turned off when drawing arcs.
- You need to pay attention to clockwise and counterclockwise directions when specifying points in an arc or you will get surprising results. The only two Arc options that draw arcs in any direction are 3 Point (the default), and Start, END, DIR. All other options draw arcs in a counterclockwise direction unless you specify a negative value.
- A good way to decide which arc drawing option to use is to ask yourself what information you have to draw the arc and whether you want to use the center or start point as your first specification point. After you have answered these questions, go to the Arc menu and pick the most appropriate option.

- The best option for drawing an arc depends on the drawing problem to be solved. The 3 point option is often used when drawing land contours because you don't have information that would be required to use any of the other options. The Start, End, Direction method is used when laying out roads and driveways, where a specific turning radius is required. For drawing arcs with a low rise, the 3 Point and Start, End, Dir options work well because they allow the center of the arc to be off the screen.
- If you respond with a ⏎ after re-entering the Arc command the new arc will start from the endpoint of a previously drawn line or arc. (This is similar to using the ⏎ after reentering the Line command.)

● Donut

Draws solid circles and donut shapes.

Using the Donut Command

Donuts are drawn by specifying the inside diameter, the outside diameter, and the center of the donut.

Once you have drawn a donut, you can place multiple copies of it. To cancel the command, press Ⓕ, Ⓕ2, ↵ or the spacebar.

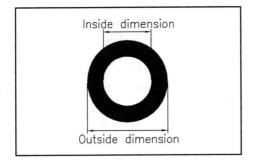

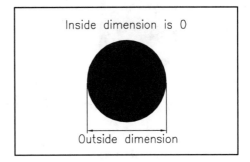

When drawing a donut, the inside dimension is the diameter of the hole and the outside dimension is the size of the donut. To draw a solid circle, specify 0 for the inside diameter, then enter the outside diameter. When Fill (covered in Chapter 9) is on, the donuts and circles are drawn solid. When Fill is off, AutoCAD draws lines instead of solid filled areas. Any changes to Fill require a regeneration of the drawing before you can see the changes on-screen. The Fill setting is on the Drawing Aids dialog box.

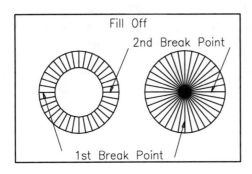

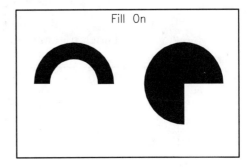

If you want only a segment of a circle or donut, turn Fill off and break the drawing at the segment lines.

● Polygon

Constructs an equal-sided polygon, given the number of sides and the radius or the specification of a single side.

Polygon Options

- Edge
- Circumscribed
- Inscribed

Using the Polygon Command

You can draw a polygon in three ways. With all three, you first specify the number of sides. In the Edge method, you specify the length of one side of the polygon. With the other two methods, AutoCAD draws the polygon inside or outside an imagined circle (you specify the radius).

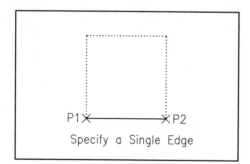

P1✕————————✕P2
Specify a Single Edge

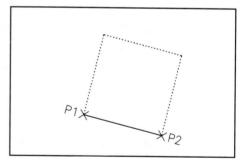

P1✕
✕P2

The Edge option automatically draws the sides of the polygon based upon the length you show on the screen. The placement of the second point determines both the length and the orientation of the polygon. You can also enter the length from the keyboard.

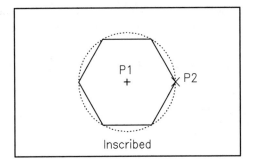

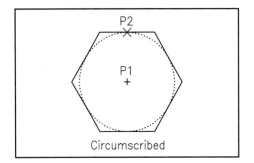

The Inscribed option inscribes the polygon in a circle. The Circumscribed option circumscribes the polygon about a circle. The placement of the second point determines the orientation of the polygon.

Polygon Notes

Polygon orientation is determined by how you select the diameter. When drawing a polygon inscribed in a circle, the point picked positions the endpoint of one of the sides. When drawing a polygon circumscribed about a circle, the point picked will be the midpoint of one of the sides. If you enter the diameter as a value, the side of the polygon is drawn parallel to the x-axis.

● Point

Draws a pixel-sized point unless changed in Point Style. Points are used to mark locations that you want to reference.

Using the Point Command

Because the small size of the default point makes it difficult to see, AutoCAD provides many sizes and styles. There are 20 styles from which to select a point most appropriate for your application. Point sizes can be set as a percentage of the screen size or in absolute units.

Point styles and sizes are found in the dialog box brought up by Settings ➤ Point Style.

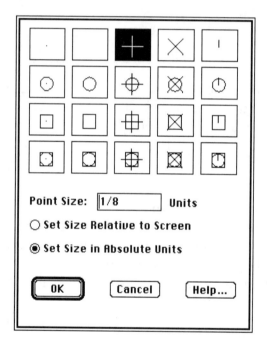

T I P

Only one style or size can be used at a time. Changes in style or size take effect only after you regenerate a drawing. Setting size in relation to the screen can sometimes produce giant points if you change your limits. It is more predictable to set the size in absolute units.

● Rectangle

Draws a rectangle of any proportion.

Using Rectangle

Follow the directions on the icon—pick two points that define the diagonal of the rectangle.

TUTORIAL

● Drawing a Furniture Library

With this lesson, you will start building a furniture library. You'll draw a desk, a workstation, and chairs, which you will use in planning an office you'll design in later chapters. Do not copy the dimensions or text shown on the illustration into your drawing.

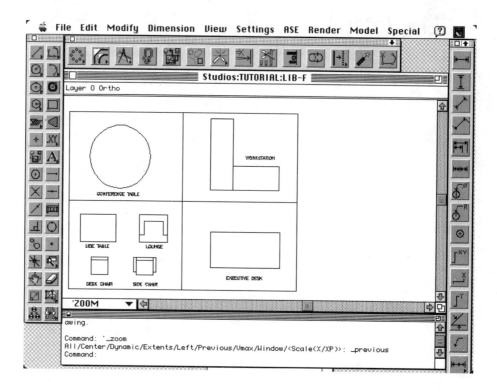

1. Start AutoCAD by double-clicking on the AutoCAD icon.

2. Name the drawing.

> Command: **File ➤ New**
> *Click on New Drawing Name, select the Tutorial folder, and name the drawing LIB-F, then click on Save*

3. Select **Settings ➤ Units Control**, and set the following:

> Units: **Architectural**
> Precision:0′-0″ ⏎ *Accept the default precision of 0′-0″*

4. Select **Settings ➤ Drawing Aids**, and set the following:

> Snap: X and Y: **3″** and **On**
> Grid: X and Y: **0** and **On** (This means that it will follow the snap settings)
> Ortho: **On**
> Solid Fill: **On**
> Quick Text: **Off**
> Blips: **Off**
> Highlight: **On**

5. Set the Limits for your drawing. Select **Settings ➤ Drawing Limits**, and set the following:

> ON/OFF/<Lower left corner> <0′-0″,0′-0″>: **-1′,-1′** (Sets limits slightly below 0,0)
> Upper right corner <1′-0″,0′-9″>: **21′,17′**

6. Remember to Zoom All to see the extent of the new setting.

> Command: **ZOOM ➤ ALL**

7. Turn off the UCS icon.

> **Settings ➤ UCS ➤ Icon Off**

8. Turn your coordinate readout on by pressing F6 until you get the angle distance readout.

9. Make a border using the Rectangle command.

Command: **RECTANGLE**
First point: **0,0**   *Enter the coordinates from the keyboard*
Second point: **20',15'**

10. Divide the screen into four quadrants, as shown in the drawing. Use the Osnap override MID to pick the midpoints of the boundary lines (Osnap is covered in the next chapter and you may want to refer to it). You use Osnap overrides to snap to special points on your entities. In this case, AutoCAD finds the midpoints of the lines without your having to measure them. When you select an Osnap, AutoCAD echoes the Osnap that you have picked in the command window.

11. Select LINE ➤ 1 **Segment** and do the following:

*Click on the **MID**point Osnap*
From point: MID of   *Pick the bottom line of the border*
*Click on the **MID**point Osnap*
To point: Mid of   *Pick the top line of the border*

Command: **LINE ➤ 1 Segment**
*Click on the **MID**point Osnap*
From point: **MID** of   *Pick the left line of the border*
*Click on the **MID**point Osnap*
To point: **MID** of   *Pick the right line of the border*

12. Zoom to the lower-left quadrant to start drawing the chairs.

Command: **ZOOM ➤ WINDOW**
First corner: Other corner: *Window the lower-left quadrant*

13. Draw the desk chair, using the dimensions and grid shown in the drawing for reference. Drawing on the grid is easy, because snap and grid have the same increment. Always set the snap and grid to work for you.

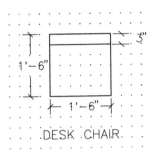

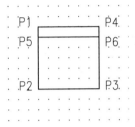

Command: **LINE ➤ 1 Segment**
From point: *Pick point 1*
To point: *Pick point 2*
To point: *Pick point 3*
To point: *Pick point 4* To point: **C** (To close the figure)

Command: **LINE ➤ Segment**
From point: *Pick point 5*
To point: *Pick point 6*

14. Draw the side chair next to the desk chair, using the same dimensions as those for the desk chair. Add the side arms, using the dimensions shown in the following drawing:

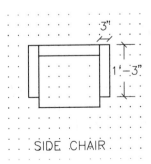

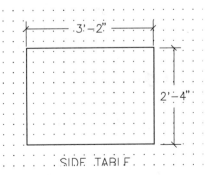

Check the coordinate readout to make sure that the lines you draw are the same length as those shown in the drawing.

15. Move your cursor to the upper-left portion of your screen, and use the same technique to draw the side table. Use the dimensions shown in the illustration (above), and check the coordinate readout for the line lengths.

16. Change your snap settings. Select **Settings ➤ Drawing Aids,** and set the following:

Snap: X and Y: **1″** and **On**

17. Move your cursor to the upper-right portion of your screen, and draw the lounge chair. Follow the points and use the dimensions shown in the illustration:

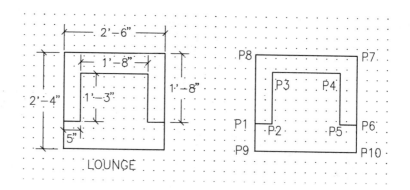

Command: **LINE ➤ Segments**
From point: *Pick point 1*
To point: *Pick points 2 to 10 in sequence*
To point: *Return to point 6*
To point: ⏎

18. Zoom to the lower-right quadrant to start drawing the executive desk. Either use Zoom Previous and then Zoom Window or Zoom Dynamic; you could even use Pan.

19. Draw the executive desk, using the dimensions shown in the illustration:

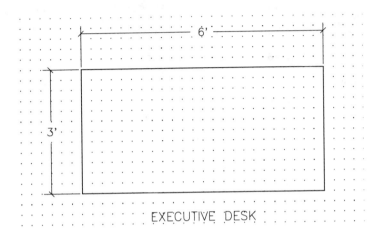

EXECUTIVE DESK

20. Zoom to the upper-left quadrant to draw the conference table.

21. Draw the conference table using the diameter option of the Circle command.

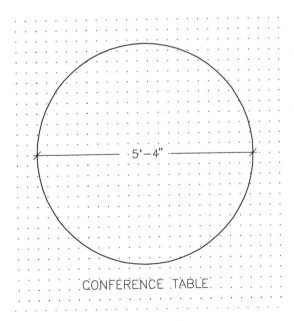

CONFERENCE TABLE

Command: **CIRCLE ➤ Center, Diameter**
3P/2P/TTR/<Center point>: *Pick a point in the center of the screen*
Diameter: **5'4** *Enter dimension from the keyboard.*

22. Zoom to the upper-right quadrant to draw the workstation.

Command: **ZOOM ➤ Window**

23. Draw the workstation, using the dimensions shown in the illustration:

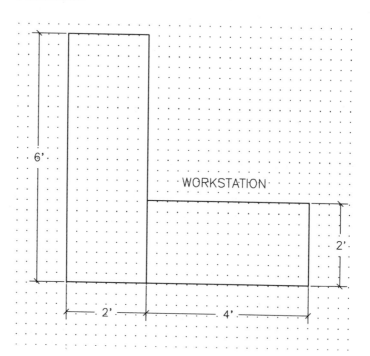

24. You have drawn the furniture that you will make symbols of later and use in laying out your furniture plan. Quit AutoCAD and Save Changes.

7

Drawing Aids

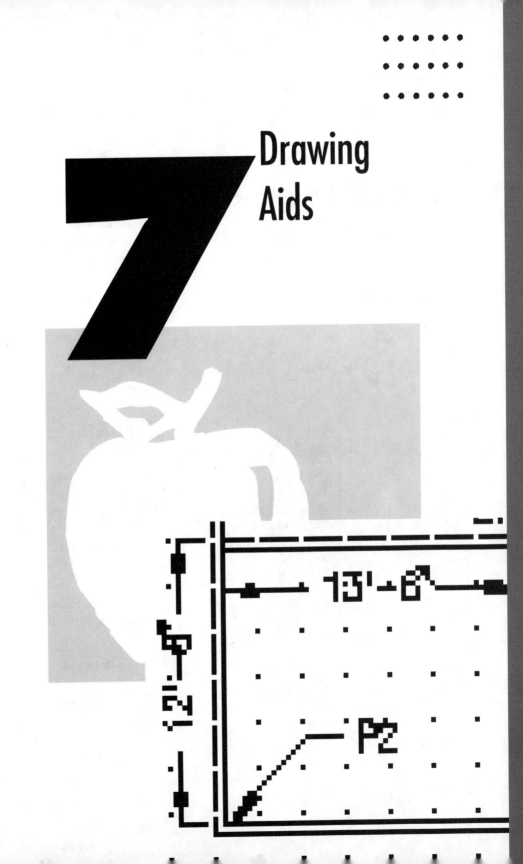

There are some drawing tools that will help you with drawing, editing, and cleaning up your drawings. For the beginner, learning Osnaps and Filters often seems like an additional complication, but to the pro, these tools make drawing quicker, easier, and more accurate.

- Osnap
- Undo/U
- Redo
- Filters .XY
- Object Filters

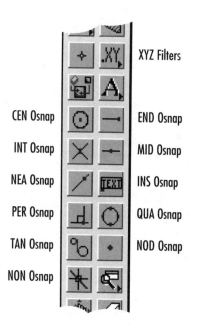

● Osnap

The Osnap command (short for object snap) makes it easier to pick specific points on entities, such as endpoints and midpoints of lines and centers of circles and arcs. It does this by allowing you to pre-specify the kind of point you want to pick and giving you a large enough target box to make picking easier.

Osnap Options

- ENDpoint
- TANgent
- INTersection
- NODe
- MIDpoint
- INSert
- CENter
- NEArest
- QUAdrant
- QUIck
- PERpendicular
- NONe

Using the Osnap Command

There are two forms of the Osnap command. Running Osnaps stay active until you turn them off. Osnap Overrides stay active for one instance only and will *override* any running Osnaps that have been set. Osnap overrides are used often and are easily accessed from the Tool Palette.

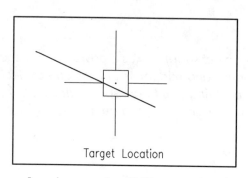

Target Location

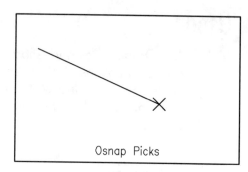

Osnap Picks

In selecting the ENDpoint Osnap, the target can be placed anywhere between the middle of a line and the desired endpoint.

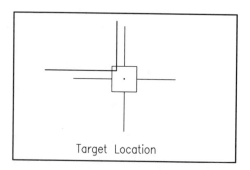

Target Location

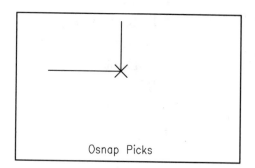

Osnap Picks

In selecting the INTersection Osnap, both lines comprising the intersection must be within the target.

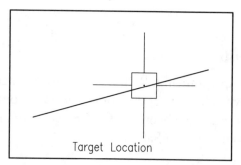

Target Location

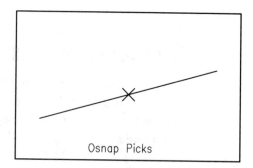

Osnap Picks

The MIDpoint Osnap finds the midpoint of a line; it can also find the midpoint of an arc. The target can be placed anywhere on the entity.

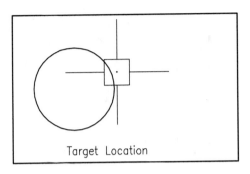

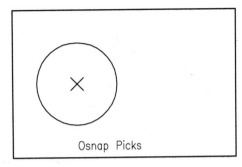

The CENter Osnap finds the center of a circle. The target can be placed anywhere on the circle's perimeter. The CENter Osnap can also be used to pick the center of an arc.

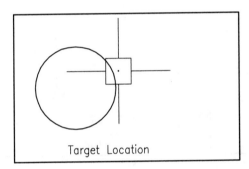

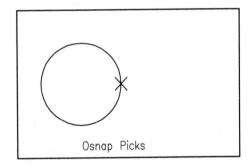

The QUAdrant Osnap finds the points on a circle or an arc that indicate their cardinal quadrants—0, 90, 180, and 270 degrees. The target should be placed on the perimeter of the circle, nearest to the quadrant point desired.

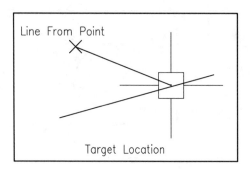
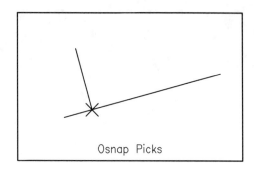

The PERpendicular Osnap is usually used to draw a line perpendicular to the start point. It can also be used to start a line perpendicular *from* the start point. The target can be placed anywhere on the entity that the line is being drawn to.

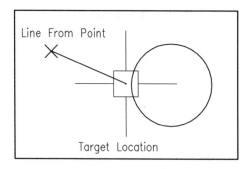
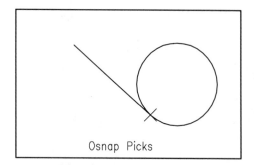

The TANgent Osnap snaps a line to a point where it is tangent to a circle. There are two tangents possible from a point to a circle. Either side of the circle can be specified.

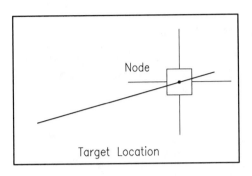

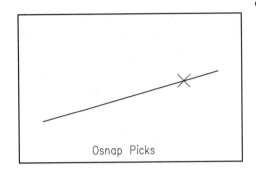

The NODe Osnap snaps to a point. The point must be inside the target box.

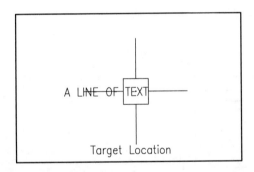

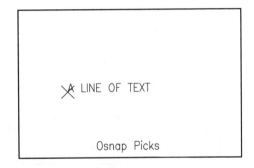

The INSert Osnap snaps to the insertion point of a line of text. The target can be placed anywhere on the line of text. This mode also snaps to the insertion point of a block.

The NEArest Osnap snaps to a point on an entity that is nearest to the cross hairs.

The QUIck option modifies any of the other Osnap modes except INTersection. When your drawings are large, this option speeds up selection.

Running Osnaps and Aperture Size

Running Osnaps are set in the dialog box brought up by choosing **Settings ➤ Object Snap**. You can change the size of the Osnap target box by using the slider in the Aperture Size area of the Osnap dialog box.

```
┌─Select Settings────────────────┐
│  ☐ Endpoint      ☐ Insertion   │
│  ☐ Midpoint      ☐ Perpendicular│
│  ☐ Center        ☐ Tangent     │
│  ☐ Node          ☐ Nearest     │
│  ☐ Quadrant      ☐ Quick       │
│  ☐ Intersection                │
└────────────────────────────────┘
┌─Aperture Size──────────────────┐
│     Min     Max      ┌──────┐   │
│                      │  ☐   │   │
│  ◄ ▐███▌        ►    └──────┘   │
└────────────────────────────────┘
   ( OK )   ( Cancel )   ( Help... )
```

Osnap Notes

- You can tell that you have Osnap turned on when an outline box appears around the cross hairs.
- You can set more than one running Osnap.

● Undo

*This command allows you to step back sequentially and undo previous commands. It is accessed under the Edit menu. Sometimes it is faster to type **U** or enter ⌘+Z.*

Undo Options

- ● Number
- ● Mark
- ● Back

Using the Undo Command

When you select Undo from the Edit menu you are using the U version of the command, which is single undo. Typing the word **Undo** offers other useful options.

If you type a number after typing Undo, AutoCAD undoes that number of previous commands.

Mark will mark a point in your drawing process so that you can return to that point should you decide not to go with the changes, a very useful option when trying out new designs. To use the Mark option, type **Undo** and then **M** for *Mark* at a point in your drawing session that you might want to go back to. Continue drawing. If you decide to undo the changes, type **Undo** and then **B** for *Back* and you will be returned to that point in you drawing when you issued the Mark option. You may use as many marks as you wish. Marks are discarded when you save a drawing.

Undo Notes

- ● If you use Undo too many times, you can use Redo to undo the last undone command. Redo will redo only one Undo.

- Other options for this command, such as Auto, Control, Group, and End, are used when working with menu macros and large drawings; they are outside the scope of this book.
- The U option used inside a command is different from U used as a command. When used inside a command, it undoes the last step taken while inside that command. When used as a separate command, it undoes *all* the steps taken in the last command. It is possible to undo to the beginning of your drawing session. AutoCAD warns you if this will be the result of your Undo.

● Redo

The Redo command in the Edit menu reverses the effect of the last undone command. Redo will redo only one Undo.

● Filters .XY

Not a command but a way of constructing a point by giving x, y, and z coordinates separately instead of all at once. You can enter the coordinates in any order that is convenient to the construction of the point. You can use filters to construct points in either 2-D or 3-D space.

Filter Options

- .X
- .Y
- .Z
- .XY
- .XZ
- .YZ

Using Filters

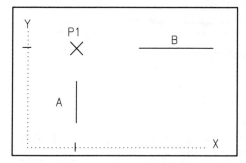 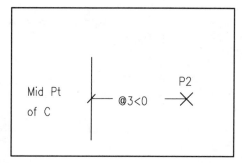

With filters you can derive the coordinates of point P1 from the x-coordinate of the vertical line A and the y-coordinate of the horizontal line B. By using Osnaps in combination with relative coordinates, you can use filters to place a point, P2, a specific distance from the midpoint of line C.

Filter Notes

- Filters can be used to start lines a specific distance from an existing object without drawing construction lines.
- When using filters in 3-D space, use the .XY filter to pick a point in the x-y plane and then specify the z-coordinate.

Object Filters

Object Filters are great aids in cleaning up drawings. Sometimes you will want to move entities from one layer to another; you might want to edit blocks that are on many layers; or you might want to change the dimension of all occurrences of an entity. Manually performing this kind of editing is not a problem with a drawing the size of the one in this book where there are only a few entities. However, it does become a problem with large drawings worked on by many people. AutoCAD has made selecting entities easy with Object Filters.

The procedure is as follows:

● Select **Special ➤ Object Filter** to access the dialog box.

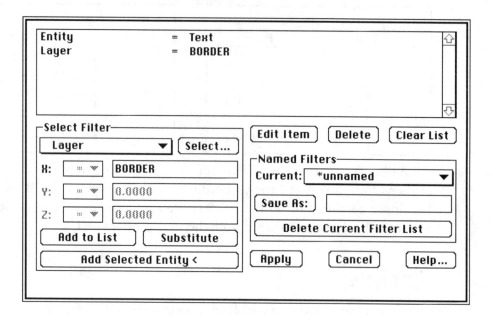

● Under **Select Filter**, scroll through the pop-up list box to find the entity you want.

● Click on the **Add to List** button—the item appears above in the list box.

● You can continue adding and modifying the items, each time clicking on the **Add to List** button. For example, you could pick all text on the layer Border.

● When you have finished your selection, Click on the **Apply** button.

- The dialog box will disappear and you will be back in the graphic screen and the Select object prompt will appear in the Command Window. To select, you may window objects on the screen or type **All**, which will apply the filter to everything except entities on frozen layers. Only the filtered items will be selected, all other entities will be filtered out. While entities will be selected on locked layers, you cannot edit them.

- ⏎ to finish the selection.

- Now you can use any of your editing commands, and when you are prompted to Select objects, respond with **P** to get the previous filtered set.

TUTORIAL

● Drawing Walls

In this exercise you will be using relative coordinates, Osnaps, and the Double Lines command, also referred to as DLINE, to draw walls for an office in the drawing named PLAN. You set up your drawing environment for this drawing in Chapter 5.

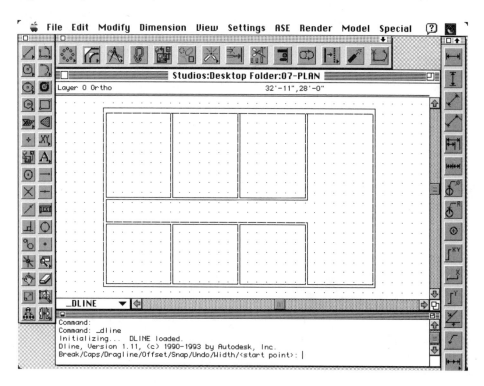

1. Locate your PLAN drawing and start AutoCAD by dragging and dropping the Plan drawing on the AutoCAD icon.

2. If Layer 0 is not the current layer, make it so.

3. When using the Double Line command, you must set its options before drawing lines. These options are reset each time you want to change the wall width or the side for drawing the wall. Set the options for Width, Dragline, and Caps.

Command: **LINE ➤ Double Lines**
Break/Caps/Dragline/Offset/Snap/Undo/Width <start point>: **W**
New DLINE width <0>: **6**
Break/Caps/Dragline/Offset/Snap/Undo/Width <start point>: **D**
Set dragline position to Left/Center/Right/<Offset from center = 0>: **L**
Break/Caps/Dragline/Offset/Snap/Undo/Width <start point>: **C**
Draw which endcaps? Both/End/None/Start/<Auto>: ⏎

4. Stay in the DLINE command and start drawing the perimeter walls by typing in the coordinates.

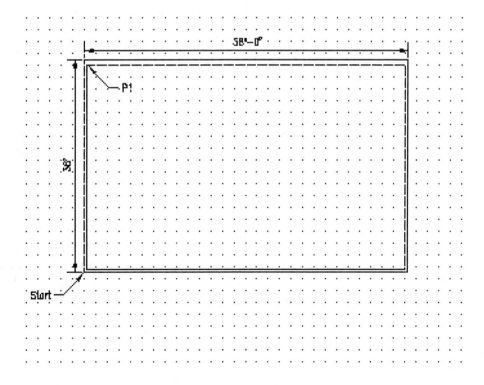

Break/Caps/Dragline/Offset/Snap/Undo/Width <start point>: **12',17'**
Next point: **@36'<90** (AutoCAD repeats the line above, but you are
only concerned with the next point)

5. Stay in the DLINE command but change the width option and
draw the top wall.

Arc/Break/CAps/CLose/Dragline/Snap/Undo/Width <start point>: **W**
New DLINE width: <6> **12**
Next point: **@56'6<0**

6. Continue to stay in the DLINE command, reset the width and
continue drawing walls.

Arc/Break/CAps/CLose/Dragline/Snap/Undo/Width <start point>: **W**
New DLINE width: <12> **6**
Next point: **@36'<270**
Next point: **CL** (Will close the polygon)

7. Now draw the interior partitions on the upper part of the plan.
Zoom into the drawing to get a closer view. The Offset option
aids in starting a wall and requires that you pick a point, indicate
a direction, and type in a distance. This requires less typing than
entering coordinates. Use the Osnap override END to select the
base points from which you will offset your walls. The Offset option only starts the wall. To continue drawing the wall, you will
have to use relative coordinates to place the points. Set the Caps
option for Start so the partition wall will not break into the exterior window wall. You can re-pick the command by clicking on
the command pop-up list on the lower-left portion of your
screen. This is an easy way to pick commands that you have already used. If your target box for Osnap is too large, change it.
Under Settings, select Object Snap and use the slider bars to
change the aperture size.

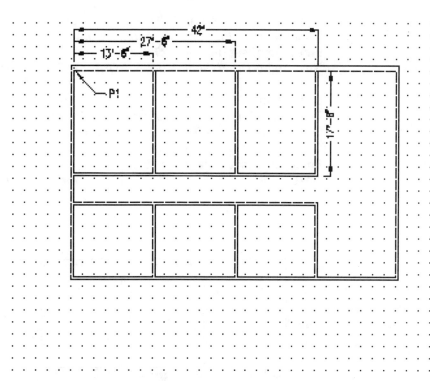

Command: **DLINE**
Break/Caps/Dragline/Offset/Snap/Undo/Width <start point>: **C**
Draw which endcaps? Both/End/None/Start/<Auto> **S**
Break/Caps/Dragline/Offset/Snap/Undo/Width <start point>: **O**
Offset from: *Pick point P1 (Use END Osnap)*
Offset toward: *Pick any point to the right*
Enter the offset distance: **42'**
Next point: **@17'6<270**
Next point: **@42'<180**

8. Change the dragline to Right to work with dimensions.

Command: **DLINE**
Break/Caps/Dragline/Offset/Snap/Undo/Width <start point>: **D**
Set dragline position to Left/Center/Right/<Offset from
center = <–3>: **R**
Break/Caps/Dragline/Offset/Snap/Undo/Width <start point>: **O**

Offset from: *Pick point P1* (Use END Osnap)
Offset toward: *Pick any point to the right*
Enter the offset distance: **27'6**
Next point: *Draw the line down to meet the horizontal wall*

Command: **DLINE**
Break/Caps/Dragline/Offset/Snap/Undo/Width <start point>: **O**
Offset from: *Pick point P1* (Use END Osnap)
Offset toward: *Pick any point to the right*
Enter the offset distance: **13'6**
Next point: *Draw the line down to meet the horizontal wall*

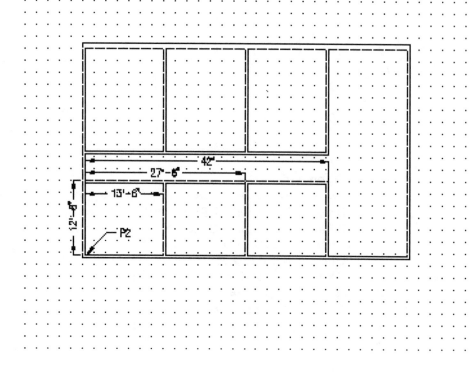

9. Draw the partitions on the lower part of the plan. Set the
dragline to Left and set Caps to Auto.

Command: **DLINE**
Break/Caps/Dragline/Offset/Snap/Undo/Width <start point>: **D**
Set dragline position to Left/Center/Right/<Offset from
center = +3>: **L**
Break/Caps/Dragline/Offset/Snap/Undo/Width <start point>: **C**
Draw which endcaps? Both/End/None/Start/<Auto>: **A** (Type A even
though is shown as the default)
Break/Caps/Dragline/Offset/Snap/Undo/Width <start point>: **O**
Offset from: *Pick point P2* (Use END Osnap)
Offset toward: *Pick a point in the upwards direction*
Enter the offset distance: **12′ 6**
Next point: **@42′<0**
Next point: *Draw the line down to meet the horizontal wall*

Command: **DLINE**
Break/Caps/Dragline/Offset/Snap/Undo/Width <start point>: **O**
Offset from: *Pick point P2* (Use END Osnap)
Direction: *Pick a point to the right*
Distance: **27′6**
Next point: *Draw the line upward, perpendicular to the
horizontal wall*

Command: **DLINE**
Break/Caps/Dragline/Offset/Snap/Undo/Width <start point>: **O**
Offset from: *Pick point P2* (Use END Osnap)
Direction: *Pick a point to the right*
Distance: **13′6**
Next point: *Draw the line upward, perpendicular to the
horizontal wall*

10. Quit AutoCAD and save changes. You have drawn the walls in
the plan by using the Double Lines command with the offset option and by entering relative coordinates. If you were drawing a
plan on your own, you could use the coordinate readout for the
wall lengths. In later chapters you will add doors, windows, and
furniture to this drawing.

8

Have It
Your Way

Mac users have been accustomed to personalizing the look and feel of their programs. AutoCAD also offers options to modify the program to your preferences. This chapter covers simple ways to personalize AutoCAD. The two menus we will use are the Edit menu and the Settings menu.

```
┌─────────────────────────────────┐
│ Edit  Modify  Dimension         │
├─────────────────────────────────┤
│  Undo                      ⌘Z    │
│  Redo                            │
├─────────────────────────────────┤
│  Cut                       ⌘H    │
│  Copy                      ⌘C    │
│  Paste                     ⌘U    │
│  Clear                           │
├─────────────────────────────────┤
│  Command Window             ▶    │
│  Show Tools                      │
├─────────────────────────────────┤
│  Preferences...                  │
└─────────────────────────────────┘
```

```
┌─────────────────────────────────┐
│ Settings  ASE  Render           │
├─────────────────────────────────┤
│  Drawing Aids...                 │
│  Layer Control...                │
│  Object Snap...                  │
├─────────────────────────────────┤
│  Entity Modes...                 │
│  Point Style...                  │
├─────────────────────────────────┤
│  Dimension Style...              │
│  Units Control...                │
├─────────────────────────────────┤
│  UCS                        ▶    │
├─────────────────────────────────┤
│  Selection Settings...           │
│  Grips...                        │
├─────────────────────────────────┤
│  Drawing Limits                  │
├─────────────────────────────────┤
│  Menu Style                 ▶    │
└─────────────────────────────────┘
```

- Changing how the screen looks
- Changing the looks of icons
- Changing the menus
- Changing ways to make selections

● Preferences

When you first configured AutoCAD, you had an opportunity to set prefer-ences. If you just did a plain vanilla installation and accepted all the defaults, you can go back now and tweak the program. You reach this dialog box by choosing **Edit ➤ Preferences**.

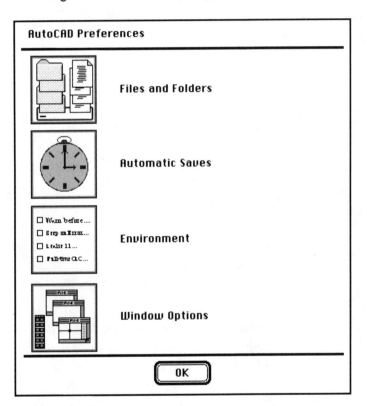

Window Options

This section contains settings that change how your screen looks (the other options are covered in Appendix A). It deals with menus, cursor style, and color. Click on the Window Options button to access the options.

```
┌─────────────────────────────────────────────┐
│ Window Options                                │
├─────────────────────────────────────────────┤
│ Graphics Window :                             │
│                                               │
│ Crosshair Style :                             │
│ ○ Full Screen          ⊠ Status Line          │
│ ◉ Small                ☐ Screen Menu          │
│ ───────────────────────────────────────────  │
│ Background Colors :                           │
│                                               │
│ Graphics Window    ┌──────────┐               │
│                    └──────────┘               │
│ Tool Palettes      ┌──────────┐               │
│                    └──────────┘               │
│ ───────────────────────────────────────────  │
│           ( Cancel )   ( OK )                 │
└─────────────────────────────────────────────┘
```

Here you can adjust the following settings:

- Crosshair Style
- Status Line
- Screen Menu
- Background Colors

Crosshair Style

The default is the full screen crosshair cursor. This one makes it easy to align the entities that you are editing with other entities on the screen. The alternate cursor style is Small, which has short crosshair.

Status Line

This is generally left on; it provides information on the current layer, tells whether you have Snap or Ortho on, and most importantly, gives the coordinate readout. The only reason I can think of for turning off the status line would be to eliminate it when taking pictures of the screen.

Screen Menu

This will get you the old style side screen menu. It contains *all* the commands. Unless you are an old time user, though, I would leave this off and use the icons and pull-down menus.

Background (Screen) Colors

Both screen color and background color for the tool palettes are changed by clicking on their respective boxes to access the color wheel dialog box. Color is modified for each by using the standard Apple color wheel and brightness scroll bar.

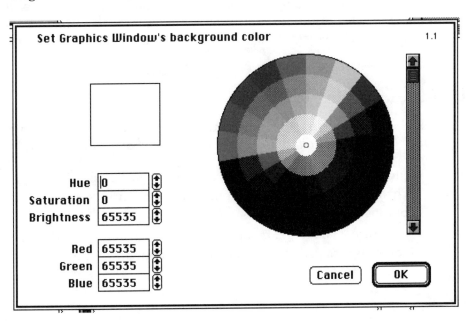

Most users find a white screen too glaring, preferring a black or dark-gray shade.

● Menu Styles

Settings ➤ *Menu Styles brings up a dialog box where you can change the icons menus for Modify and Dimension into text menus. The Tool Palette icon may not be changed, though. Examples of the text style appear in Appendix B.*

● Command Window

With **Edit** ➤ **Command Window** *you can turn the Command Window on and off. Since this is the area where AutoCAD prompts you for what to do next, you should probably leave it on, unless you are an expert user and are familiar with the responses required, or you want to take pictures of the screen and don't want the command window to appear in the picture.*

● Pick Box and Aperture

Both boxes must be sized right for your work: too large, and unwanted lines are selected; too small, and it's difficult to see what you are picking.

Pick box   The target box that appears when picking objects, is changed in the dialog box brought up with **Settings** ➤ **Selection Settings**.

Aperture   The target box that appears when you have an Osnap active, is changed in the dialog box brought up with **Settings** ➤ **Object Snap**.

● Grips

Using grips is another way to select objects for editing, in which entities have their own object snaps (grips are square markers appearing at significant points on entities). Macintosh users may be familiar with the use of grips from other Macintosh drawing programs. Grips are useful when you want to do multiple editing operations on entities.

Grips Options

- Stretch
- Move
- Rotate
- Scale
- Mirror
- Copy
- Undo
- eXit

Using Grips

When grips are turned on, objects that are selected for editing will have out-line squares located at their end, mid, and center points. The grip selected will depend on what kind of editing you want to do. If you want to rotate an object around its midpoint, you would select the midpoint grip; if you want to rotate an object around its endpoint, you would select the endpoint grip. Only five editing commands work with grips: Stretch, Move, Rotate, Scale, and Mirror.

To use grips you must have the following settings *on*:

- Noun/Verb
- Implied Windowing
- Grips

To reach the Grips dialog box, select **Settings ➤ Grips**.

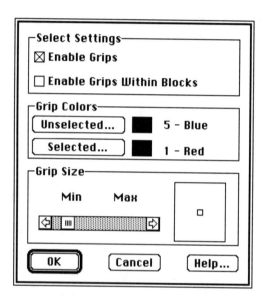

Grips can occur in three states:

Warm Blue outline squares appear all over the objects you have selected for editing.

Hot Selecting a grip turns it red and it is now a hot grip. Once a grip is hot, you have the choice of the grip editing commands. The commands appear in order, Stretch, Move, Rotate, Scale, and Mirror, and each one offers the additional option of Copy. Press the spacebar to cycle through the five grip modes until you see the one you want to use.

Cold These are grips on entities that are not selected. These grips can be used as object snapping points. You de-select entities by Shift-clicking on them.

You can try this brief exercise. The object is to move the midpoint of the line onto the center of the circle using grips.

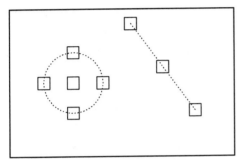 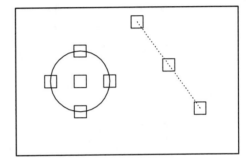

Both circle and line are selected and grips appear on the entities. Shift-click on the circumference of the circle (not the grips). That entity is de-selected but the cold grips remain as snapping points.

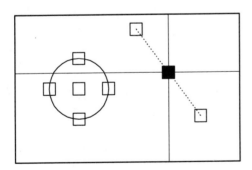 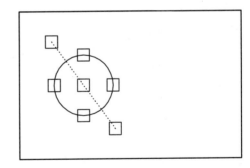

Click on the midpoint grip of the line, and it will become a hot grip. Press the spacebar until Move appears. Move the line over the center of the circle. The line will snap to the center grip on the circle.

Grips Notes

- Objects must first be selected to activate grips.
- Pressing ⌘+. (period) twice or Ctrl-C twice will remove the grips from your drawing.
- You can change the grip size and color in the Grips dialog box.
- Don't enable grips within blocks—this places too many grips on the screen, making it hard to see the actual drawing.
- You can select more than one grip for editing if you hold down the Shift key before you select the first grip and continue holding it down while selecting the grips. A second click on the last grip, without holding down the Shift key, will activate the editing commands.
- You can continue editing by clicking on the grip again to make it hot and cycling through the editing commands.

9

Area Fill Commands

SECTION   WORK POINT

The area-fill commands cover the area you specify with a solid fill or with one of the many textures available in AutoCAD's hatch patterns.

- Bhatch (Hatch)
- Solid
- Fill

● Bhatch

Fills a specified area with a pattern. You can choose from the 65 hatch patterns that AutoCAD provides or you can define your own simple line pattern. Bhatch is a complete reworking of the old Hatch command. It will find boundaries, remember the last hatch used, and let you preview the hatch before you actually apply it. When using Bhatch you will switch between two dialog boxes in addition to the dialog boxes showing the hatches. The Bhatch icon is found on the Tool palette. Click it to bring up the first dialog box.

Bhatch Options

- Pick points
- Select objects

- Preview hatch
- Apply hatch
- View selections
- Stored hatch pattern
- Copy existing hatch
- User defined pattern spacing
- Hatching style

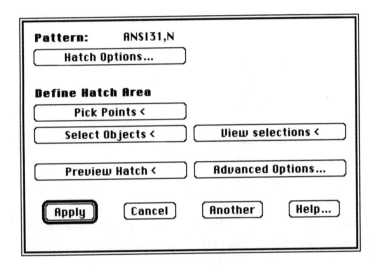

The first dialog box contains options for:

- Specifying the location for the hatch, by picking internal points in a closed region or by picking entities as in the original hatch command.
- Previewing and applying the hatch, permitting you to see what the hatch looks like before committing to it.

● Accessing the other hatch options.

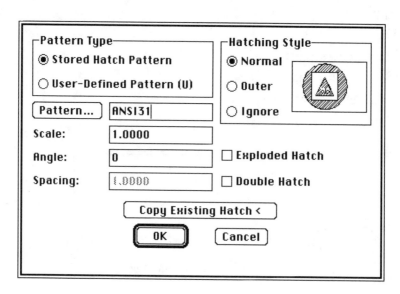

Selecting Hatch Options will bring up the second dialog box, which contains options for:

● Accessing AutoCAD's hatch patterns, hatch scale, and rotation.
● User-defined hatch patterns and options for spacing and double hatching.
● Copying an existing hatch (only for Release 12 hatches).
● Hatching style—options available when using Select Object mode. When using Pick Point mode, keep option on Normal.

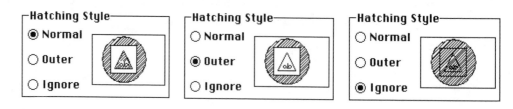

Using the Bhatch Command

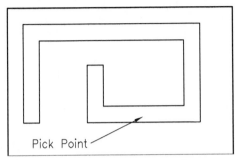
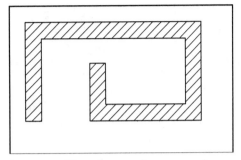

When you pick a point inside an enclosed region, Bhatch searches your drawing data and defines the boundary and hatches within it. For complicated or large regions, pick your point near one of the lines creating the boundary.

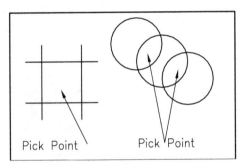
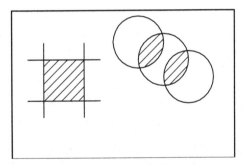

For Bhatch to work, the regions must be completely enclosed. Extraneous lines are ignored when Bhatch constructs a boundary.

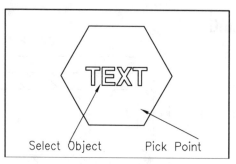

Select Object   Pick Point

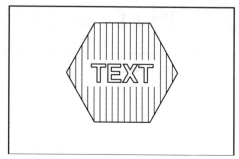

To ignore text inside of an area, pick a point inside the region and then use the Select Object mode to pick the text. You can also use the Hatch command and select the area. The old Hatch command, in its Normal mode would not hatch over text.

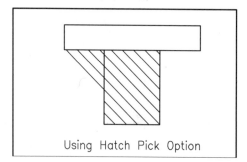

Using Hatch Pick Option

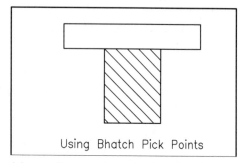

Using Bhatch Pick Points

In the old Hatch command, hatch would overflow unless the border was defined with exact segments. Bhatch creates its own boundary and avoids all these problems. Complete examples of the hatch library can be found in Appendix B, but here are a few of the standard hatch patterns.

Standard Hatch Patterns

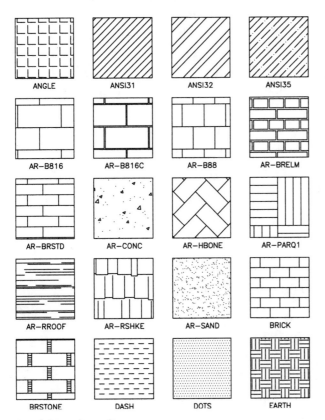

Bhatch Notes

The hatch patterns are reproduced at the angle illustrated. If you want to change this, enter a new angle in the Angle box in the dialog box.

One common error is to specify too small a scale for the hatch pattern. Many of the patterns are symbols for materials, such as brass (ANSI34) and steel (ANSI32). The size of these patterns has been designed for 1″=1″ scale for use in mechanical drafting. If you are designing in 1/8″=1′ scale (or 1″=96″) and want to use these hatches, you must multiply the hatch scale factor by 96 to compensate for the reduction that will be made when you plot the drawing. Architectural hatches, those that have an *AR* prefix, are actual textures or surfaces drawn at full scale, and as such, can be entered at the full-scale value of 1.

Hatch acts as a block. To erase a hatch, select any line in the hatch pattern. A hatch can be exploded into its component parts for editing; however, it will revert to layer 0 regardless of the layer it was on originally, and exploding it can substantially increase the size of your drawing.

T I P   Because hatches slow down the time it takes to regenerate your drawing, it is a good practice to put them on a separate layer so that layer can be frozen. The Bhatch makes it easy to poche walls. It should be done after openings for doors and windows are made.

● Solid

Produces a solid-filled area that is bounded by straight line segments.

Using the Solid Command

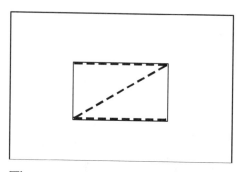 

The area to be filled is specified by picking points in the shape of the letter Z. AutoCAD fills the areas in triangular sections.

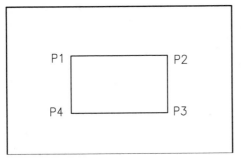 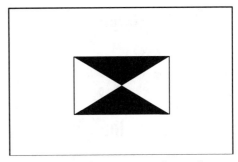

If you get a "bow tie," you incorrectly selected the points by picking them sequentially around the perimeter.

Solid Notes

- For a drawing to be solid, the auxiliary command Fill must be turned on. However, drawings with Fill on take longer to display after regeneration, so it is a good practice to keep Fill off while you are drawing.

- Create a border you can snap to when creating a solid. Eyeballing can lead to jaggies.

- To erase a solid area, it is easiest to use Undo immediately after you have created it; otherwise, use Erase with a crossing window (the solid will become lined), and then use R to remove any lines that you do not want erased. Redraw will bring back the border lines.

- AutoCAD prompts, "Third point, Fourth point" to allow you to continue to fill in more complex areas. If you get unexpected results this way, start the command again and work on the sections separately.

- To fill curved sections, use wide plines (discussed in Chapter 11).

● Fill

Fills in wide plines, donuts, solids, and arrows.

Fill Options

- On
- Off

Using the Fill Command

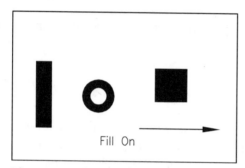

Fill On

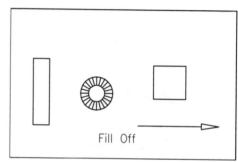

Fill Off

If you turn Solid Fill on, objects will appear solid. If you turn Fill off, only the outline of the entity will be drawn.

Changes in Fill options are only visible after you regenerate your drawing. Fill can be either on or off, but it will affect all the items in a drawing.

N O T E   Drawings with Fill turned on take longer to regenerate, so Fill is generally left off until plotting. Objects with Fill turned on appear solid only in plan views.

TUTORIAL

● Drawing Architectural Symbols

In this lesson, you will use the Polygon, Point, Donut, Hatch, and Solid commands to create four architectural symbols: a north arrow, a column-line symbol, a section symbol, and a work point symbol.

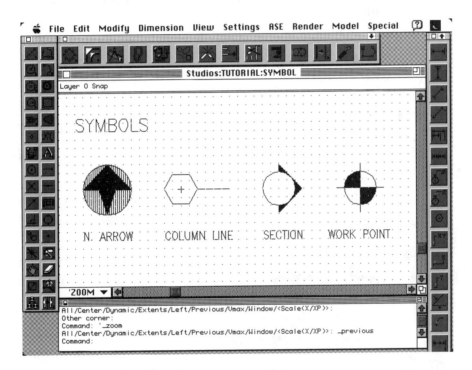

These symbols are not used in the PLAN drawing, but they are included to provide an exercise in using the commands. The snap and grid settings make it easy to locate points, but this lesson also makes use of filters and Osnap overrides to demonstrate their use. It is a long lesson—remember to save frequently.

1. Start a new drawing called **SYMBOL**.

2. Establish the following settings:

Units: **Architectural**
Precision: **1/4**
Limits: Lower left **0,0**; Upper right **6,3**
Snap: **1/4** *and set to* **Off**
Grid: **0',0"** *and set to* **On** (To follow snap setting)
Blips: **Off**
[F6] (Coords On)
[F4] (Ortho On)
UCS Icon: **Off**
Zoom: **All**

Drawing the North Arrow

3. Start the north arrow by drawing a circle with a diameter of 3/4″.

Command: **CIRCLE ➤ Center Diameter**
3P/2P/TTR/<Center point>: *Select a point around the right side of the screen*
Diameter: **3/4**

4. Zoom in so that the circle fills the screen. Start to become aware of when you need to zoom in or out in a drawing. You will be prompted in this lesson, but in later lessons it will be left to your discretion.

Command: **ZOOM ➤ Window**

5. Use the *running* Osnap for the QUAdrant mode because you will be drawing to the QUAdrant of the circle a number of times, and use the Osnap *overrides* to override the quadrant Osnap for those modes that are needed only once.

Command: **SETTINGS ➤ Object Snap ➤ Quadrant**

6. Draw the top part of the arrow using the Osnap target to pick the points. The QUAdrant Osnap remains active until it is canceled. The CENter Osnap override will override the QUAdrant Osnap for a single pick. Remember, it is not necessary to pick the points exactly when using Osnaps.

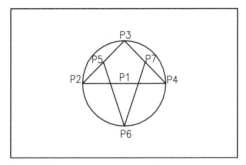

Command: **LINE ➤ Segments**
From point: *Pick a point on the perimeter of the circle*
(Use CEN Osnap)
To point: *Pick a point near P2*
To point: *Pick a point near P3*
To point: *Pick a point near P4*
To point: **C** (To close the polygon)

7. Begin another line for the bottom of the arrow. For these points use the MIDpoint Osnap override.

Command: **LINE ➤ Segments**
From point: *Pick a point near P5* (Use MID Osnap)
To point: *Pick a point near P6*
To point: *Pick a point near P7* (Use MID Osnap)
To point: ⏎

8. You are finished with the outline of the north arrow symbol, now you will add a hatch pattern and a solid fill to complete the design.

Command: **BHATCH**

9. Before you can apply a hatch, you must specify the hatch style, scale, and rotation. This is done through three different dialog boxes. As you enter the information, the appropriate dialog box will appear automatically. Click on **Hatch Options** (a new dialog box appears). Check to see that Stored Hatch Patterns is on.

10. Click on **Pattern** (this will bring up the hatch library).

11. Click on the hatch called **LINE** (click on Next until you find it). Once you select the hatch you enter scale and angle in the next dialog box.

12. In the Scale box, enter **1/4**. In the Angle box, enter **90**. Click the **OK** button. Now the original dialog box appears for you to pick and apply the hatch.

13. Click on **Pick Points**.

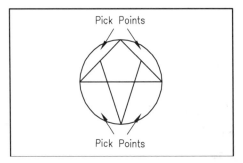
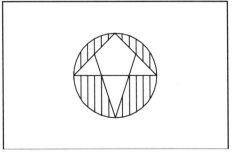

Select internal point: *Pick the points as indicated in the drawing.*
Analyzing the selected data
Select internal point: ⏎ (When you have finished picking the points)
Click on **Preview** (To see the hatch before you apply it)
Press ⏎ to continue (This will return you to the dialog box)
Select Apply (If you were satisfied with the preview, this will apply the hatch)

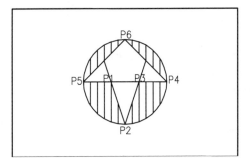

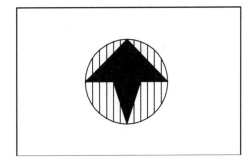

14. Fill the arrow using the Solid command, utilizing the running QUAdrant Osnap to pick the exact points. Set Fill to On if it is not already turned on.

Command: **Settings ➤ Drawing Aids**
Solid Fill: **On**

Command: **SOLID** (Type this one in)
First point: *Pick point 1* (Use INT Osnap)
Second point: *Pick point 2* (The QUAdrant Osnap resumes)
Third point: *Pick point 3* (Use INT Osnap)
Fourth point: ⏎ (There isn't any)
Third point: ⏎ (To terminate the command)

15. Use the Solid command again and fill in the other section of the arrow.

Command: **SOLID**
First point: *Pick point 4*
Second point: *Pick point 5*
Third point: *Pick point 6*
Fourth point: ⏎
Third point: ⏎ (To terminate the command)

You now have a north arrow that can be made into a block, inserted into drawings and rotated to indicate the north direction in a plan.

Drawing the Column-Line

16. Start the column-line symbol by drawing a hexagon to the right of the north arrow. Make sure to turn your snap on because you will be drawing to the grid.

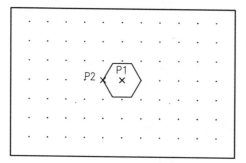

Command: **POLYGON ➤ Inscribed**
Number of sides: **6**
Edge/<Center of polygon>: *Pick point 1*
Radius of circle: *Pick point 2*

17. Draw a line from the right point of the hexagon to indicate column direction.

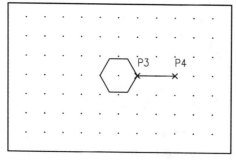

Command: **LINE ➤ 1 Segment**
From point: *Pick point 3*
To point: *Pick point 4*

18. Mark the center of the hexagon with a point for future insertion of a letter. Select a complex point style so that the point will be visible. First set the style from the dialog box.

Command: **Settings ➤ Point Style**
Style: *Click on the style that looks like a plus sign*
Point Size: **1/16**
Set Size to Absolute Units: **On**

19. Use the filters right next to the Point icon to place the point in the center of the hexagon. You could simply place the point on the grid, but these instructions will give you practice using filters. First you will be prompted for X value and second for YZ (it is okay to enter just the Y value). If you find it difficult to pick certain points, toggle Snap off (press F3). It is considered good practice to keep snap on, turning it off only when it doesn't permit you to pick a point.

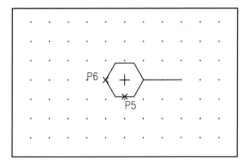

Command: **POINT**
Command: **XY Filter ➤ X**
Pick point 5 (Use MID Osnap—this is the X value)
Pick point 6 (Use END Osnap—this is the Y value)

Drawing the Section Symbol

20. Start the section identification symbol by drawing a circle. Turn Osnap off and toggle Snap back on (press ⬚F3⬚).

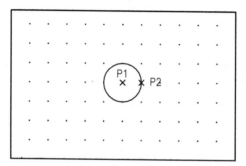

Command: **CIRCLE** ➤ **Radius**
3P/2P/TTR/<Center point>: *Pick point 1*
Radius: *Pick point 2*

21. Draw a square around the circle.

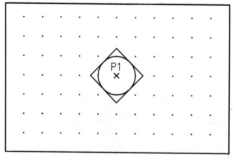

Command: **POLYGON** ➤ **Circumscribed**
Number of sides: **4**
Edge/<Center of polygon>: *Pick point 1*
Radius of circle: **@1/4<45** (This will draw and rotate the square)

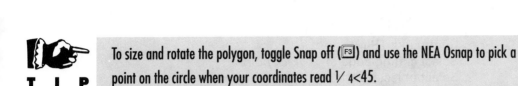
22. Draw a line bisecting the symbol. Pick the point with the help of the ENDpoint Osnap Toggle Snap off (press F3).

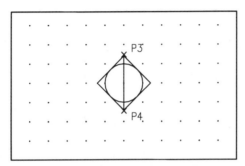

Command: **LINE ➤ 1 Segment**
From point: *Pick point 3* (Use END Osnap)
To point: *Pick point 4* (Use END Osnap)

23. Zoom in to see more detail.

Command: **ZOOM ➤ Window**

24. Use the Trim command to erase half of the polygon. (A full explanation of the Trim command is given in Chapter 10).

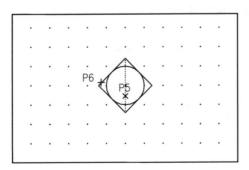

Command: **TRIM**
Select cutting edge(s)...   *Pick point 5*
Select objects: ⏎
<Select object to trim>/Undo: *Pick point 6*
<Select object to trim>/Undo: ⏎

25. Use the Trim command to erase the line through the circle.

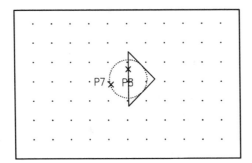

Command: **TRIM**
Select cutting edge(s)...   *Pick point 7* (The circle is the cutting edge)
Select objects: ⏎
<Select object to trim>/Undo: *Pick point 8*
<Select object to trim>/Undo: ⏎

26. Use a hatch pattern to shade the arrow points. The pattern,
Line, has already been used for the previous symbol and is listed
on the line marked Patterns. The previous angle is okay but you
will have to change the scale.

Command: **BHATCH**

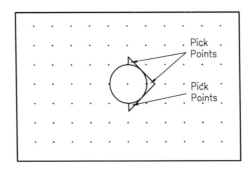

27. Click on **Hatch Options** and set the scale to 1/16. Click the **OK** button and then click on **Pick Points** (the dialog box goes away).

Select internal point: *Pick the three points as shown*
Select internal point: ⏎ (When you have finished picking the points)

28. Click on **Preview**. Press ⏎ to return to the dialog box. Click on Apply if you were satisfied with the preview.

Drawing the Work Point

29. The next symbol you will draw is referred to as a *work point* or a *datum point*. Start by drawing a circle. Toggle Snap on (press F3).

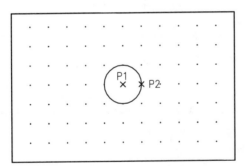

Command: **CIRCLE** ➤ **Radius**
3P/2P/TTR/<Center point>: *Pick point 1*
Radius: *Pick point 2*

30. Zoom in to work on the symbol.

Command: **ZOOM** ➤ **Window**

31. Use the Donut command to draw the filled sections.

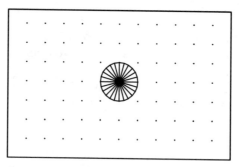

Command: **DONUT**
Inside diameter <0'-0">: **0**
Outside diameter <0'-0">: **1/2**
Center of doughnut: *Pick the same center as that for the circle then press* ⏎ *to finish the Donut command*

32. Turn Fill off to make it easier to work with the donut.

Command: **SETTINGS ➤ Drawing Aids**
Solid Fill: **OFF**

33. To see the effect, you have to regenerate the drawing.

Command: **REGEN** (Type it)
Regenerating drawing.

34. Change the snap spacing to aid in drawing the crossing lines. These lines extend ¹/₈" on either side of the circle.

Command: **SETTINGS ➤ Drawing Aids**
Snap: X and Y: **1/8**

35. Draw the first and second crossing lines, snapping to the grid.

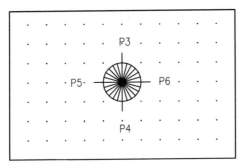

Command: **LINE ➤ 1 Segment**
From point: *Pick point 3*
To point: *Pick point 4*

Command: **LINE➤ 1 Segment**
From point: *Pick point 5*
To point: *Pick point 6*

36. Use the Trim command to erase parts of the donut.

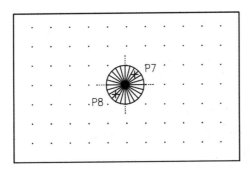

Command: **TRIM**
Select cutting edge(s)... *Pick one of the crossing lines*
Select objects: 1 selected, 1 found   *Pick the other crossing line*
Select objects: ⏎
<Select object to trim>/Undo: *Pick point 7*

<Select object to trim>/Undo: *Pick point 8*
<Select object to trim>/Undo: ⏎

Sections of the donut are trimmed:

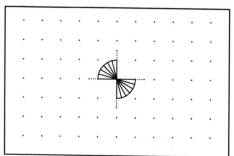

37. Use Redraw to restore the missing pieces of the symbol.

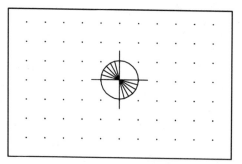

Command: **VIEW ➤ REDRAW**

38. Zoom back to the full view and turn on Fill.

Command: **SETTINGS ➤ Drawing Aids**
Solid Fill: **ON**

39. Regenerate the screen to see the effect of Fill turned on. Your work point drawing should now look like the full-screen image at the beginning of the tutorial.

Command: **REGEN** (Type it)

40. Quit AutoCAD and Save Changes.

10

Erasing and Moving Objects

As soon as you have drawn some objects, you will probably want to move, erase, or copy some of them. In this chapter you will learn about these basic editing commands plus some more advanced ones. Some of the more powerful editing commands are covered in Chapter 13. The commands that are marked with [pf] are those that work in both the pick-first and command-first mode.

- Erase [pf]
- Break
- Trim
- Extend
- Move [pf]
- Copy [pf]
- Offset
- Mirror [pf]
- Rotate

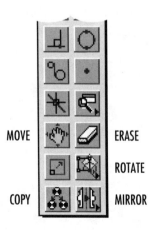

MOVE   ERASE

     ROTATE

COPY   MIRROR

OFFSET

BREAK

EXTEND

TRIM

● Erase

Erases whatever object or group of objects is selected, such as lines, circles, and polylines. It will not erase parts of these entities. (To erase parts of entities, use the Break command.) The effectiveness of this command is enhanced by using the selection sets in specifying what objects are to be erased. You may want to review selection sets in Chapter 2.

Using the Erase Command

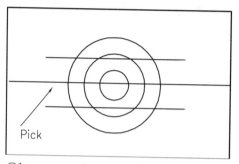 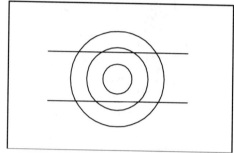

Objects can be erased simply by picking them and choosing Exit ➤ Erase.

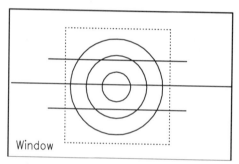 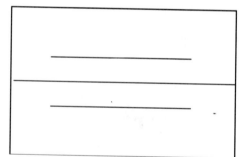

Specific groups of objects can be erased by selecting them with the Window option. Only objects *completely* within the window area are erased. This would also apply to the Window Polygon.

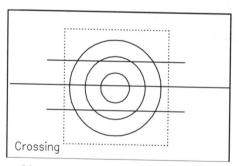 

You can also select objects by using the Crossing option. *All* objects inside of this box and any objects crossed by the box are erased.

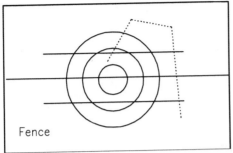 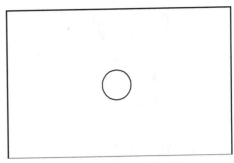

Fence

Fence is another selection mode that can be used to erase objects. The Fence option is similar to a very thin Crossing Window or Crossing Polygon. Fence works well in tight spots where it would be difficult to get a window or polygon in.

Erase Notes

Using **Undo** inside of the Erase command will de-select the last entity picked in case you have picked one in error.

Sometimes, when erasing, the remaining lines will look as though they were broken or partly erased—this is normal. Use the Redraw command to restore the complete appearance of these lines.

● Break

You can use the Break command to erase part of a line, a pline, a circle, or an arc. You can also use it to cut these objects without erasing any part of them.

Break Options

- Select Object, 2nd Point
- Select Object, Two Points
- At Selected Point

Using the Break Command

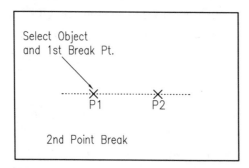
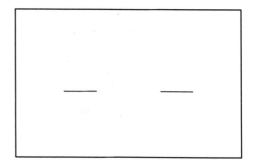

In the Select Object, 2nd Point option, the point you use to select the object becomes the first point of the break; you then select the endpoint of the break. This option requires you to pick only those two points. The section between is erased after you press ⏎.

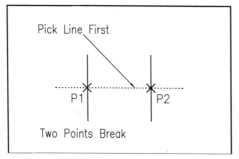
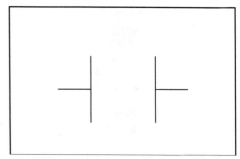

The Select Object, Two Points break allows you to indicate the object to be broken before you find the first and second points. You use this option when the points where you want to break are too close to other lines. First, pick the object that you want to break, then pick the two points for the break.

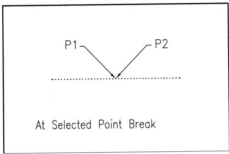

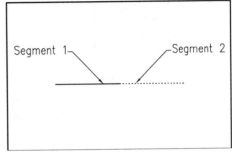

The At Selected Points cuts a line without erasing it, because the first and second points are the same.

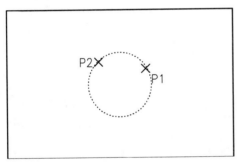

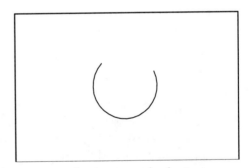

To break a circle, you select the break points in the counterclockwise direction.

● Trim

Erases those parts of objects that intersect the cutting plane on the side of the cutting line you specify. If you have selected an object in error while you are trimming, you can type **Undo** *to deselect the object.*

Using the Trim Command

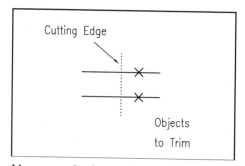

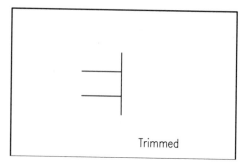

You are asked to select a cutting edge; after you press ⏎, you are prompted to select objects to trim. You can select objects on either side of the cutting edge.

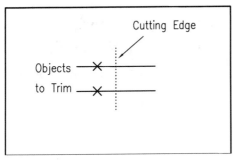

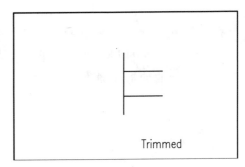

The point you specify determines what sections are erased.

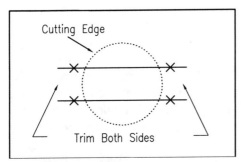

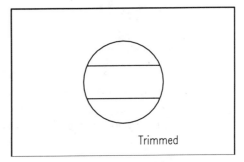

A cutting edge can be something other than a straight line; circles, arcs, and even polygons work fine.

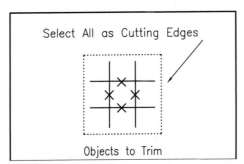

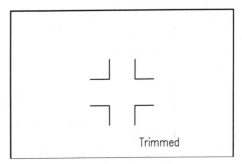

You can have more than one cutting edge. An object that you select as a cutting edge can itself be an object to be trimmed.

T I P

A common error is to forget to press ⏎ after selecting the cutting edge. After you make your selection, you must press ⏎ to complete the selection before you select the objects to be trimmed. Also, you cannot use a block as a cutting edge or an object to be trimmed.

● Extend

Extends lines, plines, and arcs to meet specified boundary edges. You can se-lect more than one boundary at a time, but you must pick each object you want to extend individually with your cursor. It is similar to the Trim command in that you must pick an edge before proceeding with the command.

Using the Extend Command

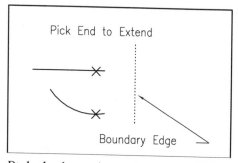

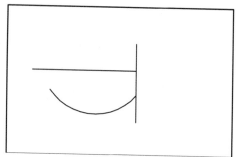

Pick the boundary edge, press ⏎, and select the objects you want to extend.

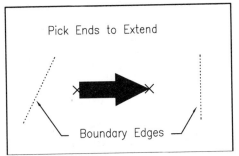

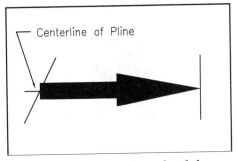

You may have more than one boundary edge. You must pick each of the ends you want to extend. Wide plines are extended to their centerlines. Tapered plines have their points extended to meet the boundary line.

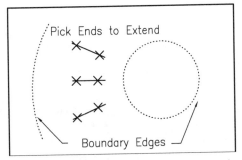

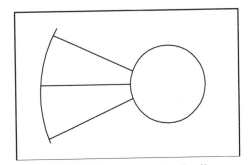

Arcs and circles can act as boundary lines. Again, you must individually select each end you want to extend.

T I P

One common error is forgetting to press ⏎ after making a boundary selection (it is also a common error with the Trim command). Boundary edges and objects you want to extend must be separated by pressing ⏎. You don't have to pick endpoints when selecting the objects you want to extend, just the side of the line that is closest to the boundary edge.

● Move

Moves objects from one location on the drawing to another. You can indicate the distance on the screen by moving your cursor or by typing in the x and y displacements.

Using the Move Command

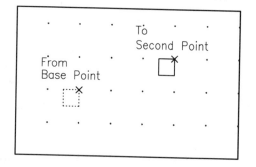

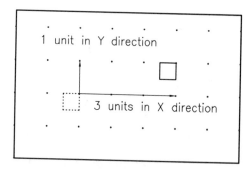

After you select the objects to be moved and they are highlighted, Auto-CAD prompts with *Base point or displacement*. The base point is the point *from* which you want to move the object and can be visualized as the handle on the object you want to move. After you have indicated the point, the next prompt is *Second point of displacement*. This is the point *to* which you want to move the object. You can simply think of this as the From/To method. The second method (see the second drawing) involves typing the displacement vector. When prompted for *Base point of displacement*, type in the distance you want to move the object in the x and y directions. When prompted for *Second point of displacement*, simply press ⏎.

Move Notes

- When groups of objects are moved, they keep the same relationship to one another that they had before being moved.
- You can move objects in 3-D space by indicating a z value for elevation.

T I P If you move something and it disappears, select Undo and try again. What you probably did was incorrectly enter the point where you wanted the object moved to as the *from* point. If you want to find the object, you can use Zoom, All; it should be there in outer space.

● Copy

Structured very much like the Move command, except that it gives you the option of making more than one copy of an object. Copy has one option: Multiple.

Using the Copy Command

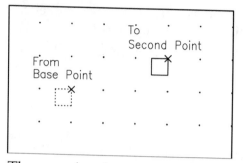 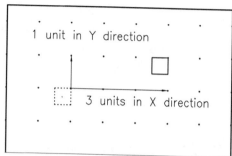

The procedure for copying single objects is the same as for moving them. The From/To method makes a copy from one place to another. The base point is the point on the object you are copying, and the second point is the point where you want the copied object to appear. The other method for copying objects is to type in the displacement vector (see the second drawing), as you do in the Move command. To the first prompt for *Base point of displacement*, type in the x,y vector value, remembering to use the minus sign if the values go in a negative direction. Respond to the prompt *Second point of displacement* by pressing ⏎.

When you select the Multiple option, pick the first point on the object and continue picking multiple second-point locations on the screen. When groups of objects are copied, they keep the same relationship to one another that they had before being copied.

Copy Notes

- The response to the *Select object* prompt can be Previous, in which case the original object is copied, or Last, in which case the last object placed or created is copied.
- As in the Move command, **Undo** undoes the last operation.
- Specifying x, y, and z coordinates copies an object in 3-D space.

● Offset

Copies lines and arcs parallel to the existing entity. Closed polylines, polygons, and circles are offset in a "nesting" fashion. The distance to be offset can be indicated by screen pointing or by specifying a distance and direction.

Offset Options

- Through
- Offset distance

Using the Offset Command

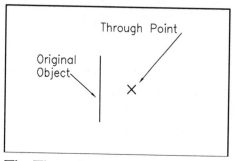
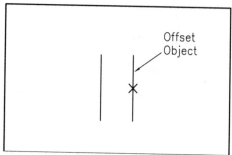

The Through option (the default) asks you to select an object and a point through which you want the duplicated object to pass. Entities are set parallel to the existing object. The prompt repeats, so you can continue selecting objects and various points to copy through. You can terminate the command by pressing ⏎.

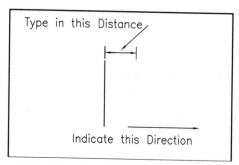
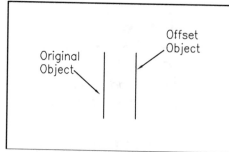

The Distance option asks you to select the offset distance, the object, and the side to be offset. When asked for the side to offset, you indicate the direction; the actual distance has already been specified. This distance remains in effect until you reenter the command and specify another distance or the Through option.

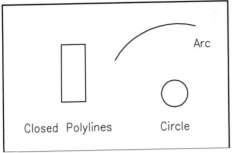

Closed polylines, polygons, circles, and arcs are offset in a "nesting" fashion.

Offset Notes

- You must explicitly select the object to be offset; you cannot use *P* for Previous or *L* for Last.
- Using Offset is the only way you can make concentric circles and arcs.
- When you get the prompt *Offset distance or Through <Through>*, and you want to use the Through option you must respond with a ⏎ to accept the default. If you type in a number, it will be used as the offset distance.

● Mirror

Makes a mirror image of an object. The location of the new image is controlled by the mirror line. You are offered the choice of deleting old objects or not.

Using the Mirror Command

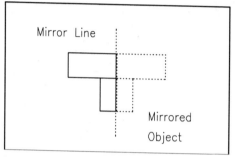

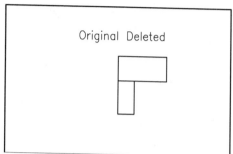

To specify a mirror line, select two points to indicate the reflection plane. If you want your mirror line to be perfectly orthogonal, press F8 to toggle the Ortho mode on. If you press **Y** after the prompt *Delete old objects*, the original object will be erased, leaving only the mirrored one. The default option leaves the old object.

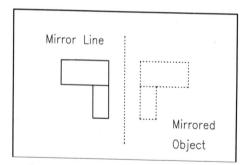

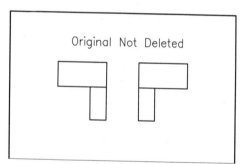

It may help to think of the mirror line as a reflecting mirror. Aside from reflecting the actual object, it also reflects the space between that object and the mirror.

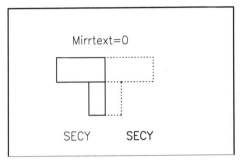

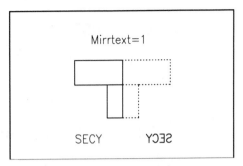

Text will be mirrored unless you set the variable Mirrtext to 0. Mirrtext is a system variable. To change it, type **Mirrtext** and change the value to 0.

Mirror Notes

- AutoCAD's default value will cause text inside of blocks and dimensions to be mirrored, along with the object mirrored.
- Mirrored blocks cannot be exploded with the AutoCAD explode command. However, there are Lisp programs that will do this, and AutoCAD provides one in the Samples directory (see Chapter 16 on Fine Tuning Your Drawing Environment). Exploded blocks revert to the original drawing and are no longer "glued together" as a single entity.

● Rotate

Rotates an object to a new orientation about a selected base point.

Rotate Options

- Rotation Angle
- Reference

Using the Rotate Command

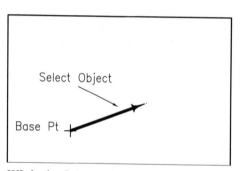

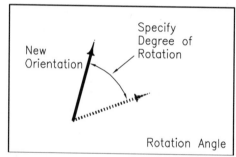

With the Rotation Angle option (the default), after you have selected the object to be rotated and have specified the base point, enter the number of degrees you want to rotate the object; remember that + is counterclockwise and − is clockwise. You can also use your cursor to drag the object into position.

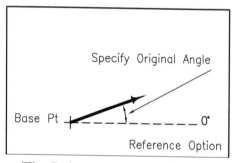

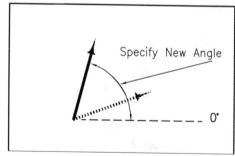

The Reference option allows you to type in the original angle (the angle you are moving *from*) and then the new angle (the angle you are moving *to*). You must first indicate the base point.

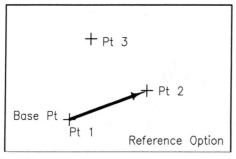
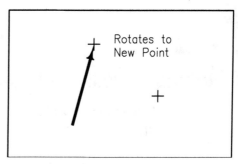

You can also indicate the rotation on the screen with the Reference option. First, point to the base point and then the endpoint of the object, which will indicate its angle. Then, pick the new point.

Rotate Notes

- When you drag an object into position, you can get a readout of the angle if you have your coordinates toggled on (press ⟦F6⟧). Dragging is particularly useful if you don't know the angle of the original object.
- To find the angle of an object, use the List command under **Special ➤ Inquiry**. It gives you all the vital statistics on an object.

TUTORIAL
• Making a Closet and Editing a Wall

In this lesson you will add a closet to your plan and edit out a wall section using the editing commands you have learned in this chapter.

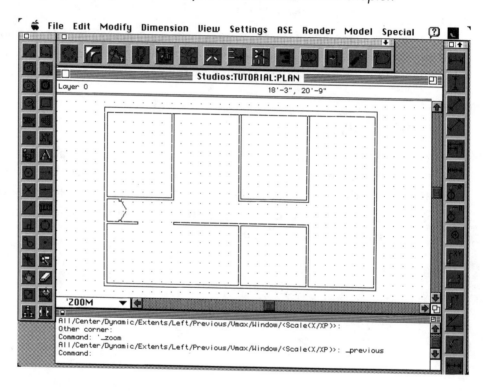

1. Open the PLAN drawing.

2. To make a closet at the left end of the corridor, copy the inside wall line out into the corridor.

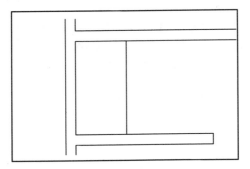

Command: **COPY**
Select objects: *Pick wall*
<Base point or displacement>/Multiple: **30,0**
Second point of displacement: ⏎

3. Use the Offset command to copy this line 6 inches to the right to form the outer wall of the closet. You could use Copy again but this will let you try out the Offset command.

Command: **OFFSET**
Offset distance of Through<Through>: **6**
Select object to offset: *Pick the last line you drew*
Side to offset?: *Pick any point to the right*
Select object to offset: ⏎

4. Zoom in and trim the wall intersections. Toggle snap if necessary.

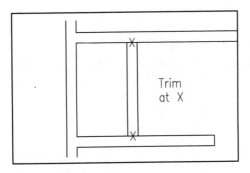

Trim
at X

Command: **TRIM**
Select cutting edge(s)...   *Select the two walls you just made*
Select objects: ⏎
<Select object to trim>/Undo: *Pick the wall intersections*

5. You will use relative coordinates to draw the jamb 4 inches from the corner, but first you have to use the ID command to make the corner the last point. Ignore numerical values.

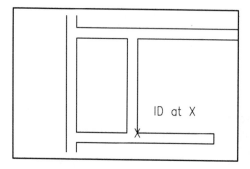

Command: **Special ➤ Inquiry ➤ ID Point**
Point: *Select point* X (Use INT Osnap)

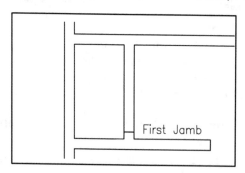

Command: **LINE ➤ 1 Segment**
From point: **@4<90** (Draws a line starting 4″ from the ID point)
To point: *Pick inside wall of closet* (Use PER Osnap)

6. Mirror the line to the other side using the midpoint of the wall line in the back of the closet.

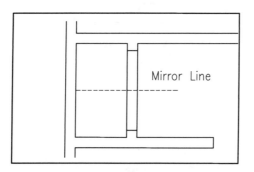

Mirror Line

Command: **MIRROR ➤ 2D**
First point of mirror line: *Pick wall line in back of closet*
(Use MID Osnap)
Second point: *Any point horizontally*
Delete old objects? <N>: ⏎

7. Trim the double lines back to the jambs.

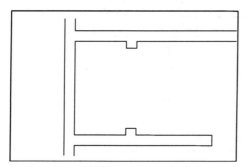

Command: **TRIM**
Select cutting edge(s)... *Pick both jambs*
<Select object to trim:>/Undo: *Pick the lines between the jambs*

8. Draw the first of the double doors by using filters.

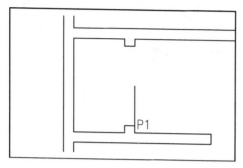

Command: **LINE ➤ 1 Segment**
From point: *Pick P1* (Use the END Osnap)
Select: **.X** (From the XY Filter icon)
To point: .X of @ (Specifies the x filter point)
(need YZ): *Pick the midpoint of the back wall of the closet as the y filter point* (Use MID Osnap—Z is not needed)

9. Rotate the door 30 degrees and mirror it.

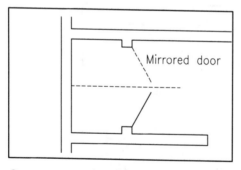

Command: **ROTATE ➤ 2D**
Select objects: **L**
Base point: *Pick the end of the door near the jamb* (Use END Osnap)
<Rotation angle>/Reference: **–30**

Command: **MIRROR ➤ 2D**
Select objects: *Pick door*
First point of mirror line: MID of *Pick back wall of closet*

Second point: (See drawing)
Delete old objects? <N>: ⏎

10. Now you will do some wall editing. The order in which editing is done will show you how some of the editing commands work. For example, by capping the wall first, you can make use of the Trim command to trim out the line between the two capped points. Start by erasing the wall as shown.

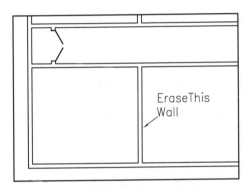

Command: **ERASE** *Pick wall lines*

11. Draw a line to cap the right wall.

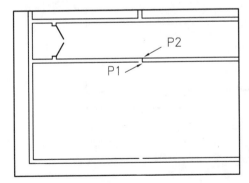

Command: **LINE ➤ 1 Segment**
From point: *Pick P1* (Use END Osnap)
To point: *Pick P2* (Use PER Osnap)

12. Now you will take out part of the wall to make an entrance to the corridor; use the Break command.

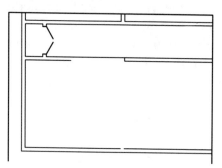

Command: **BREAK ➤ Select Object, Two Points**
Select object: *Pick the broken wall line*
Enter first point: *Pick the END point* (Use the END Osnap)
Enter second point: @–7',3"

13. Draw a line to cap the left wall.

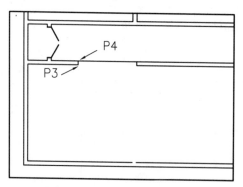

Command: **LINE ➤ 1 Segment**
From point: *Pick P3* (Use END Osnap)
To point: *Pick P4* (Use PER Osnap)

14. Trim out the wall between the two end caps.

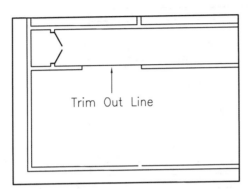

Trim Out Line

Command: **TRIM**
Select cutting edge(s)...   *Pick both caps*
<Select object to trim:>/Undo: *Pick the line between the caps*

15. The wall line on the lower part of the plan has a break in it from when you removed the wall. The proper way to "heal" the wall, is to make it a continuous line (as opposed to adding a line between the two line segments).

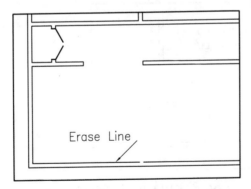

Erase Line

Command: **ERASE** *Pick the left wall segment*

16. Extend the remaining line to meet the corner.

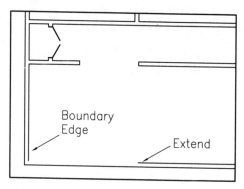

Command: **EXTEND**
Select boundary edge(s): *Pick boundary*
Select Object: ⏎
<Select objects to extend:>/Undo: *Pick wall segment*

17. Use the same combination of commands—Erase, Extend, Trim— to remove the wall between the two offices on the upper part of the plan.

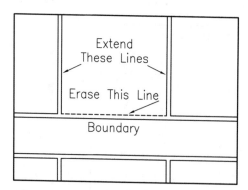

Command: **ERASE** *Pick the line indicated*

Command: **EXTEND**
Select boundary edge(s): *Pick boundary*
Select Object: ⏎
<Select objects to extend>:/Undo: *Pick the side walls*

18. Trim out the line between the walls.

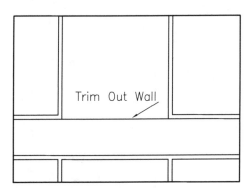

Command: **TRIM**
Select cutting edge(s)...   *Pick the wall you just extended*
<Select object to trim:>/Undo: *Pick the line between the walls*

19. Your drawing should look like the one at the beginning of the tutorial. Quit AutoCAD and Save Changes. You will continue in the following chapters to add the window wall and doors.

11

Drawing and Editing Polylines

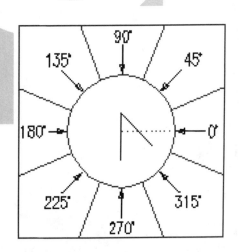

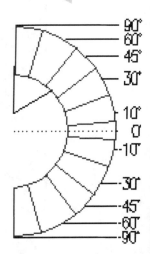

Polylines, or *plines,* are lines endowed with many properties. You edit plines with special commands. In this book we will deal
with the simpler modifications to plines.

- Pline/Polyline
- Pedit

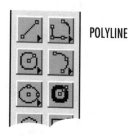 POLYLINE

DDMODIFY

PEDIT

● Pline/Polyline

A polyline can be a line segment, an arc, or a combination of both. It can have uniform or varying width. When one is drawn as connected segments, it acts as a single object. There is a special option for drawing 3-D polylines, but the examples in this book use only 2-D polylines. 3-D polylines can be drawn anywhere in x,y,z space.

Pline Options

- Width
- Halfwidth
- Arc
- Length
- Undo
- Close

Using the Pline Command

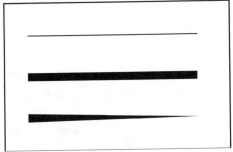
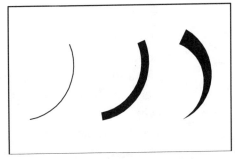

A line or arc drawn with the Pline command can have 0 width (in which case it looks like a regular line or arc), uniform width, or different beginning and ending widths.

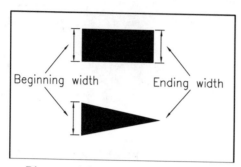
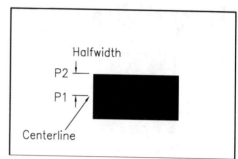

Pline width is specified by a beginning width and an ending width. Tapers are produced by specifying different beginning and ending widths. The Halfwidth option is useful when you are specifying a width using the screen cursor instead of typing in the value. For a pline having width, the cursor is attached to the pline's centerline. With the Halfwidth option, width is indicated by a rubber-banding line from the centerline of the pline to a point indicating its edge.

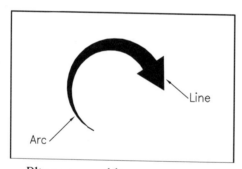
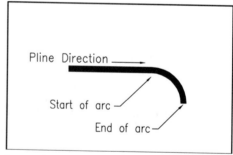

Pline arcs and lines can be combined; the widths of each can be varied to produce complex shapes. The default option for pline arcs is Start point, Endpoint, and Direction. Occasionally you may be surprised by the direction in which the arc is drawn—AutoCAD determines it from the last line or arc drawn.

Since you have already indicated a starting point, those Arc options for drawing arcs which begin with Start are available—Angle, Center, and 3-point (referred to as Second); you must, however, enter your choice from the keyboard.

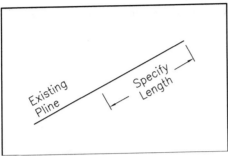

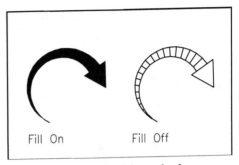

Fill On   Fill Off

   The Length option (L) draws a line segment of a specified length that continues in the same direction as the previous segment. (Do not confuse this with entering *L* for Line in the arc portion of the Line command; this changes you from arc drawing to line drawing.) When Fill is on, wide plines are drawn solid. When Fill is off, the individual segments are shown. Any change to Fill requires a regen before the change can appear on the screen.

   Using Undo inside the Pline command is the same as using Undo in the Line command—it steps you back and erases one segment at a time. The Close option also works the same in the Pline command as it does in the Line command—it closes a polygon by drawing a pline from the last point to the starting point.

Pline Notes

- As with the Line command, with Pline you must specify the starting point before any other specification is accepted.
- Plines are very useful in area calculations since both the perimeter and enclosed area can be accessed through the List and Area commands. Plines are often used in mapping applications to draw contour lines and roads.
- The Break command works on plines as it does on other entities.
- To change regular lines and arcs into plines or to modify the widths of plines, use the Pedit command.
- Plines can be disassembled into their component lines and arcs with the Explode command. When exploded, plines revert to 0 width.

- With a closed pline, the Fillet command works on all the vertices at one time.

● Pedit

Has many options to edit 2-D polylines, 3-D polylines, and meshes. This book covers the options that perform editing functions on the whole 2-D polyline and briefly explores the use of Grips to edit the vertices of polylines.

Pedit Options

- Close
- Join
- Width
- Fit curve
- Spline curve
- Decurve
- Ltype gen
- Undo
- eXit

Using the Pedit Command

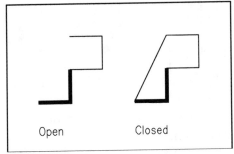

Open   Closed

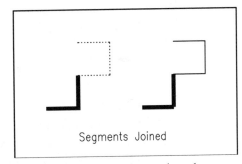

Segments Joined

Plines behave differently depending upon whether they are open or closed. Plines that have been used to make an enclosed form and whose last segment has been drawn with the Close (C) option are considered closed plines, and, as such, act as single objects or entities. When you choose the Pedit command and select the pline to edit, AutoCAD already knows whether the pline selected is open or closed. If the pline is closed, you are offered the Open option; if it is open, you are offered the Close option.

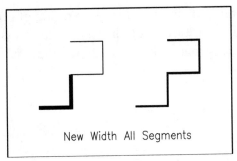

New Width All Segments

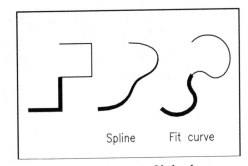

Spline   Fit curve

The Join option lets you join other plines to an existing one. If the lines you select are not plines, you are given the option of turning them into plines. For plines to be joined, they must meet at *exactly* the same point.

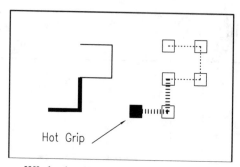

Hot Grip

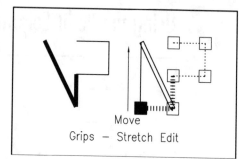

Move

Grips — Stretch Edit

With the Width option, you can select a new width for the entire pline. This new width will affect *all* the segments of the pline.

The Fit curve option replaces the straight lines between the vertices with arcs and results in a strongly curved line. The Spline curve option gives a smoother curve by "pulling" the line toward the vertices instead of forcing the line to pass through them.

Pedit will edit vertices in a polyline, but a much easier way to do simple vertex editing is by using grips. First you turn on Grips if not already on; select the polyline; make the grip hot at the vertex you want to edit and then move the grip to a new place. By using the shift key you can edit more that one vertex at a time.

The command Ddmodify offers a dialog box for easy editing of polylines. Polylines are just one of the many entities that Ddmodify edits. As you probably guessed by now, the *Dd* means that a dialog box is attached to the command.

```
┌─Properties──────────────────────────────────────────────────┐
│ [ Color... ] ■  BYLAYER          [ Layer... ]  0             │
│ [ Linetype... ]  BYLAYER         Thickness:  [ 0" ]         │
└─────────────────────────────────────────────────────────────┘

Polyline Type: 2D polyline       Entity Handle: None

┌─Vertex Listing─┐  ┌─Fit/Smooth─┐  ┌─Mesh─────────┐  ┌─Polyline─┐
│ Vertex:1 [Next]│  │ ◉ None     │  │ M:  ☐ Closed │  │ ☒ Closed │
│                │  │ ○ Quadratic│  │              │  │ ☐ LT Gen │
│ X: 86'-6"      │  │ ○ Cubic    │  │ N:  ☐ Closed │  │          │
│                │  │ ○ Bezier   │  │ U: [    ]    │  │          │
│ Y: 29'         │  │            │  │              │  │          │
│                │  │ ○ Curve Fit│  │ U: [    ]    │  │          │
│ Z: 0"          │  │            │  │              │  │          │
└────────────────┘  └────────────┘  └──────────────┘  └──────────┘

        ( OK )    ( Cancel )    ( Help... )
```

- The Decurve option undoes the effect of both of the curve options and makes the lines straight again.

- Ltype gen, when set to one (1), will make linetypes made with polylines look better by making the linetype continuous around all the vertices.

- The Undo option allows you to undo the last Pedit operation while remaining in the Pedit command.

- The Exit option exits you from the Pedit command.

TUTORIAL

● Drawing a Door and Window Unit

In this lesson, you will use plines to make drawings of a door and a window unit to use in your PLAN drawing. In the next chapter, you will turn these drawings into blocks. Blocks are drawings that have been "glued" together to make a cohesive symbol, which is both easier to use and cuts down on the size of your drawing database.

You will be doing two different kinds of drawings that you will make into blocks: The first is a window unit designed to be used as a full-size block; the second is a door designed to be a unit or 1″ symbol.

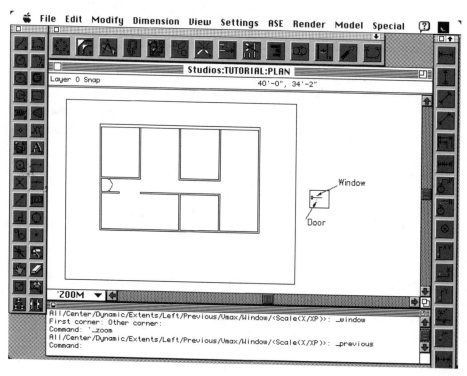

N O T E

Because of your growing familiarity with AutoCAD, commands that have already been covered appear in a condensed form. New commands and commands that may be confusing appear in full. (This lesson uses DDmodify, which is covered in Chapter 13; it is used to change the properties of plines.) The grid settings are sized to accommodate the dimensions in the drawing for ease of drawing. Use your own judgment about when to zoom; remember to use Osnaps to help you place points; and to press ⏎ to end your selection when you use the Verb-Noun form of command.

1. Use the right side of your Plan drawing to draw these symbols. These symbols will be small, so to help you find them make a square about 6'x6' (or 3 grid units by 3 grid units). Zoom in to the square.

2. Change the following settings:

Command: **Settings ➤ Drawing Aids**
Grid: X and Y: **0**
Snap: X and Y: **6"**

3. Start the drawing for the window unit, following the dimensions in the illustration. Use Pline to draw the column.

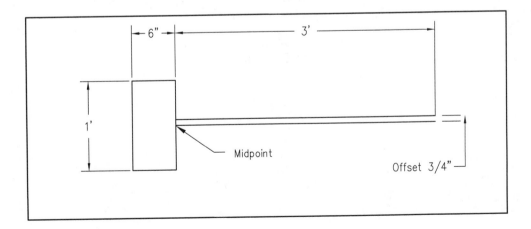

Command: **PLINE ➤ 2D Polyline**
From point: *Start the column*
Endpoint of line: *Continue drawing the three other corners of the column and finish with C*

4. Use the LINE ➤ 1 Segment command to draw the glass line 3' long from the midpoint of the side of the column.

5. Offset the glass line 3/4".

Command: **OFFSET**
Offset distance or Through <Through>: **3/4**
Select object to offset: *Pick line*
Side to offset ?: *Any point in the y direction*

6. You want these two glass lines to appear at the top of the window frame, as they are shown in the 3-D drawing at the beginning of the book. To get this effect, you must copy both lines upward 8' in the z direction.

Command: **COPY**
Select objects: *Select both lines*
<Base point or displacement>/Multiple: **0,0,8'**
Second point of displacement: ⏎

7. To give the column height, you have to change its property of thickness. Use the Ddmodify dialog box and enter the new value in the Thickness edit box.

Command: **Ddmodify**
Select objects: *Select the column*
Thickness: **8'**

8. You may want to see the results in 3-D. This topic is covered in Chapter 18, but for a quick look use the dialog box in Viewpoint to set the view. Click on the compass to rotate the dials (on some machines the dial may be off center). You can zoom in this view as you can in your plan view.

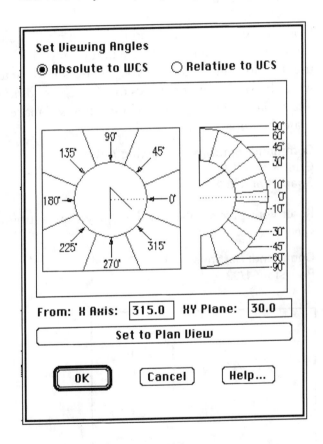

Command: **View ➤ Viewpoint ➤ Presets**
From: X Axis: **315.0**
XY Plane: **30.0**

9. To return to your plan view:

Command: **View ➤ Plan View ➤ Current UCS** (or type
PLAN and ⏎)

Drawing the Door Symbol

10. Doors have varying sizes and instead of making a drawing for
each door size, you will make a unit door of 1 inch. When you
use the block in a drawing, you will obtain the actual height and
width by specifying multiples of 1″, such as 30 *inches wide* and 96
inches high. Changing your snap settings will make it easier to
draw the door.

Command: **Settings ➤ Drawing Aids**
Grid: X and Y: **0**
Snap: X and Y: **1″**

11. Reset your precision so it will display the fraction when you
specify it.

Command: **Settings ➤ Units Control**
Precision: **1/32**

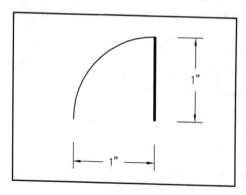

12. Use Pline to draw a door that will have some thickness.

Command: **PLINE ➤ 2D Polyline**
From point: *Start on a grid point* (Pt. 1)
Current line-width is 0'-0"
Arc/Close/Halfwidth/Length/Undo/Width/<Endpoint of line>: **W**
Starting width <0'-0">: **1/32**
Ending width <0'-0 1/32">: ⏎
Endpoint of line: **Pt 2**

13. Draw an arc for the door swing.

Command: **ARC ➤ Start, Center, Angle**
Start point: **Pt 2**
Center: **Pt 1**
Included angle: **90**

14. The height of the door must be *1 inch* so that you can multiply it later to get the actual door height. To do this, use the Ddmodify command to change its height as you did for the column. This time pick the command from the pop-up list box on the lower left of your screen.

Command: **DDMODIFY**
Select objects: *Pick the door only and not the swing*
Thickness: **1**

15. You have finished the door drawing. Reset your setting:

Grid = 2'
Snap = 1"
Precision = 0

16. Return to the view you saved in the VIEW settings.

Command: **View ➤ Named view ➤ Restore ➤ All**

17. Quit AutoCAD and save changes. In the next chapter you will find out how to make blocks out of the door and window drawings.

12

Making and Using Blocks

The commands described in this chapter are used to create what you have been accustomed to thinking of as symbols—items you drew using templates. If you are going to use an object more than three or four times in your drawing, it is a good practice to make a *block* out of it, because blocks take up much less space in your drawing file. A particularly useful property of blocks is that you can update them; when you update a block, all occurrences of it in a drawing are replaced with the new one.

The commands in this chapter are more complicated than the simple drawing and editing commands because they are processes that affect the entire drawing. This chapter covers both the simple uses of the commands and the techniques for using and updating blocks in drawings.

- Block
- Wblock
- Insert
- Xref
- Xbind
- Explode
- Base
- Oops

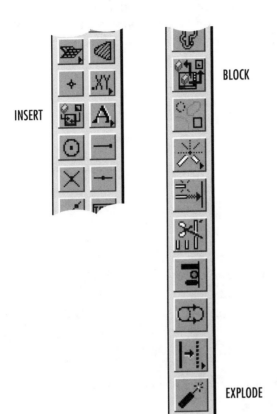

INSERT

BLOCK

EXPLODE

● Block

"Cements" together diverse entities into a single symbol after you have re-
sponded to three prompts. At that point the drawing disappears. If you want

*to reuse the original drawing, you can bring it back with the Oops command.
This command makes blocks that can be used only inside the current drawing. You must use the Wblock command to make a block that can be used in
other drawings.*

Block Options

- Block name (or ?)
- Insertion base point
- Select object

When making blocks you are asked for the following:

Block Name

Type in the name you want to give the symbol. Although you can make it as
long as 26 characters, it is a good idea to keep it fewer than 20. Spaces in file-
names and folders can cause problems so it is best to avoid them.

Insertion Base Point

The point on the block that is attached to your cursor when you insert the
block back into your drawing.

Select Object

When you select the object, make sure you get the entire object. If you do a
⏎ without selecting something, AutoCAD makes a block with nothing in it.

Using the Block Command

The Block command only makes blocks, it does not put them into a drawing.
Blocks are placed into a drawing with the Insert command. The Block command is selected by picking the icon, but all the responses must be typed in
to the command line.

Making Blocks

- When you select objects for a block, its a good idea to use a window for selection instead of individually picking each object. This way you can be sure to get the entire object. If you select something that should not be included, you can always type **R** for remove and cast out the offending object.

- A good check that you have made a block is that objects will disappear. You can bring the original drawing (not the block) back by typing the Oops command. Do not use Undo in this instance as it will un-block the block.

- An easy way to see what blocks are already in your drawing is to select the Insert icon and click on the box marked **File**. Alternately you can type **?** when asked for the block name and respond to the default <*> by pressing ⏎ (the asterisk stands for everything).

Insertion Points

- Insertion points are usually placed in the lower-left corner of the block, except when block usage would indicate otherwise. For example, circular objects, such as tables and trees, are easier to place if the insertion point is at the center.

Creating Blocks on Layer 0

- Blocks made on layer 0 carry a special adaptive quality. They take on the color and linetype of whatever layer they are inserted into. Blocks made on other layers retain the properties of the layer on which they were made.

Redefining a Block

- A block can be *redefined* inside a drawing by drawing another object and blocking it with the same name. AutoCAD warns you that a block with that name already exists. When you specify Y to redefine it, all occurrences of that block are changed (updated) to the new block. The original drawing no longer exists, having been replaced by the new one.

- If you want to substitute a block and still have the old one, you have to use the Wblock command covered in the next section.

- If you want to use an existing block as a base for the new chair drawing, it must be exploded first. Make sure that the insertion base point is the same for both blocks; otherwise, the new one will be inserted with a different orientation.

● Wblock

Writes the block definition onto your disk, allowing you to insert that block into any other drawing. You can Wblock a part of a drawing as a block or Wblock a block that already exists inside a drawing or even the entire drawing.

NOTE   Although you may distinguish blocks as symbols to be used in other drawings and different from drawings themselves, AutoCAD sees them all as drawings and assigns to them the file extension .DWG.

Wblock Options

- File name
- Block name

When making Wblocks you are asked for the following:

File Name   The file dialog box appears so that you can type in the name you want to give the block and select the appropriate folder on your hard disk.

Block Name The rules for naming blocks hold for Wblocks but here are additional options in responding to the *Block Name* :

Option	Meaning
=	Indicates that the Wblock name is the same as an existing block already in the drawing. There will be no more prompts, and the block will be written to the disk.
⏎	Equivalent to a blank response; the process that follows is similar to that for making a block. You must specify the insertion point and indicate what part of the drawing is to be Wblocked. As in the Block command, the part being Wblocked will disappear. Using the Oops command will bring it back.
*	A special response that causes the entire drawing to be written to the disk. There are no further prompts, and the drawing does not disappear. This is a quick way of purging unused items, such as blocks, layers, linetypes, and text styles. If you want to purge selectively, use the Purge command.

Using the Wblock Command

- The Wblock command writes the block definition to your disk, which means that it is now available to be inserted in any other drawing. You can Wblock a block that already exists inside the drawing or Wblock an object that has not been blocked previously.

- One of the advantages of using blocks is that you can automatically change all occurrences of a block in the drawing. *Redefining* is changing the block; *updating* is effecting the change in the drawing that contains the block.

- Blocks in drawings are like place holders. They have a name, location, and rotation. They keep these properties even after you redefine them. The name stays the same even though the block may look different.

T I P   Because drawings and blocks written to the disk are indistinguishable from one another, it is helpful to name drawings made expressly for use as blocks with some distinguishing character, such as a leading underbar. In this book, *B-* is used as a prefix for blocks, as in *B-DESK*.

● Insert

This is the command you use to bring blocks into drawings. You can insert blocks that are already in your current drawing or blocks that have been previously written to the disk. There are options that allow you to change the scale and rotation of the block at the time of insertion. The command is selected from the Insert icon and provides a dialog box to aid in locating the block you want to use.

Insert Options

- Block name (or ?)
- Insertion point
- X scale factor
- XYZ
- Corner
- Rotation

The command starts out with a dialog box.

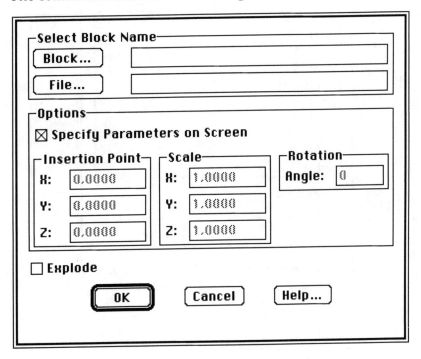

After the block is selected, it is placed in the drawing and the other options appear on the Command line.

Block Name

If the block you wish to use is in your current drawing select the **Block…** button. The blocks in your drawing will be shown in the list box.

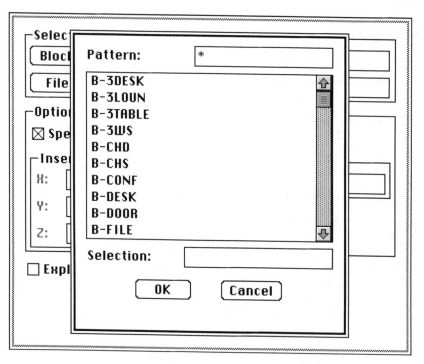

If the block you wish to use is a file on you hard disk, select the **File...** button. The file dialog box appears so you can locate the block.

```
┌─────────────────────────────────────────────────────┐
│                                                       │
│    ┌─ 🗁 BLOCK LIBRARY ▼ ─┐      ⊂⊃ Studios           │
│    │ 🗋 B-3CHRD          │ ⬆                           │
│    │ 🗋 B-3CHRS          │      ┌──────────┐           │
│    │ 🗋 B-3CHRS.dwg      │      │  Eject   │           │
│    │ 🗋 B-3DESK          │      └──────────┘           │
│    │ 🗋 B-3DFURN         │ ▓    ┌──────────┐           │
│    │ 🗋 B-3LOUN          │      │ Desktop  │           │
│    │ 🗋 B-3TABLE         │      └──────────┘           │
│    │ 🗋 B-3WS            │ ⬇   ─────────────           │
│    └────────────────────┘      ┌──────────┐           │
│                                │  Cancel  │           │
│    Select Drawing File         └──────────┘           │
│                                ┌──────────┐           │
│                                │   Open   │           │
│                                └──────────┘           │
└─────────────────────────────────────────────────────┘
```

The dialog box offers the additional option of specifying the parameters on the screen or presetting them in the dialog box. Check the option of *Specifying Parameters on Screen.* The option to preset scale, rotation, and insertion point isn't useful unless you know the coordinates for each block insertion.

The dialog box also offers the option of exploding a block. This will insert the block in its original (exploded) pieces. Do this if you want to modify the block you are inserting. Explode will return a block to its original entities and can be used at any time.

Insertion Point

The point at which you want the block placed in your drawing.

X Scale Factor

The scale in the x direction of the block as it was originally created. You will then be prompted for the Y scale factor, which defaults to the same value as the X scale factor unless you specify otherwise.

XYZ

Select this option by typing in **XYZ** if you want to specify a Z (height) scale for the block. Prompts for specific X, Y, and Z scale factors will follow.

Corner

Sizes the block by defining a rectangle.

Rotation

With the Rotation option you specify the degree of rotation or use your cursor to indicate the rotation on the screen. If you have the dynamic coordinate readout on (press F6), you can see the value of the angle (the default is 0).

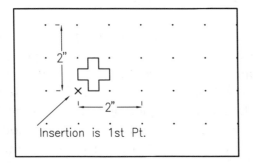

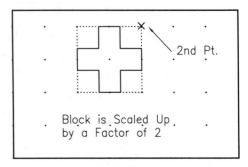

The Corner option is a visual option for specifying both the X and Y scale factors. The insertion point is taken as the first corner, and the second corner dynamically follows your cursor location, as though you were making a window. The distance from the insertion point is both the X and Y scale factor and can be positive or negative.

T I P

When redefining a block, *Block=Block* can be abbreviated to *Block=* if the block name is the same. If you get the message "Invalid File Name" when trying to insert a block, check to see that the file has a .DWG extension.

Using the Insert Command

The Insert command not only places a block in your drawing but also adds the block definition to your drawing database. The result of this is not always apparent. The following will try to explain some of the side effects inherent in block insertion.

Inserting a Block Database

Sometimes, you will want to insert an entire drawing just to bring in the blocks it contains, or to bring in layers or settings that are inside that drawing (the drawing *database*). In such a case, you don't want the actual drawing to appear in your current drawing. To insert only the database, respond to the *Insertion point* prompt by pressing ⌘+. (period), F2, or Ctrl+C.

T I P

A common beginner's error is using the Block command when they should have used the Insert command (since the prompts are similar). This can result in the original block being redefined as a blank block. You will then have to go back and remake the block from the original drawing.

Redefining Blocks from the Disk

To exchange an old block with a new one without destroying the old one, you have to use blocks that are taken from the disk. Because AutoCAD first looks for the block inside the current drawing when inserting blocks, you have to signal it to go to the disk to get the new block. Placing an = (equal sign) after the block name when inserting it instructs AutoCAD to go directly to the disk to get the block for insertion. Later in the book you will substitute a 2-D desk for a 3-D desk by using the Insert command and typing:

```
B-DESK=B-3DESK
```

When you change the design of a block and want to update it in the drawing, use the Insert command and call it from the disk by typing:

    B-BLOCK=B-BLOCK

Nested Blocks

Blocks inserted from the disk can be simple blocks or *nested* blocks. Nested blocks are blocks contained within other blocks or drawings. An example of nested blocks is the LIB-F drawing, which contains individual furniture blocks. When LIB-F is inserted into the PLAN drawing, all the blocks that are nested inside of LIB-F are also brought into the PLAN drawing.

Removing Blocks

- If you press Undo or ⌘+Z immediately after inserting a block it will be removed from your drawing.
- AutoCAD cannot remove blocks or drawings from a hard or floppy disk. You must use the Finder to effect these changes.
- You can remove *unused* blocks from your drawing with the Purge command.

T I P

When inserting blocks into drawings, occasionally a large ghost image of the block will appear. AutoCAD is dynamically scaling the block to your cursor movement—take your hand off the mouse to eliminate this confusing effect. If you click on the mouse when this scaling takes place, the block will be inserted at that, generally unusual, scale. Specify the scale and rotation for the block through the keyboard (generally three mouse clicks if you are inserting the block at the scale and angle that it was created). If you place a block on the wrong layer, use the DDmodify command to switch it to the correct layer. If you are having trouble updating a block, rename the one in your drawing, AutoCAD will then be forced to go out to the disk to bring in the block.

● Xref

Xref, which stands for external reference, allows you to bring a block (drawing) into another drawing on "temporary loan." When you edit your drawing, the latest version of the Xref drawing is loaded automatically into your current drawing.

Because the block is loaned temporarily, or externally referenced, your drawing size does not increase and the block is updated automatically in the drawing where it is inserted. This last property is of great help when updating blocks, a process that can confound even experienced users.

Xref Options

- Attach
- Bind
- Detach
- Path
- Reload
- ?

Using the Xref Command

The Attach option temporarily attaches the Xref to your current drawing. If you respond with a ~ (tilde) when asked for a name, a file dialog box appears from which you can make your choice. AutoCAD will then prompt you for the insertion point, scale, and rotation, just as in the Insert command. Nested blocks and layers that are attached along with the Xref carry the Xref's name as a prefix separated by ¦ (vertical bar). The blocks that come with the Xref are not available to be used independently unless you use Xbind. Externally referenced layers can be turned on and off but cannot be made the current layer.

The Bind option attaches the Xref to your current drawing (this is much like inserting a block). The information in the drawing database will be changed to reflect this binding and will show that there are no longer any external references and that the nested blocks have been renamed to include numbers with 0.

The Detach option removes Xrefs from your drawing.

The Path option shows the path that AutoCAD uses to find the Xref. If you change the location of the Xref'ed drawing, you can specify the new location. In the Macintosh the path is indicated by the disk name followed by the folder name, separated by colons as :Studios:Clients:Jones.

The Reload option is used when you want to update the Xref while in your current drawing. This is not a single-user function; it is used in a network environment, where someone else may be working on the Xref'ed drawing.

The ? option lists the Xrefs in your drawing.

● Xbind

Used when you do not want to bind the entire Xref, but only parts of it, such as its layer setup or blocks. These parts are referred to as independent symbols.

Xbind Options

- Block
- Dimstyle
- LAyer
- LType
- Style

TUTORIAL

● Making and Inserting Blocks

In this lesson you will convert drawings you have already made into blocks and insert them in the PLAN drawing. The door will be blocked in the drawing; the window will be Wblocked; each furniture piece will be blocked; and the entire furniture library drawing, LIB-F, will be brought into the PLAN drawing. All blocks in this book are made on layer 0, so they will take on the characteristics of whatever layer they are inserted onto.

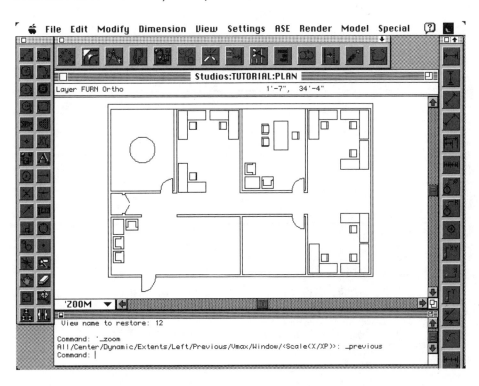

1. Open your PLAN drawing. You will block the window unit first. Because you plan to use this symbol in this drawing only, it is not necessary to write the symbol to the disk. Use XY filters to place the insertion point of the block at the center of the column.

Command: **BLOCK**
File name: **B-WINDOW**
Insertion base point: *Select .X from the XY Filter icon*
Pick midpoint of X (Use MID Osnap)
Pick midpoint of Y (Use MID Osnap)
Select objects: *Window the window unit* (Object disappears)

Use the Oops command to bring the window unit back in case you didn't make the block correctly. Do not use Undo because it will undo the block.

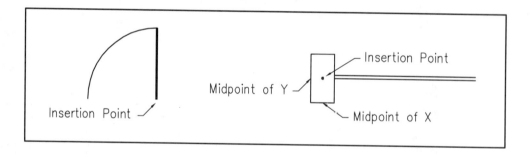

2. Wblock the door directly to the hard disk. When the dialog box appears, type in the name and make sure the destination folder is TUTORIAL.

Command: **WBLOCK**
Filename: **B-DOOR**
Block name: ⏎
Insertion base point: *Pick the hinge point*
Select objects: *Window the door and the swing* (Object disappears)

3. You will now go to the LIB-F drawing and make blocks of the furniture. Open the LIB-F drawing and save changes to the PLAN drawing.

Making Furniture Blocks

4. Block the executive desk.

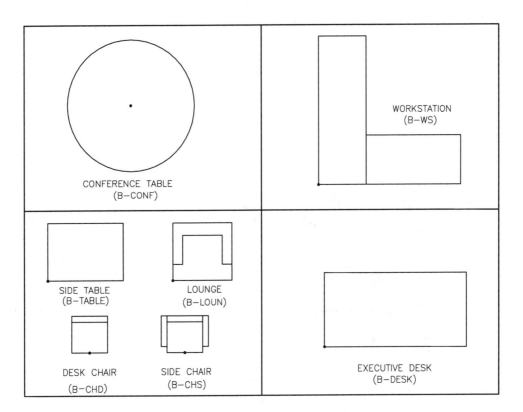

CONFERENCE TABLE
(B–CONF)

WORKSTATION
(B–WS)

SIDE TABLE
(B–TABLE)

LOUNGE
(B–LOUN)

DESK CHAIR
(B–CHD)

SIDE CHAIR
(B–CHS)

EXECUTIVE DESK
(B–DESK)

Command: **BLOCK**
Block name (or ?): **B-DESK**
Insertion base point: *Pick the point indicated by the dot*
Select object: *Window the desk* (The desk disappears)

If you want to bring the drawing back, use the Oops command. Do not use Undo, because that will undo the block.

5. Continue to make blocks out of the other furniture. The dots indicate the recommended insertion points. To simplify updating the 2-D blocks to 3-D blocks in later chapters, give the blocks the names in the parentheses. When you finish making the blocks click on the **Insert ➤ Blocks...** to check that you have made all the blocks. This is a good place to use the Command Pop-Up list to cycle between Block and Oops.

6. Instead of quitting AutoCAD you will open the PLAN drawing and Save the changes to the LIB-F drawing.

Inserting Doors

7. Make the DOOR layer current before inserting the doors.

8. Insert the B-DOOR symbol 4″ from the lower-right corner of the upper-left room using relative coordinates. First, use the ID command to set the corner of the room as the "last point" from which to specify relative distances. In the dialog box, locate the B-DOOR block in the File list box.

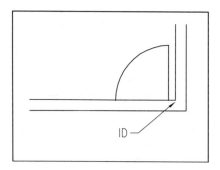

Command: **ID**
Point: *Pick the corner of the room* (Use Int Osnap)

9. Insert the door, using relative coordinates. To specify both height and width, enter **XYZ** at the prompt for the X scale factor.

Command: **INSERT ➤ File**…
Select Drawing File: **B-DOOR**
Insertion point: **@-4,0**
X scale factor <1>/Corner/XYZ: **XYZ**
X scale factor <1>/Corner: **30** (Door width)
Y scale factor (default=X): ⏎
Z scale factor (default=X): **96** (Door height)
Rotation angle <0>: ⏎

10. After inserting the door, draw the door jambs, using Osnaps to draw a line from the end of the door perpendicular to the wall and another from the end of the door swing perpendicular to the wall. These must be done accurately—otherwise the lines won't trim.

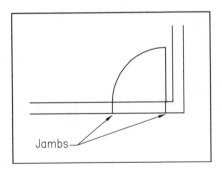

Jambs

11. Use Ddmodify to change the jamb lines to layer 0 with the rest of the walls.

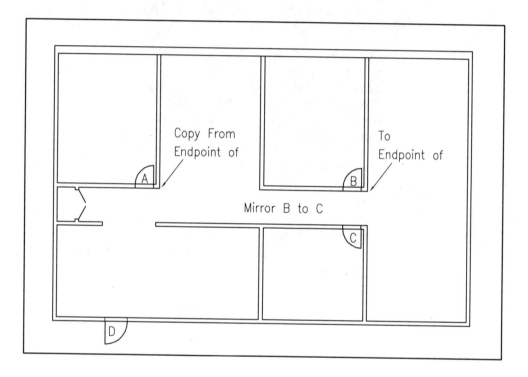

12. At this point you could insert the other door blocks, but since you have already drawn the door jambs, it is more efficient to copy and mirror both the door and the jambs: Copy door A and the jambs to the location for door B. With the End Osnap on, use the corner location of one room as the *from* point and the other corner as the *to* point.

13. Mirror door B to door C, using the midpoint of the back of the closet wall as the start of the mirror line.

14. Insert the door for the entrance. It will be 36" wide and rotated 180 degrees. Add the jambs and change the jamb lines to layer 0.

Command: **INSERT ➤ Block**...
Select Block Name (B-DOOR): ⏎ (Notice that the block now appears in the Block list)
Insertion point: *Line up door with left-hand side of corridor opening*
X scale factor <30>/Corner/XYZ: **XYZ**
X scale factor <30>/Corner: **36**
Y scale factor (default=X): ⏎
Z scale factor (default=X): **96**
Rotation angle <0>: **180**

15. Trim out the wall between the jambs.

Command: **TRIM**
Select the cutting edge(s)... *Window the whole plan* (You can always select more cutting edges than you will use)
<Select objects to trim>/Undo: *take out the walls between the doors* (This is a good time to use the Fence option)

Inserting Furniture Blocks

16. Before inserting furniture in the plan, make FURN the current layer.

17. To insert the furniture blocks, insert the LIB-F drawing in the PLAN drawing. This will bring in all the associated furniture blocks. Because you don't actually want to *place* the LIB-F drawing in the PLAN drawing, but just want to *insert* it so you can bring in the blocks, respond to the prompt for "Insertion point" by pressing F2, ⌘+. (period) or Ctrl+C. This is a standard way of inserting a whole library of blocks into a drawing.

Command: **INSERT ➤ File** ...
Select Block Name: **LIB-F** (You can see it ghosting on the screen)
Insertion point: F2

18. Place the furniture as shown in the drawing at the beginning of the tutorial. It is more efficient to place a workstation, along with its associated chair, and then to copy, mirror, and rotate them into place, than it is to place these blocks individually. If it feels easier to insert the blocks without rotating them, you can always rotate them later.

19. In the next chapter, you will complete the office layout with the help of other editing commands. Quit AutoCAD and Save changes.

13

Using and Modifying Objects

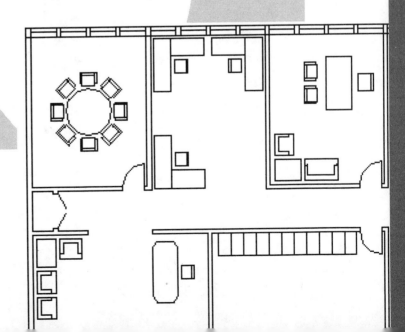

This chapter introduces you to AutoCAD's power editing commands. In using them, you will experience the advantage that the computer gives you over manual drafting.

SCALE

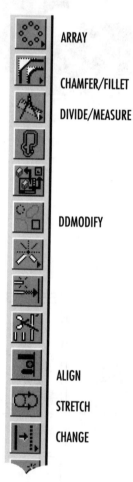

ARRAY

CHAMFER/FILLET

DIVIDE/MEASURE

DDMODIFY

ALIGN

STRETCH

CHANGE

You will be able to do things easily that were either difficult or nearly impossible to do by hand. This is truly "new drafting."

- Ddmodify [pf]
- Change [pf]
- Array [pf]
- Stretch [pf]
- Scale [pf]
- Measure
- Divide
- Fillet
- Chamfer
- Align

● Ddmodify

Ddmodify is one of three general editing commands—general in that they will change many of the properties associated with an entity. Ddmodify is the latest and the most comprehensive command for editing individual entities.

Ddmodify Options

There are four standard properties associated with most entities:

- Layer
- Linetype

- Color
- Thickness

Other options are entity specific.

Using the Ddmodify Command

The standard properties associated with entities are listed on the top section of the dialog box—color, linetype, layer and thickness. The bottom section is reserved for the properties specific to the entity that is being modified. Some of the entities that Ddmodify modifies are: Lines, Circles, Arcs, Blocks, Text, Xrefs, Points, Polylines, Viewports (in paper space), 3-D Faces, Attributes, and Dimensions (dimension has it own editing capability inside of the dimension command). Two examples are shown—Blocks and Text.

```
┌─Properties──────────────────────────────────────────────┐
│ [ Color... ] ■  BYLAYER        [ Layer... ]  DOOR        │
│ [ Linetype... ]  BYLAYER        Thickness:  [0"      ]    │
│                                                          │
│ Block Name: B-DOOR                                       │
│ ┌─At─────────────┐                                       │
│ │ [ Pick Point < ] │   H-scale: [3'    ]   Columns:  [0      ]│
│ │ H: [17'-0 5/8"] │   Y-scale: [3'    ]   Rows:     [0      ]│
│ │ Y: [7'-0 13/16"]│   Z-scale: [8'    ]   Col Spacing: [0"   ]│
│ │ Z: [0"        ] │   Rotation: [0    ]   Row Spacing: [0"   ]│
│ └───────────────┘                                        │
│ Handle: None                                             │
│              [ OK ]   [ Cancel ]   [ Help... ]           │
└──────────────────────────────────────────────────────────┘
```

In the last chapter you inserted blocks in your drawing. If you made an error in specifying the Z scale for the height, you can correct it in the dialog box which offers the option of changing the X,Y and Z scale *independently*. You can change block location by changing the coordinates, but the Pick Point option returns you to the graphic screen to make the selection and is more useful. Rotation can be changed at the same time by specifying the new angle. You can change the elevation by changing the Z value.

Properties

Color... ■ BYLAYER		Layer... BORDER	
Linetype... BYLAYER		Thickness: 0"	

Text: This is text

Origin

Pick Point <

X: 12'-9 5/8"

Y: 20'-5 3/8"

Z: 0"

Height: 1'-6"   Justify: Fit ▼

Rotation: 0   Style: STANDARD ▼

Width Factor: .85   ☐ Upside Down

Obliquing: 0   ☐ Backward

Handle: None

OK   Cancel   Help...

Ddmodify will edit a text string. Besides the standard properties, Ddmodify changes the following properties, which are specific to a string of text: Location, Height, Rotation, Width Factor, Obliquing Angle, Justification, Style, and even Upside Down and Backward. All these are options that you set when you define a text style (which is covered in Chapter 14).

T I P

It is easier to use Ddmodify than List to find information on an entity, for several reasons. First, it is quicker to pick a command from the icon than the menu bar. Second, the command window is too small to contain the information that the List command provides and so you have to zoom the window to fill size to read it. Third, listing information about an entity is generally a precursor to changing it; with Ddmodify, listing and changing can be done in one step.

● Change

The Change command actually comprises two separate commands—Change Properties and Change Points. Both of these will do multiple changes on multiple entities.

Change Properties Options

- Color
- Layer
- Linetype
- Thickness

Using the Change Properties Command

The Change Properties option acts similarly to Ddmodify except that it only modifies the four standard properties, *but* it will modify more than one entity at a time.

```
Color...   ■   BYLAYER (white)
Layer...       0
Linetype...    BYLAYER (CONTINUOUS)
Thickness:     0"

   OK          Cancel        Help...
```

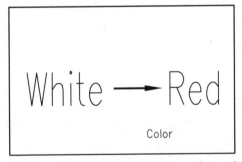

Color

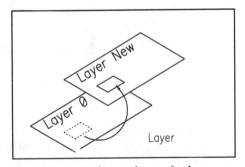

Layer

The Color option changes the color of an object, independent of what layer it is on. Don't use color this way if you expect to use color as a guide to layer identification. Set your colors by layer, and let the object take on the color of the layer. This way the color of an item will be an indication of the layer it is on. Color is also used to specify pen weight. The Layer option moves an object from one layer to another. This does not change the active layer. To do this, use the Layer command.

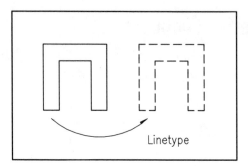

Linetype

The Linetype option changes the linetype of an object. If you are going to have more than a few special lines, it is better to assign a linetype to a layer and move those lines to that layer. Linetypes must be loaded before they can be used (see Chapter 16).

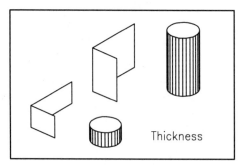

Thickness

Thickness is AutoCAD's term for what architects call height. You can use the Thickness option to give extruded height to lines, circles, arcs, plines, donuts, polygons, hatches, and even to text. Change Properties does not change the height of blocks, solids, or 3-D faces.

Using the Change Points Command

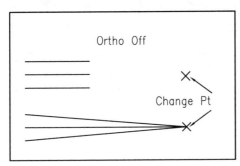

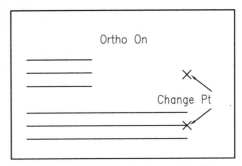

There is something that the Change Points option does that Ddmodify does not do: It will extend lines to a specified point. If the Ortho mode is on, lines that are parallel are extended to the new point but remain parallel. It will also operate on more than one entity at a time.

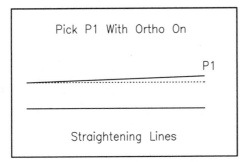

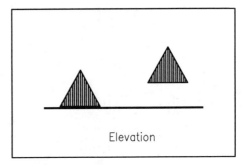

You can straighten lines that have "jogs" in them or that are not quite orthogonal by using Change Points with Ortho mode turned on and picking one end of the line as the "Change point." Use End Osnap for accuracy. Elevation of entities can be changed by using the P (Properties) option in the Change Points command. Elev will appear on the prompt line.

T I P There are a few methods for changing the elevation of multiple objects besides using Change Points. You could use the Move command to move them in the Z direction with a displacement of 0,0,n. For changing the elevation of single objects, Ddmodify works the easiest. At one time Change was used to make changes in text. Ddmodify is easier to use and provides more options. Use Ddmodify for most of your editing needs except for special cases like those above or when you want to edit multiple objects.

● Array

Repeats an object in a rectangular or circular pattern.

● Array Options
- Rectangular (R)
- Polar (P)

Using the Array Command

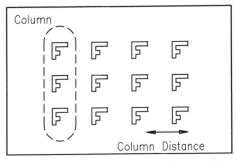

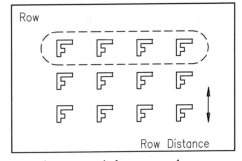

Rectangular arrays are made up of columns and rows and the spaces between each unit.

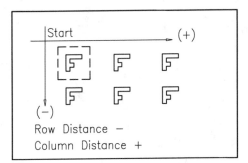

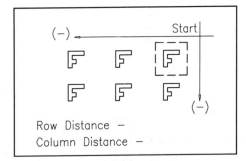

The direction for the rectangular array is determined by the negative

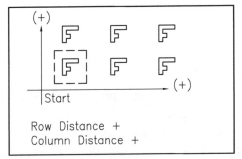

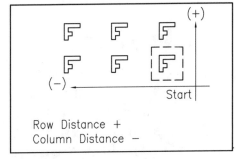

or positive values given to the row and column distances.

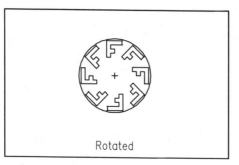

Rotated

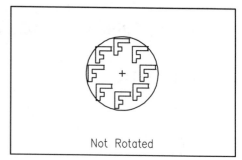

Not Rotated

In a polar array, you have the option of either rotating or not rotating objects as they are copied.

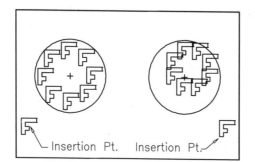

Insertion Pt.   Insertion Pt.

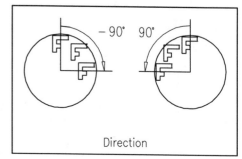

Direction

The direction for a polar array is determined by assigning a positive or negative value to the angle. If the object you are arraying is complex, you should make a block out of it so that it will be arrayed as a unit. The insertion point of the block should be at the center of the block. If the insertion point is not centered, your array could be off center.

Array Notes

There are many uses for the Array command:

- You can put a regular pattern of columns on a plan. (Nontypical columns could then be erased and inserted individually.)

- You can do seating layouts for restaurants and workstation clusters for offices. You can array lines in the z direction for items such as bookshelves.

- If you set your snap to a specific angle, you can array at an angle other than orthogonal.
- The 3-D rectangular array uses x, y, and z to produce cubic-looking configurations. This is not the way to draw stairs.

The objects placed by the Array command can be edited individually. If you are creating an array where you will not need to alter any of the objects, the Minsert command produces arrays that use less memory. They can be modified with the Ddmodify command but they can not be exploded. The Minsert command requires a block as the item to be arrayed.

● Stretch

Stretches or shrinks that portion of a drawing cut by a crossing window. Arcs, lines, plines, solids, and 3-D faces can be stretched; circles, text, and blocks cannot.

Using the Stretch Command

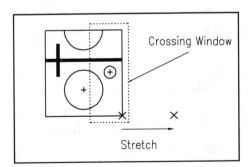
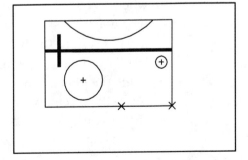

When you use the Stretch command, ends of lines and objects that are outside the crossing window are not moved. Objects completely inside the crossing window are moved along with the stretched items. Circles are considered to be inside if their centers are inside the crossing window.

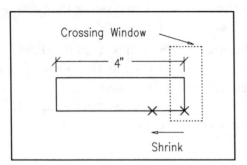 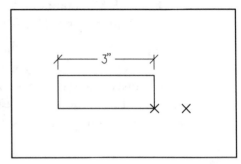

Changing the size of the object also changes the dimensioning shown if associative dimensioning is turned on (see Chapter 15).

Stretch Notes

- The Stretch command is used to alter size in one direction only. If you want to change both the x and y dimensions, use the Scale command.

- The crossing window is supplied automatically when you pick the command from the icon. If you type in the command, you must specify a crossing window to select the objects.

- You can enter the amount you want an object stretched by typing in 0,0 when asked for a base point, and the amount of displacement when asked for the new point. As an example, a base point 0,0 and new point 2,0 stretches a line 2 inches in the x direction; a new point of −2,0 shrinks the line 2 inches.

- When you are stretching an object that has dimensioning, do not include the dimension text in your box; this way, the new dimension text will be centered on the new dimension line. If your new dimension text happens to be inserted off-center, use the Hometext option in the Dim command (see Chapter 15).

When stretching, keep Ortho mode turned on to keep your lines straight.

● Scale

Changes the size of the items selected to whatever new size you specify. Changes in x and y will be identical. You can indicate the amount to be scaled by typing in a number, or you can use the screen cursor to show the amount.

Scale Options

- ● Scale factor
- ● Reference

Using the Scale Option

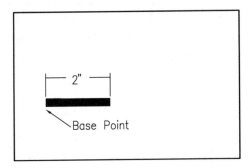

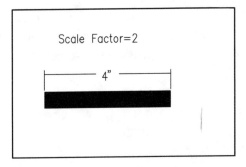

The default option asks for a scale factor. This is a single number indicating how much the item should be scaled: 2 indicates that the object should be enlarged two times. You can also move your cursor on the screen to scale dynamically: 1 unit produces an object the same size, 2 units enlarges the object two times.

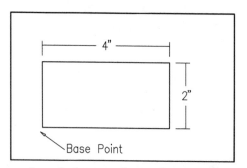
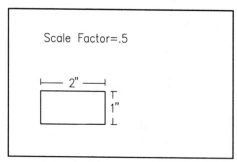

A scale factor of .5 reduces the object to one-half size.

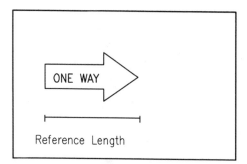
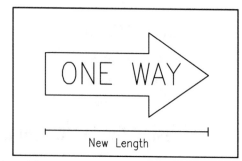

The Reference option asks for the original length (the reference length) and the new length. You can type these lengths in, or you can show the two lengths on the screen by pointing with your cursor.

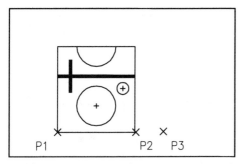

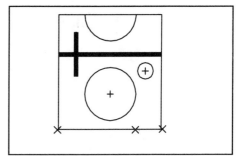

If you are using the pointing method, the first and second points indicate the reference length and the third point indicates the endpoint of the new length.

The Scale option also changes the sizes of blocks. Notice that, when scaling up a drawing, plines with width are also enlarged.

● Measure

Measures out specified lengths along lines, plines, circles, and arcs. These segments can be marked off with regular points, complex points, or blocks.

Measure Options

- Segment length
- Block

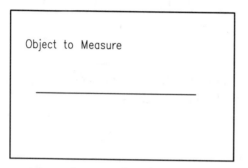
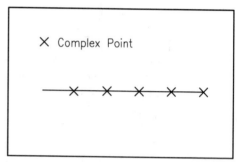

After selecting the object, you are asked for a segment length. Measuring starts nearest to the end you specify. The segments will be marked with points. These points are difficult to see, though you can use the Osnap mode *Node* to snap to them. A better solution is to redefine the standard point as a complex point (see Chapter 5).

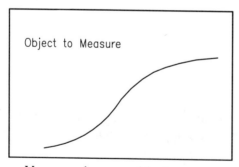
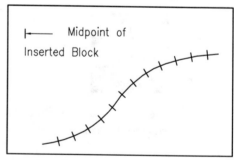

You can also use a block as a measuring marker. This block *must* be in the drawing. Generally, you will want to accept the option to align the block with the object being measured, but you also have the option not to.

T I P   You can make railroad lines by using a block for the ties or can indicate different utility lines by using a letter as a block.

● Divide

Divides lines, plines, circles, and arcs into the number of segments specified. These segments can be marked off with regular points, complex points, or blocks.

N O T E   The command forms for Measure and Divide are almost identical, except that Measure measures out specific lengths, and Divide divides an object into a specific number of segments.

Divide Options
- Segment length
- Block

Using the Divide Command

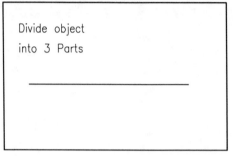 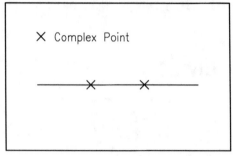

After selecting the object to be divided, you are asked for the number of segments. The segments will be marked off with points, though these are difficult to see. As in the Measure command, you can use the Osnap mode *Node* to snap to them and can use complex points to make the standard points more visible (see Chapter 5).

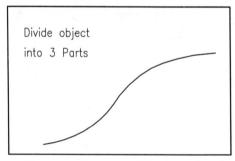 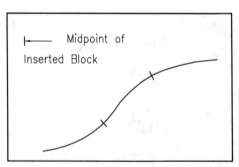

You can also use a block as the dividing marker. This block *must* be in the drawing. Generally, you will want to accept the option to align the block with the object being divided, but you also have the option not to.

● Fillet

Draws a user-specified radius curve between two lines. If the specified radius is 0, the lines chosen will automatically be trimmed or extended to meet each other.

Fillet Options

- Select two objects
- Polyline
- Radius

Using the Fillet Command

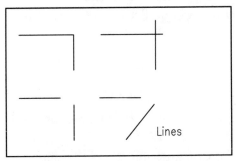

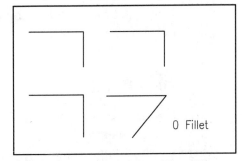

The default option asks you to select two lines you want to fillet. The Fillet command will work even if the lines selected intersect each other or do not meet. When you specify a 0 radius, the lines are trimmed at their intersection.

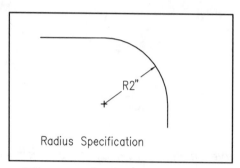

Radius Specification

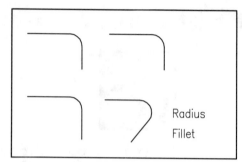

Radius
Fillet

The curve for filleting is determined by the actual radius of the fillet. Auto-CAD's default option is 0, so to draw a radius curve, you must first set the radius with the Radius option and then enter the Fillet command *again* to select the two lines.

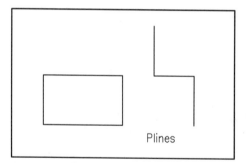

Plines

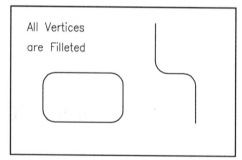

All Vertices
are Filleted

To fillet plines, select the Polyline option. Because plines are single entities, you only have to select one point to fillet all the vertices.

Fillet Notes

- You can use the Crossing option to select the ends of lines you want to fillet.
- The Fillet command also works on arcs and circles. To avoid unexpected results, the points you pick should be closest to the ends you want to fillet.
- You cannot fillet lines parallel to each other.
- If you want to undo a fillet you have made, use the Undo command.

T I P

You can use the Fillet command to make radius curves on driveways and radius edges on furniture. With a 0 radius, it will clean up wall intersections.

● Chamfer

Bevels corners; similar to the Fillet command, except that Chamfer asks for two distances and Fillet asks for a single radius. As with Fillet, if the distance specified is 0, the lines will automatically be trimmed or extended to meet each other.

Chamfer Options

- Select two objects
- Polyline
- Distance

Using the Chamfer Command

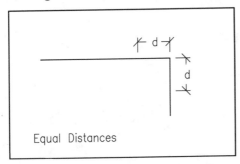

Equal Distances

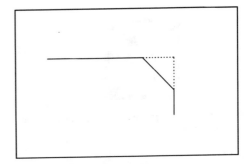

Because the AutoCAD default distance is set to 0, to get a chamfer, you first have to use the Distance option to set the amount for each side you want to trim back. You then reenter the Chamfer command, and pick the first and second lines that correspond to the distances you have specified. Distances can be equal.

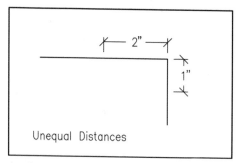

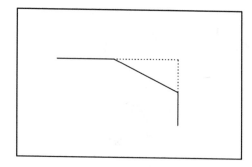

Unequal Distances

Or, distances can be different.

Chamfer Notes

- Chamfer works the same on plines as the Fillet command. To chamfer plines, select the Polyline option. Because plines are single entities, you only have to select one point to chamfer all the vertices.
- If you want to undo a bevel you have made, use the Undo command.

● Align

Align will line up an object with one, two or three different planes.

Using the Align Command

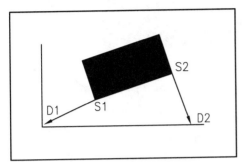 

Align can act as a combination of the Rotate and Move commands.

TUTORIAL

● Continuing Work on the Office Plan

In this lesson you will use some of the new editing commands you have learned about to continue refining your office plan. First, open the PLAN drawing.

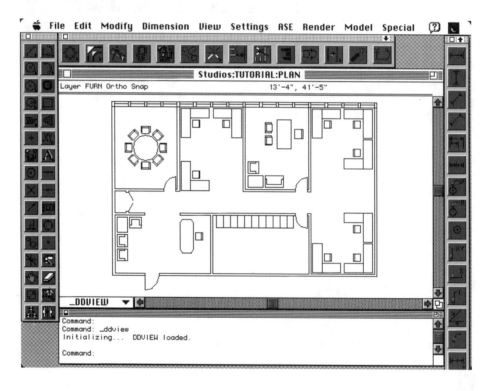

1. Make Window the current layer.

2. The window wall will be made by inserting the window block you made in Chapter 11 and arraying it. You could use the End Osnap to simply place the block, but to have an opportunity to see how the Align command works, insert the block off to the side and rotate it. You will then use the Align command to put it in place.

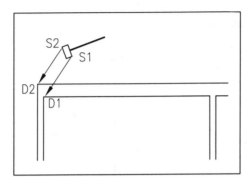

Command: **INSERT GRAPHIC ➤ ...Block**
Block name (or ?): **B-WINDOW**
Insertion point: *Choose point near building*
X scale factor <1>/Corner /XYZ: ⏎
Y scale factor (default=X): ⏎
Rotation angle <0>: **20** ⏎

Command: **ALIGN**
Select objects: *Pick window block*
1st source point: *Pick corner S1 of the column* (Use END Osnap for all points)
1st destination point: *Pick corner of building D1*
2nd source point: *Pick corner S2 of the column*
2nd destination point: *Pick the outside corner of the building D2*
3d source point: ⏎ (You need to press ⏎ twice to terminate the command)
<2d> or transformation: ⏎

3. Array the block to make the window wall. You will make one more unit than you need because you need a column at the end.

Command: **ARRAY ➤ 2D**
Select objects: *Pick the window block*
Rectangular or Polar array (R/P): **R**

Number of rows (---) <1>: ⏎
Number of columns (|||) <1>: **17**
Distance between columns (|||): **42**

4. Explode the last window block and erase the two glass lines. The block will change color because it reverts to layer 0.

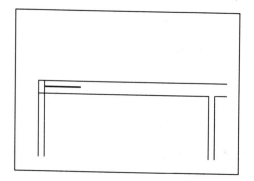
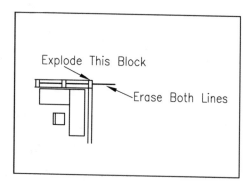

5. Change the column to the WINDOW layer and set the current layer to FURN because you will be inserting furniture into your drawing.

6. Insert the side chair, B-CHS, as shown. Use the polar array to place chairs around the conference table. Use the center of the table as the center of the array.

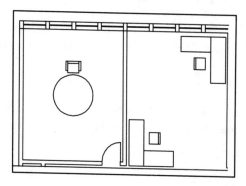
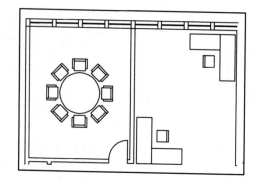

Command: **ARRAY ➤ 2D**
Select object: **L** (This will pick the chair you just inserted)
Rectangular or Polar Array (R/P): **P**
Center point of array: *Use CEN Osnap*
Number of items: **8**
Angle to fill (+=ccw, −=cw) <360>: ⏎
Rotate objects as they are copied? <Y>: ⏎

7. Scale up the desk chair in the executive office.

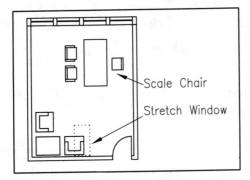 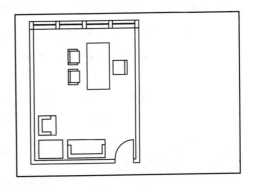

Scale Chair
Stretch Window

Command: **SCALE**
Select object: *Pick the chair*
Base point: *Pick the center of the chair*
<Scale factor>/Reference: **1.25**

8. Before you can stretch the lounge chair into a sofa, you will first
have to explode the lounge block. The block reverts to layer 0.
Change it back to the FURN layer. Use Change ➤ Properties
instead of Ddmodify because the sofa, when exploded, has
many lines.

9. Stretch the lounge chair.

Command: **STRETCH**
Select objects: *Window the part you want to stretch*
Base point: *Select right corner of lounge chair*
New point: *Move cursor 2′6″ in the 0 direction* (It helps to have Ortho on)

NOTE It would be more efficient to *insert* the chair block with a scale of 1.25 and the lounge with an X scale of 2 and a Y scale of 1; however, doing it this way gives you the opportunity to use the new editing commands you learned in this chapter.

10. You will now use the Stretch command to *move* a wall. This technique leaves no breaks in the wall.

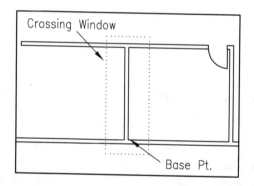
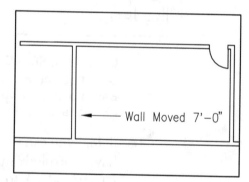

Crossing Window

Base Pt.

Wall Moved 7'-0"

Command: **STRETCH**
Select objects: *Window as shown*
Base point: *Select corner*
New point: *Move cursor 7′-0″ in the 180 degrees direction* (It helps to have Ortho on)

11. You will use the Measure command to make the row of files in the file room but first you must create the file block. Draw the file using the Rectangle command and then make a block out of it and name it B-FILE.

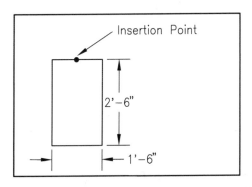 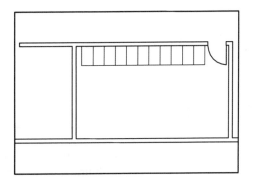

Command: Rectangle
First Corner: *Anywhere*
Other Corner: **@1'6,2'6**

12. Use the Block option of the Measure command and specify the file block.

Command: MEASURE
Select object to measure: *Pick the upper wall*
<Segment length>/Block: **B**
Block name to insert: **B-FILE**
Align block with object? <Y>: ⏎
Segment length: **1'6** (width of file cabinet)

13. The last task remaining is to make the reception desk. Use Line
➤ Segments, follow the dimensions in the drawing, and chamfer

the corners as shown. The long side is picked first to match the longer chamfer distance.

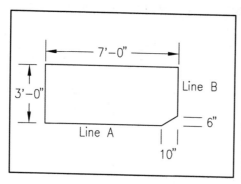 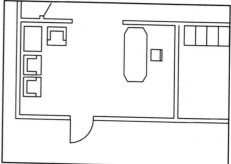

Command: **CHAMFER**
Polyline/Distances/<Select first line>: **D**
Select first chamfer distance: **10**
Enter second chamfer distance: **6**

14. Start the Chamfer command again.

Command: **CHAMFER**
Polyline/Distances/<Select first line>: *Pick line A*
Select second line: *Pick line B*

15. Finish off the other three corners, following the same procedure—picking the longer side first. When finished with the desk, rotate it into place and add a chair. At this point you have a complete 2-D office plan. Only two objects, the doors and windows, are in 3-D; the rest will be redrawn in 3-D in Chapter 18.

16. You have made and used the door and window block successfully, so erase the original ones on the side of your drawing.

14

Adding Text to Your Drawings

📁 AutoCAD Releas

- 📁 ADS
- 📁 ASI
- 📁 Fonts
- 📁 IGESFont
- 📁 Plot Files
- 📁 Sample
- 📁 Source

No more lettering guides, Leroy pens, and ink smudges—AutoCAD provides a wide variety of fonts, sizes, and spacings for you to use with text in your drawings. If there aren't enough typefaces to suit you, there is a large assortment provided by third-party software vendors.

- Dynamic Text/Dtext
- Import Text
- Set Style
- Quicktext

Dynamic text import text set style

● Dynamic Text/Dtext

Allows you to place notes on drawings, import text from word processing programs, and create different text styles using a variety of fonts.

Dtext Options

- Start point
- Justify
- Style

Using the Dtext Command

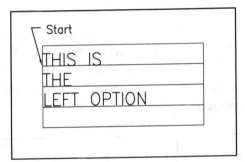

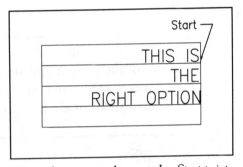

The default option is left-justified text; you start it by responding to the *Start point* prompt by indicating where you want the text to begin. You will be prompted for a height, unless the text style you are using already has the height specified (see "Set Style"), and for rotation. The square marker on the screen indicates your letter size. For all other types of justification, you must first select the Justify option. The right-justified option places text so that the right-hand margin is aligned.

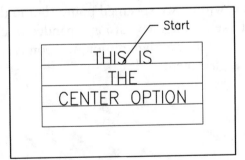

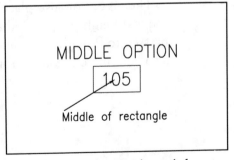

The Center option centers each line of text after you have selected the center point. The Middle option places the midpoint of a single line of text at the point you specify. This is particularly useful for placing numbers and letters inside of callouts for items such as room numbers and column indicators.

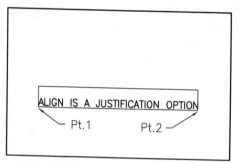 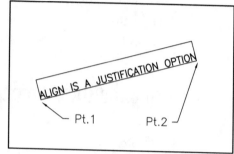

The Align option places text within two specified points, using the proportions of the current text style. Height is not required for the placement because it is predicated on the style proportion. The points specified also determine the angle for text placement.

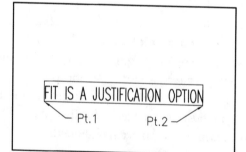 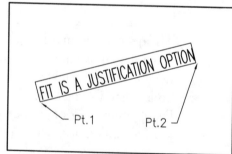

The Fit option also places text within two specified points, but in this case the text height is specified and fixed while the width is expanded or compressed to fit within the space. As with the Align option, the points specified also determine the angle for text placement.

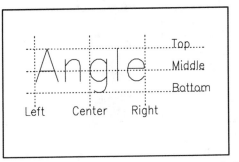

The BEST one.

The %%uBEST%%u one.

75°

75%%d

The alphabet soup—TL/TC/TR/ML/MC/MR/BL/BC/BR—lists the justification options available, which allow for greater precision in placing text. The letters indicate top, middle, or bottom horizontal placement and right, center, or left vertical placement.

The double percent sign (%%) allows you to insert some special symbol codes in your text:

Code	Format/Symbol
%%u	Underscore—you must indicate both on and off
%%o	Overscore—you must indicate both on and off
%%d	Degree symbol
%%p	Plus and minus tolerance symbol
%%c	Circle diameter symbol

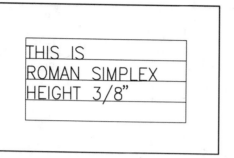
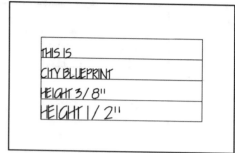

PostScript fonts are sized for printing and not for drafting. To make their heights approximate text sized in inches, they have to be made approximately one third larger. Depending upon your need for accuracy, you may want to enter PostScript text heights in decimals, as shown in this list of equivalents:

Standard Text Size	Equivalent PostScript	1/4" Plotted	1/8" Plotted
1/16"	.0833	4"	8"
3/32"	.1250	6"	12"
1/8"	.1666	8"	16"
1/4"	.3332	16"	32"

The Style option allows you to select a style for your text from those styles already designed (see "Set Style"). If you are going to change styles, you should select this option before picking the Justify option. If you don't remember the names of the styles you have made you can get a list of them by typing Style, responding with a ? and then ⏎ when prompted to get a list of the styles in your drawing.

Dtext Notes

Text is entered the same way as you normally do when you type.

- The Backspace key erases a letter at a time, up to the start of the current entry.

- The ⏎ key terminates a text line and starts another one directly under the previous line.
- Because a single ⏎ is the indication for a new line, two ⏎s are necessary to indicate the end of text entry.
- The type of justification you specify remains in effect until you reenter the Dtext command. The justification will revert to left if you move your cursor and pick another location.
- If you have chosen anything else except the left-justified default option, the actual text placement, such as centered or right-justified, will not occur until you have finished the command.
- In both the Aligned and Fit options, the points picked indicate the rotation, so you will not get a rotation prompt for either of these commands. The right-, center-, and left-justified options are used for multiple lines of text, and the Align, Fit, and Middle options are used to place single lines of text.
- The Text command is the older command for placing text and has almost been supplanted by Dtext, because Dtext is easier to use. Text is now mainly used when you want to use a script to import a text file.

T I P

You only have to specify the first letter of the option when making your selection. You usually pick the starting point for text with your screen cursor, but you can also type in absolute coordinates. Although you usually type in the text height, you can also specify it on the screen by entering two points. This can be particularly useful when using PostScript fonts where the numerical size is about one-third smaller than standard AutoCAD text.

● Import Text

When you select Import Text, the Asctext Lisp program is automatically loaded. It has numerous options to modify the text you are importing. You are prompted for each option offered and the file is inserted after the last prompt.

Using Import Text

The text file you are importing must be in "Text Only" or Ascii format. Most word processor programs will save text files in Text Only format. Before you bring the file into AutoCAD set the style for the incoming file.

When you select Import Text you will get the following prompts:

```
Start point or Center/Middle/Right/?:
Height <.2000>: (Set height here unless predefined in the text style)
Rotation angle <0>:
Change text options? <N>: (If you enter Y you will get the following
additional prompts)
Distance between lines/<Auto>: (Auto is a good choice to start)
First line to read/<1>: (You can select where in the document to start)
Number of lines to read/<All>: (And where to end)
Underscore each line? <N>: (Does it by entering the %% code for un-
derline. To underscore a few lines, use Line)
Overscore each line? <N>: (Overkill)
Change text case? Upper/Lower <N>: (All of one or the other)
Set up columns? <N>: (Easier to format the columns in the
text editor)
```

Making Changes to Text in a Drawing

The ability to change text is important, because text is frequently entered in the wrong size or with spelling mistakes or other errors. Ddmodify will change text location, height, spelling, or style type. Changes cannot, however, be made globally; each line of text must be handled individually.

Changing Text with a LISP Program

There are many LISP programs that deal with text modifications—some from Autodesk, many from third-party vendors. Autodesk provides one called *Chtext* in the Support folder. It can change the height, width, justification, location, or style of multiple lines of text, or replace a string of text globally. Bringing Lisp programs into AutoCAD is covered in Chapter 16 but the description of the Chtext program is covered here.

Start the program by typing **CHT**.

You can select specific text or window the drawing. The program will ignore everything except text entities. The main prompt and options are as follows:

Height/Justification/Location/Rotation/Style/Text/Undo/Width:

Height Indicate new height for all text entities. If you are not sure of the current height type **L**. It does the best it can when there are multiple heights. It states a minimum, maximum, and an average height.

Justification The options are

Aligned/Center/Fit/Left/Middle/Right.

Location Active text is highlighted and the cursor is attached to the insertion point of each line of text. Pick points for new location.

Rotation New rotation angle.

Style Prompts for a new style name for all text or selected entities. Type L to get a list of styles in your selection. If you haven't created the style, you can use the Set Style (which functions transparently) and set one on the fly and then return to Chtext.

Text This option will search and replace text, individually or globally, much as word processing programs do. You can also choose to retype lines of text.

Width Allows you to expand or compress text as you can do when you specify a style.

Plotting Text Size

Text size, along with hatches, dimension components, and linetypes, is sensitive to final plotting size. Because plotting reduces the drawing by the scale amount, text size has to be increased by the same amount. For example, the architectural scale $1/8''=1'$ translated into inches is $1''=96''$. This number, *96*, is the *scale factor*—the multiplier used to multiply text to compensate for the plotting scale reduction.

The chart below shows how to specify the appropriate text heights in AutoCAD for the three sizes of text commonly used in architectural drawings:

Drawing Scale	Scale Factor	Plotted Text Size	AutoCAD Text Height
$1/8''=1'$	96	$3/32''$	$9''$
		$1/8''$	$12''$
		$1/4''$	$24''$
$1/4''=1'$	48	$3/32''$	$4.5''$
		$1/8''$	$6''$
		$1/4''$	$12''$

In *paper space* text is sized to the actual size on the plotted sheet (this will be covered in Chapter 18).

● Set Style

Lets you design how your text will look. The font, width, and obliquing options are used to style text. Font selection includes standard AutoCAD and fifteen PostScript type 1 fonts. Examples of these fonts are in Appendix B.

Style Options

- Text style name
- Font file

- Width factor
- Height
- Obliquing factor
- Backwards
- Upsidedown
- Vertical

Using the Style Command

The icon screens showing the font appear as soon as you choose Set Style. The name of the font that you select becomes the style name.

By modifying the width factor, you can give text an expanded or condensed look.

When you specify a height for a style, you will not get a height prompt when using the Dtext command. If you specify a 0 height, you will be prompted for the height each time you enter the Dtext command.

The obliquing angle affects the forward or backward slant of the lettering.

There are three lesser-used options that you may like to explore: Backwards, Upsidedown, and Vertical. They modify the orientation of text.

Style Notes

Beginners often confuse the Style *command* with the Style *option* in the Dtext command. The Style command designs how text will look. The Style option in the Dtext command only *selects* an existing style.

When you create a style, it becomes the current style.

The style that is set in the prototype drawing is called *Standard*. It uses TXT as its font, which because of its simplicity, is the most efficient one for AutoCAD to draw. Many users find the square zeros that this font produces unaesthetic and substitute it with the Roman Simplex text font.

You can globally change the font in a style already used in your drawing by redefining the style and selecting a different font. At the next regeneration, all the text with that style name will be changed to reflect the newly defined style. Height, width, and obliquing angle cannot be changed globally this way.

You can use this technique to "style up" a drawing before plotting: Define styles using the TXT font (because it is more efficient) and then redefine them with a more complex font when the drawing is completed.

If you want to have more than one style using the same font enter Style from the keyboard. You will be asked for a style name. Provide a name and then select a font by opening the font file. The rest of the procedure is the same as when you select the command from the icon.

```
┌─────────────────────────────────────────────────┐
│  📁 AutoCAD Release 12 ▼          ⊂⊃ Kong         │
│  ┌──────────────────────────┐  ┌──────────────┐  │
│  │ 🗀 ADS                 ⬆ │  │    Eject     │  │
│  │ 🗀 ASI                ▓  │  └──────────────┘  │
│  │ 🗀 Fonts              ▓  │  ┌──────────────┐  │
│  │ 🗀 IGESFont           ▓  │  │   Desktop    │  │
│  │ 🗀 Plot Files            │  └──────────────┘  │
│  │ 🗀 Sample                │  ┌──────────────┐  │
│  │ 🗀 Source                │  │    Cancel    │  │
│  │ 🗀 Support            ⬇ │  └──────────────┘  │
│  └──────────────────────────┘  ┌──────────────┐  │
│                                │     Open     │  │
│  Select Font File              └──────────────┘  │
└─────────────────────────────────────────────────┘
```

TIP   To find out what styles you have in your drawing, type **Style**, then a question mark, and when prompted for "Text style(s) to list <*>" respond with a ⏎.

● Qtext

Temporarily replaces text in a drawing with rectangular boxes.

Using the Qtext Command

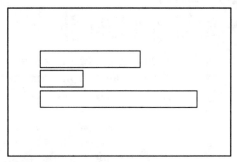

```
THIS IS
THE
QTEXT EFFECT
```

Text slows down the time it takes for AutoCAD to display your drawing. The Qtext command offers a way to deal with this by temporarily replacing text with rectangular boxes, allowing you to see the text location without actually drawing in the text. You must use the Regen command before the effects of Qtext can be seen.

N O T E

Attribute handling is beyond the scope of this book. An *attribute* is text information that is incorporated into a block to be used to retrieve data on the block. George Omura's book *Mastering AutoCAD Release 12*, SYBEX, 1992, although a book on the DOS platform, gives an excellent exposition on using attributes.

TUTORIAL

● Making a Title Block

In this lesson you will use the Text and Style commands to design a title block. Use the dimensions and the grid to help place lines and text. You can personalize your own title block by substituting your own name, office, and projects.

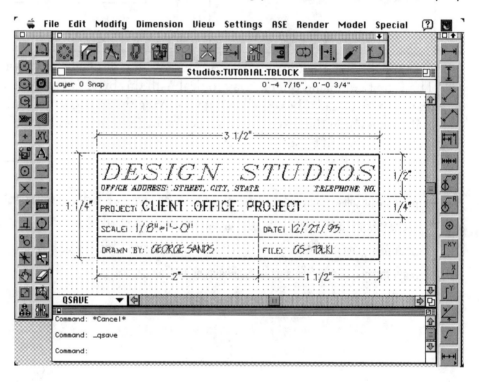

1. Start a new drawing called TBLOCK, and use the following settings:

Limits: **0,0; 6,3**
Units: Architectural
Precision: **1/32**

Snap: X and Y: **1/16** *and* ***On***
Grid: X and Y: **0** *and* ***On***
Blips: **Off**
Ortho: **On**
Coords: **On**

2. Using the dimensions shown in the lesson drawing, draw a border for the title block with a pline width of .01.

3. Use the Line command to draw the other divisions inside the border.

Creating Styles

The chart that follows gives the settings for all the text in the title block. As you become familiar with the operation of the Style and Dtext commands, you may find this chart easier to use than the step-by-step directions.

TEXT	STYLE OPTIONS	DTEXT OPTIONS
DESIGN	Style = Italic Complex Height = 0 Width = .9	Justified = Fit Height = 3/16
OFFICE ADDRESS	Same as above	Height = 1/16
TELEPHONE NO.	Same as above	Height = 1/16 Justified = Right
CLIENT	Style = Romand Duplex Height = 1/8 Width = .85	
SCALE:	Style = Standard Height = 0 Width = 1	Height = 1/16
1/8"=1'-0"	Style = City Blueprint Height = 1/8 Width = 1	
All text is left justified unless indicated otherwise. Allow 1/16 minimum allowance above and below text.		

4. Create the style for *Design Studios.* Leave the height at 0, because you will want to vary it using the Dtext command.

Command: **SET STYLE** (Select from tool palette)
New style: *Select from icon menu*
New style: **Italic Complex**
Height <0'-0">: ⏎
Width factor <1.00>: **.90**
Obliquing angle <0>: ⏎
Backwards? <N>: ⏎
Upsidedown? <N>: ⏎
Vertical? <N>: ⏎

Italic Complex is now the current text style.

5. Create a style for the project name. The height will be set because it will be used only at that size.

Command: **SET STYLE**
New style: *Select from icon menu*
Font file <txt>: **ROMAN Duplex**
Height <0'-0">: **1/8**
Width factor <1.00>: **.85**
Obliquing angle <0>: ⏎
Backwards? <N>: ⏎
Upsidedown? <N>: ⏎
Vertical? <N>: ⏎

Roman Duplex is now the current text style.

6. Create a style for the text you will use to fill in the information about the drawing.

Command: **SET STYLE**
New style: *Select from icon menu*
Font file <txt>: **City Blueprint**
Height: **1/8**
Width factor <1.00>: ⏎
Obliquing angle <0>: ⏎
Backwards? <N>: ⏎
Upside-down? <N>: ⏎

City Blueprint is now the current text style.

7. For the labels in the title block, use the existing default style, Standard.

Entering Text

8. Use the Dtext command to place the labels for the title block.

Command: **DTEXT**
Justify/Style/<Start point>: **S**
Style name: **STANDARD**
Justify/Style/<Start point>: *Indicate starting point for "Drawn by:"*
Height: **1/16**
Rotation angle <0>: ⏎

Text: DRAWN BY: *Move cursor over to the next location*
Text: FILE: *Continue to move cursor and place text*
Text: DATE:
Text: SCALE:
Text: PROJECT:
Text: ⏎ ⏎

9. Place the office name, *DESIGN STUDIOS,* using the Italic Complex style. Use the fit justification option in Dtext. The text will be expanded to fit the space.

Command: **DTEXT** Justify/Style/<Start point>: **S**
Style name: **ITALICC** (Style name is abbreviated)
Justify/Style/<Start point>: **J**
Align/Fit/Center/Middle/Right/TL/TC/TR/ML/MC/MR/BL/BC/BR: **F**
First text line point: *Bottom of D in Design*
Second text line point: *Bottom of last S in Studios*
Height: **3/16**
Text: **DESIGN STUDIOS** ⏎
Text: ⏎

10. Use the same style to place *OFFICE ADDRESS*. Reenter the Dtext command, and set the height to $1/16$. By picking a starting point for the text, the text will be left-justified automatically, because it is the default option. To place *TELEPHONE*, right-justify the text.

11. Fill in the name of the project using the Roman Duplex style.

> Command: **DTEXT** Justify/Style/<Start point>: **S**
> Style name: **ROMAN Duplex** (Style name is abbreviated)
> Justify/Style/<Startpoint>: *Start text*
> Rotation angle <0>: ⏎
> Text: **CLIENT OFFICE PROJECT** ⏎
> Text: ⏎

12. Continue using the Dtext command to place text using the style and height, following the settings as indicated in the chart. City Blueprint is not abbreviated.

13. Before ending the drawing, use the Base command to set the lower right-hand corner of the title block as the new base point. This way, when you insert the title block into a drawing, the corner of the title block will be lined up with your cursor, making it easier to place the block. Room labels will be added to your drawing in paper space in Chapter 19.

15

Getting Information

Inquiry

Calculat

Xref

This group of commands is useful in finding the vital statistics about a drawing—when it was created and the style and expertise of the office it came from. It can be helpful when you have to continue work on someone else's drawing or in troubleshooting your own.

- List/Ddmodify
- Status
- ID
- Distance
- Area
- Time

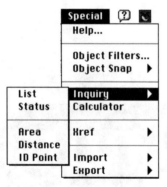

● List/Ddmodify

Provides information specific to the entity selected.

Using the List/Ddmodify Comma

Ddmodify has all but supplanted the List command for information on: what the entity is; what layer it is on; its dimensions; and its location. If the entity is a block, it provides the object's name, scale, and rotation...and it does so in a well-organized dialog box. List does the same in the command window. You may find a few things that List provides that Ddmodify does not, such as the width of polylines.

● Status

Gives you information about the drawing environment.

Using the Status Command

The Status command gives you a lot of information all in one place, such as: your drawing limits; the current status of Snap, Grid, and Osnap; and the settings of your current layer, linetype, and color. Much of this is easily available in other places but the information that you will find most useful here is:

- The number of entities in the drawing
- Model and Paper space limits
- Your current display
- The elevation currently set
- The insertion base
- The disk space available

Status Notes

- When odd things happen in your drawing, using Status is a good way to start checking. For instance, if your cursor is behaving strangely you might have an Osnap on or you may have set your Snap to 1' with your limits set to 1',9 (the result is that your cursor won't move).
- If you seem to have lost your drawing, check to see that the numbers after the *Display shows* prompt are somewhere near those specified in your limits; otherwise, you have wildly exceeded your limits and are in outer space.
- When you open an existing drawing that looks to be blank and you are sure that there was a drawing there, check the number of entities in the drawing. If there are numbers there, start zooming around to find them or check to see that your layers are on.
- Insertion base is usually 0,0 but not always. The insertion base of the title block drawing is not 0,0 because you changed it to the lower-right corner of the title block.

● ID

Gives the coordinates of a point you select or places a blip at a coordinate location you specify.

Using the ID Command

If you pick a point on the drawing, ID will print the x, y, and z coordinates. The reverse is also true: If you specify coordinates, ID will place a blip there.

● Distance

Gives you the distance between two points you select.

Using the Distance Command

To use the Distance command, pick two points that encompass the distance you want to know. If the line is continuous, you can use the Ddmodify or List command, but if the line is in segments or you want to find the distance between two points, you must use the Distance command.

NOTE If you are typing the command, it is *Dist*, not *Distance*. Distance is a variable that is an internal AutoCAD value.

● Area

Gives the area, both in square inches and square feet, and the perimeter of the space enclosed by the points you select.

Area Options

- First point
- Add
- Subtract
- Entity

Using the Area Command

If you want to find the area of a space, respond to the *First point* and *Next point* prompts by selecting points on the perimeter.

If you plan to subtract spaces from a total area, select Add option first to get the total area, then, select the Subtract option and pick the area to subtract. If you want to find the areas enclosed by polylines and entities such as circles and polygons, select the Entity option of the command.

T I P In calculating area and perimeter, AutoCAD assumes the polygon to be closed by an imaginary line from the first point to the last; therefore, it is not necessary for you to close the polygon when specifying the perimeter.

● Time

A useful command that shows the start date for the drawing and how much time has been spent in the drawing.

Time Options

ON   Turning Display to ON sets the Elapsed timer to recording time if it has been set previously to OFF.

OFF   Turning Display to OFF turns off the Elapsed timer.

Reset   Allows you to reset the Elapsed timer.

Using the Time Command

The Time command provides the following information:

Drawing Created	The date and time you first created the drawing or Save As to create a new drawing or Wblock the drawing.
Drawing Last Updated	The last time you were in the drawing editor
Time in Drawing Editor	The total time you have spent in the drawing; this timer cannot be turned off
Elapsed Timer	An additional timer that can be reset, and turned off or on (you can use it like a stopwatch to keep track of how long some procedures take)

The Time display uses the 24-hour clock. The timer is set to On as soon as you enter the drawing editor. Time is not accumulated if you quit a drawing or while you are plotting, but it is if you leave your drawing on and go to lunch.

TUTORIAL

Finding the Area of the Office

In this lesson you will use the Area command to find the area of the office, and then subtract the corridor area from the total area.

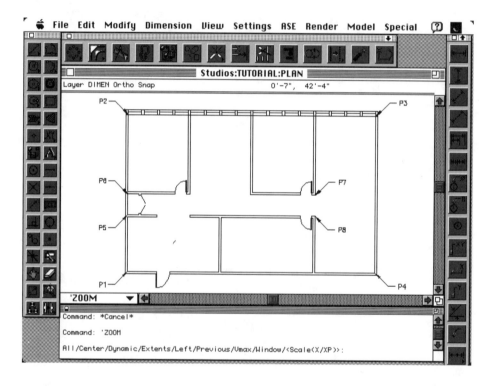

1. Open the PLAN drawing and set an INTersection Osnap to help you make accurate picks. Turn the furniture layer off and use a small view box in Zoom Dynamic to zoom the corners. Because you will be subtracting an area from the total space, you must first enter *A for Add* to let AutoCAD hold the total for additional input. Refer to the drawing for the locations of the points.

Command: **AREA**
<First point>/Entity/Add/Subtract: **A**
<First point>/Entity/Subtract: **P1**
(ADD mode) Next point: **P2**
(ADD mode) Next point: **P3**
(ADD mode) Next point: **P4** ⏎

Area=275724 square in. (1914.75 square ft.), Perimeter=180'-0"
Total area=275724 square in. (1914.75 square ft.)

2. Remain in the Area command and enter *S* for *Subtract* to subtract the corridor area.

<First point>/Entity/Subtract: **S**
<First point>/Entity/Add: **P5**
(SUBTRACT mode) Next point: **P6**
(SUBTRACT mode) Next point: **P7**
(SUBTRACT mode) Next point: **P8** ⏎

Area=27216 square in. (189.00 square ft.), Perimeter=93'-0"
Total area=28508 square in. (1725.75 square ft.)

<First point>/Entity/Add: ⏎

If you want, you can continue to find the areas of other spaces. When you have finished, quit AutoCAD.

16

Fine-tuning

🗀 **Support**

☒ Solid Fill

☐ Quick Text

☒ Blips

☒ Highlight

X Spacing	1.7321
Y Spacing	1.0000
Snap Angle	0
X Base	0.0000
Y Base	0.0000

X Spa...

Y Spa...

─Isom...

☒ On

⦿ Lef...

(OK)   (Cancel)   (Help...)

X **The commands** covered in this chapter provide additional control over your drawing environment. Although some of these are not used in this book, a knowledge of them will make various drawing tasks easier, provide you with additional linetypes, allow you to change some of the variables to better suit your needs, and to access Lisp programs. A number of these commands must be entered from the keyboard.

- Applications
- System variables (Setvar)
- UCS Icon
- Linetype
- Ltscale
- Snap (Rotate and Isometric)
- Isoplane
- Elev
- Viewres

● Applications

Applications, under the File menu, brings up a dialog box for you to select and load Lisp programs.

Using Applications

When you select Applications, a dialog box appears for you to add files.

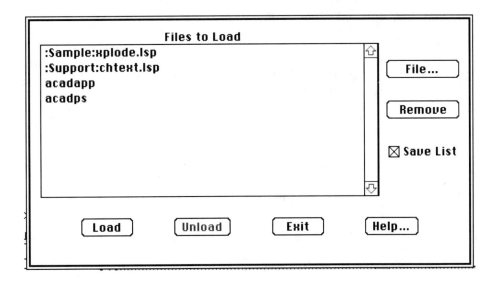

Click on the File button to select the Lisp applications that you wish to load. Once the file appears in the list box, you load it by clicking on the Load button.

The Support and Sample folders in the AutoCAD folder are rich sources of helpful programs—you are already familiar with Chtext, which is in the Support folder shown below.

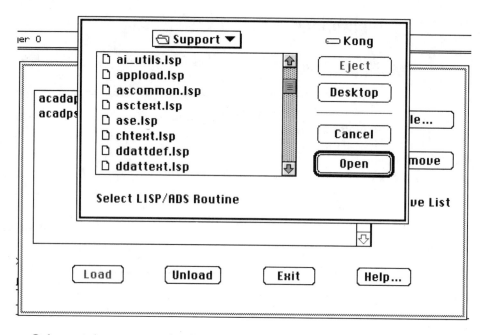

Other applications in the Sample folder that you may want to investigate are:

ddlayer.lsp   Deletes all entities on a layer (does not purge your drawing)

xplode.lsp   Explodes mirrored blocks

T I P   You can use TeachText to open and read Lisp files. A description of the program appears at the beginning of the file.

● System Variables—Setvar

The system variables are the values that control some of the functions of Auto-CAD. Many of these can be set by the user; some are "read-only" and cannot be changed.

Using the System Variables

To access the system variables, type in the name of the one you want to change at the command prompt.

Most of these variables are stored in the current drawings; a few, such as Aperture and Pickbox, are saved in the configuration file, which means that their values carry over to your other drawings.

Variable	Function
Aperture	Size, in pixels, of the Osnap target box. You can set the size by the number of pixels, sometimes more precise than by the slider.
Pickbox	Size, in pixels, of the box used for object selection.
Mirrtext	0=text mirrored; 1=text not mirrored.
Unitmode	0=displays feet and inches with a dash between feet and inches, as in 1'-3 3/4"; 1=displays feet and inches as required for input, with the dash used to separate whole from fractional inches, as in 1'3-3/4" (remember, leading zeros and the inch mark are not required for input).

Variable	Function
Coords	0=absolute coordinate display updated on pick only; 1=absolute coordinates continuously updated; 2=distance and angle from last point is displayed (this is the one you want, and if you have trouble setting it with the function keys, do it with Coords).
Splframe	0=does not display invisible edges of 3D faces; 1=displays the invisible edges of 3D faces.

● UCS Icon

The orientation of the UCS icon provides clues to where you are in 3-D space. The x and y on the icon point in the positive direction of the x and y axes in the current user coordinate system. There is also an icon that lets you know when you are in paper space, which is the space you use when setting up your drawing for plotting.

UCS Icon Options

On	Turns UCS icon on
Off	Turns UCS icon off
A (All)	Effects icon changes in all viewports instead of just the current one
N (Noorigin)	Default setting; when on, the icon is located at the lower-left corner of the viewport

OR (Origin)   Places the UCS icon at the 0,0,0
                            origin. If the origin is off the screen,
                            the icon is placed at the default
                            location

Using the UCS Icon Command

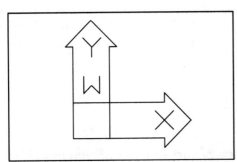 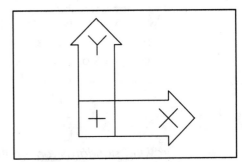

When you are in the world coordinate system, there is a *W* on the icon.
When the icon is displayed at the UCS origin, there is a plus mark (+) in the
corner of the icon.

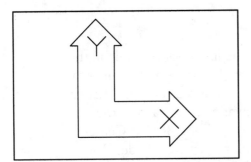 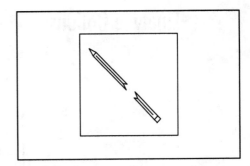

When your view is from below, the corner box does not appear in the
icon. When your view is edge-on (or within one degree of edge-on), the
icon is replaced with the image of a broken pencil. This alerts you that you
may have difficulty placing points in that view.

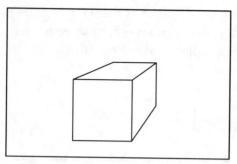
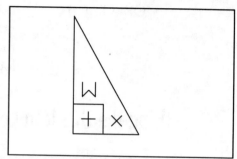

When you activate the Distance option, perspective is turned on and the perspective icon appears on the screen. When you are in paper space, the triangle appears on the screen.

● Linetype

Drawing standards require the use of various types of lines to indicate items such as hidden objects, property lines, and centerlines. The Linetype command provides access to an assortment of linetypes. The examples of AutoCAD's linetypes are in Appendix B.

Linetype Options

?	Lists the linetypes available in the linetype file; the standard linetypes are stored in ACAD.LIN. There are three varieties for each of the following types: Border, Center, Dashdot, Dashed, Divide, Dot, Hidden, Phantom.
Load	Asks for the name of the linetype to load. If you type an asterisk (*), AutoCAD will load all the linetypes.

| Create | Prompts you in creating a custom linetype. |
| Set | Sets the linetype for all subsequent entities. It is strongly recommended that this option not be used; instead, use the "by layer" procedure when assigning linetypes. This way, items that have special linetypes assigned to them can be managed using the Layer command. |

Linetype Notes

- The Linetype command must be entered from the keyboard. To see a display of available linetypes, type **linetype**, then ?, and then press↵.
- To load linetypes, Type Linetype, then type load and then press ↵. You can then either type in the linetype you want or you can type * to have all the linetypes loaded.
- When assigning linetypes to layers from the dialog box, the linetypes must already have been loaded; however, if you enter the Layer command from the keyboard you can type in the linetype you want.

● Ltscale

Modifies the scale of the linetype to fit the scale of the drawing.

Using the Ltscale Command

The scales of linetypes (except for Continuous) are affected by the scale at which you will be plotting your drawing. The "magic" number is about one-third of the scale factor. You can fine-tune how the linetype looks by adjusting the linetype scale, but one-third is a good place to start. (Example: Plot scale: $1/8 = 1'$; Scale factor: 96; Ltscale: 32.)

If one of the non-continuous linetypes looks continuous, check the Ltscale. The chances are that the scale is too small.

Changes to linetypes require a regeneration of the drawing. If you have turned Regenauto off, you must manually request a regen before the changes will appear on screen.

● Snap—Rotate and Isometric

The Snap command provides two additional options that are useful to know about: the ability to rotate the grid from 90 through −90 degrees and an isometric grid to use when doing isometric drawing. You can set both of these in the Drawing Aids dialog box brought up by Settings ➤ Drawing Aids.

Modes	Snap		Grid	
☐ Ortho	☐ On		☐ On	
☒ Solid Fill	X Spacing	1.7321	X Spacing	0.0000
☐ Quick Text	Y Spacing	1.0000	Y Spacing	0.0000
	Snap Angle	0	**Isometric Snap/Grid**	
☒ Blips	X Base	0.0000	☒ On	
☒ Highlight	Y Base	0.0000	◉ Left ○ Top ○ Right	

[OK]   [Cancel]   [Help...]

Snap Options

- Rotate
- Style

Using the Snap Command

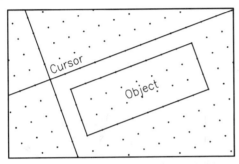 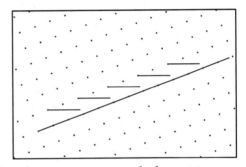

The Rotate option rotates both the grid and cursor at any angle from 90 through −90 degrees. When set in this mode, Ortho is orthogonal to the angle set. This option also allows you to relocate the grid to line up with a point in your drawing when you specify a new base point. The drawing on the right shows how arrays done with a rotated snap will follow the rotation angle.

T I P

Rotating the snap is extremely useful when drawing anything that is not oriented at right angles. You can align the grid with an existing object by responding to the *Base point* and *Rotation angle* prompts by picking two points on the object.

● Isoplane

Cycles through the three different isoplanes. The isometric grid must be set to Isometric, and Ortho mode must be set to On.

Isoplane Options

- Left
- Top
- Right

Using the Isoplane Command

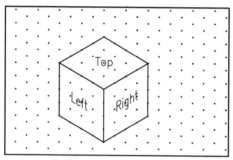 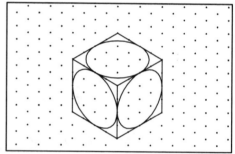

When doing an isometric drawing, it is helpful to be able to move into a different isoplane without getting out of a drawing command. Because it is important to be able to toggle between the planes transparently, there are various ways to do this:

- Press Ctrl-E or F7 (to cycle through the planes).
- Pick Left, Top, or Right in the Drawing Aids dialog box under the Settings pull-down menu.

Circles can be drawn using the Isocircle option Ellipse. When inserting circles, you must make sure that the appropriate Iso plane is activated.

Isometric drawings are 2-D representations of 3-D objects using set drawing angles: 30, 90, 0 and 210, 270, and 330. They have no 3-D view because they have no z component.

● Elev

Sets the elevation, and thickness if desired, of subsequent entities that you draw.

Using the Elev Command

This command must be entered from the keyboard. If you want to change the elevation of *existing* entities, use Ddmodify for single entities or the Move or Change Points command for multiple entities. In the Move command change the z-coordinate by displacing it in the direction desired. The Elev option in the Change command disappeared in a prior release of AutoCAD and was brought back by popular demand. Examples of the various techniques follow. Use the one that suits you best.

Command: **MOVE**
Select object: *Pick the object or objects*
Base point of displacement: **0,0,–6** (Moves the object 6 inches down)
Second point of displacement: ⏎

The example for Change Points:

Command: **CHANGE ➤ Points**
Select objects: *Pick object*
Properties/<Change point>: **P**
Change what property (Color/Elev/LAyer/LType/Thickness)?: **E**
New elevation <0'-0">: **6** (Moves the object 6 inches upwards)
Change what property (Color/Elev/LAyer/LType/Thickness)?: ⏎

NOTE When setting an elevation for drawing entities, it is easy to forget that you have the setting on. If you are drawing only a few entities at a different elevation, it may be better to elevate them with the Ddmodify or Move command. Another way of setting elevation and thickness is by selecting Entity Creation on the Options pull-down menu.

● Viewres

Controls whether your zooms are done at redraw or regen speed and how many sections will be drawn to display arcs, circles, or linetypes.

Viewres Options

- Yes
- No
- Enter circle zoom percent

Using the Viewres Command

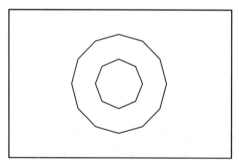
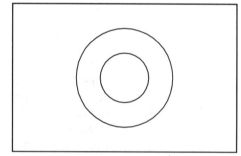

The Yes option gives you zooms done at redraw speed. The No option gives you zooms done at regen speed. The default value for circle zoom percent is 100. The larger the number is, the more segments are used to draw curves and the longer it takes to redraw the image.

Viewres Notes

If you don't want your circles to look like polygons, you can increase the number for circle zoom percent to 500, without slowing down the display time.

Sometimes your linetypes, such as dashed and hidden, will look like solid lines. If this is not caused by an incorrectly set Ltscale (which sets the scale of the linetype), increasing the circle zoom percent will produce a more accurate screen view of the linetype. Regardless of how polygon-like your circles and arcs appear on the screen, they will plot perfectly rounded.

Why wouldn't you always want fast zooms? The trade-off is how your drawing looks on the screen. Without fast zooms, you can get better display resolution, but it takes longer to update your screen.

17

Adding Dimensions

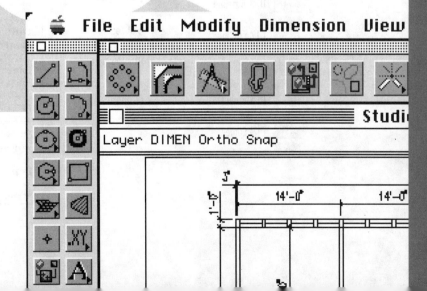

File Edit Modify Dimension View

Studi

Layer DIMEN Ortho Snap

14'-0"   14'-0"

AutoCAD has a very rich dimensioning palette. The task of dimensioning is easy because AutoCAD already knows the lengths, angles, and radii of the objects you have drawn. It involves letting AutoCAD know what you want dimensioned and where you want the dimensions placed. Although AutoCAD starts out with certain dimension variables set, you can create a dimensioning style specifically designed for your office by changing these settings in the dimension dialog boxes. Dimensions can be grouped into three major categories:

- Dimension types
- Dimension editing
- Dimension variables

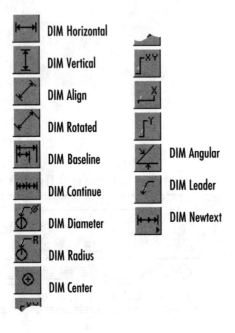

● Dimension Types

*The general format for using the dimensioning commands is to click on the di-
mension type, indicate the item you want dimensioned, drag the dimension
line to where you want it drawn, and approve the dimension value that Auto-
CAD displays by pressing ⏎. You can click on the Zoom icon and zoom in
for accurate placement of your dimensions.*

Dimension Type Commands

HORizontal	DIAmeter
VERtical	RADius
CONtinue	ANGular
BASeline	CENter
ALIgned	LEAder
ROTated	ORDinate

Using Dimension Types

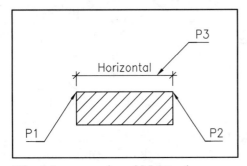

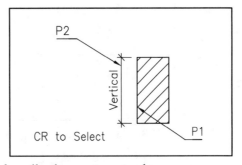

The Horizontal and Vertical commands handle dimensions in the same way.
The examples shown here work equally well for Horizontal and Vertical.
Click on the appropriate dimension icon, specify the first point (P1) and the
second point (P2) on the distance to be dimensioned, and then drag the dimension line to the location you want (P3). Alternatively, you can press ⏎

at the first prompt and select the line to be dimensioned instead of indicating the actual points.

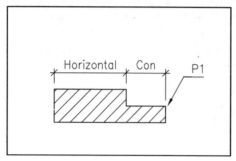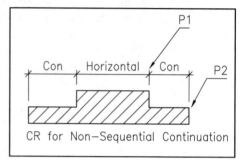

The Continue command continues a string of dimensions from an existing Vertical or Horizontal dimension by selecting the next point (P1) to be dimensioned. If the Continue dimension does not immediately follow the previous Horizontal or Vertical dimension, press ⏎ to select a point on or near the extension line from which you want to continue dimensioning. Then pick the point you want to dimension to. The Continue command works in any direction.

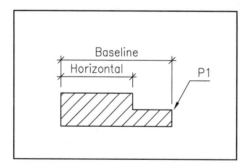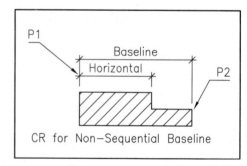

The Baseline command works the same way as Continue except that all dimensions begin at the same baseline. As with the Continue dimension, if the Baseline dimension does not immediately follow the previous Horizontal or Vertical dimension, press ⏎ to select a point on or near the baseline, and then pick the next point to be dimensioned.

With the Align command, you can either pick the line to which you want to align the dimension or specifically pick the endpoints of that line. The

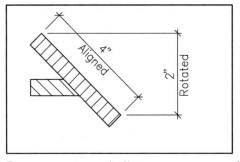

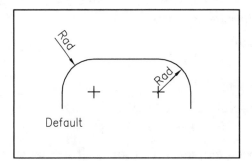

Rotate command allows you to specify the angle for the dimension line. The Diameter command has three styles, depending on how the dimension variables are set. The point at which you select the circle determines the location of the dimension.

The Radius command also depends upon how the dimension variables are set. Select the arc to be dimensioned; as with circles, the point you pick de-

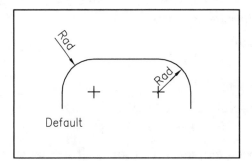

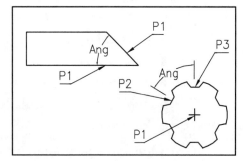

termines the placement of the dimension. The default leader line is drawn on the outside of the arc. If you want the leader drawn on the inside, pick the point with your cursor.

With the Angle command, you can select two lines forming the angle. If you respond by pressing ⏎, you can pick a vertex and a first and a second endpoint defining the angle. The vertex can be the center of the circle, but it need not be. A third command (not shown) allows you to pick a circle or an arc plus another point for the angle dimension.

The Center command draws center marks or center lines for circles or arcs, depending on the settings for these features in the Extension Lines dialog box. The Leader command draws leader lines. It works like the Line

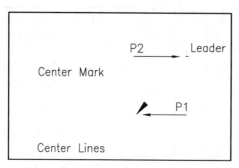

Default	Type	Effect
<4'–2">	CR	4'–2"
<4'–2">	14'–0"	14'–0"
<4'–2">	<>max	4'–2" max
<4'–2">	verify	verify
<4'–2">	Space+CR	

command, starts with an arrowhead, and ends with the shoulder and dimension text. A space plus a ⏎ suppresses the dimension default. An Undo at the *2nd point* prompt suppresses the shoulder. Leaders are not associative dimension entities (covered later in this chapter) and cannot be modified or changed when their associated object is modified. However, the text portion of the leader can be changed with Ddmodify. The term *dimension text* refers to both numerical and text entries for dimensions. There are a variety of responses to the default prompt, *Dimension text <Default>* (see the right-hand drawing):

- Press ⏎ to accept the default.
- Type in a new value.
- Type text before or after <> to add text to dimensions.
- Type in text (particularly useful with leaders).
- Press the spacebar and then ⏎ to produce a blank.

   Ordinate dimensioning is specific to machine tooling. It specifies x and y dimensions from a 0,0 base point.

● Editing—Associative Dimensions

The associative dimension commands will work on all your dimensions unless you have turned off Dimaso, you have exploded the dimension, or the entity is a leader. Associative dimensions are changed automatically when the features that they are associated with change. These editing commands offer tools to modify and manage dimensions. Both new and previous names for the commands are included.

Editing Commands

- Oblique Dimension (OBLique)
- Move Text (TEDit)
- Rotate Text (TROtate)
- Update Dimensions (UPDate)
- Home Position (HOMetext)
- Change Text (NEWtext)

Using the Editing Commands

These commands are found at the bottom of the Dimension icon menu under Newtext.

Oblique modifies an existing dimension so that the extension lines are perpendicular to the direction of the dimension. This command is very useful when dimensioning isometric drawings. Move Text starts a new paragraph.

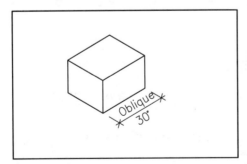

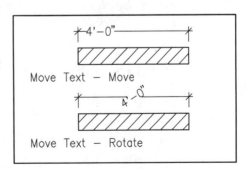

This command is used to make crowded dimensions more readable.

The other commands do the following:

Rotate Text   Rotates more than one line of dimension text.

Update Dimensions   Updates an existing dimension to the current dimension style, dimension variables, current text style, and units setting.

Home Position   Returns dimension text to its default position.

Change Text   Changes the content of the text on dimensions.

T I P

The current format of the dimension command is to call a single dimension action and then return you to the Command line. If you wish to keep the Dimension command active until you call for an Exit, as previous releases did, type **Dim** and specify the dimension option you want.

● Dimension Variables

Because AutoCAD is used in different disciplines—architecture, mechanical engineering, interior design—the dimensions require different styling. For example, a part that is being machined to a –0.002 tolerance requires a very different dimensioning format from a site plan being dimensioned in miles or meters. By changing the values of the dimension variables, you can set up these kinds of formats.

Using Dimension Variables

Dimension variables are set in the dimension dialog box that relates to that dimension feature:

- Dimension Line (the line the dimension text appears on)

- Extension Lines (lines extending from the dimensioned object to the dimension line)
- Arrows (includes ticks, dots, and arrowheads)
- Text Location (above, below, align with dimension, or always horizontal)
- Text Format (alternate dimension, 0 inches, 0 feet, tolerance)
- Color (color assignment for the different dimension features—for pen assignment)
- Features (a combination of the first four dialog boxes)

The default settings of each of these is shown with the units setting on architectural so the values are fractions instead of decimal. The dimension variables that each box controls are listed for those who are familiar with these settings. Using these settings is covered in the tutorial section of this chapter.

Style: *UNNAMED

Feature Scaling: `1.00000`

☐ **Use Paper Space Scaling**

Dimension Line Color: `BYBLOCK` ▉

┌─**Dimension Line**─────────
☐ **Force Interior Lines**

☐ **Basic Dimension**

Text Gap: `3/32"`

Baseline Increment: `3/8"`

[**OK**] [**Cancel**] [**Help...**]

Dimscale, Dimclrd, Dimoxd, Dimtofl, Dimgap, Dimdli

```
Style: *UNNAMED
Feature Scaling:        1.00000
☐ Use Paper Space Scaling
Extension Line Color:   BYBLOCK   ■
┌─Extension Lines──────────────────────┐
│ Extension Above Line:  3/16"         │
│ Feature Offset:        1/16"         │
│ Visibility │ Draw Both        ▼ │   │
│ Center Mark Size:      3/32"         │
│ ☐ Mark with Center Lines             │
└──────────────────────────────────────┘
  ( OK )   ( Cancel )   ( Help... )
```

Dimscale, Dimclre, Dimexe, Dimexo, Dimse1, Dimse2

```
Style: *UNNAMED
Feature Scaling:        1.00000
☐ Use Paper Space Scaling
Dimension Line Color:   BYBLOCK   ■
┌─Arrows────────────────────────────────┐
│ ⦿ Arrow  ○ Tick  ○ Dot  ○ User        │
│ Arrow Size:         3/16"             │
│ User Arrow:         <default>         │
│ ☐ Separate Arrows                     │
│ First Arrow:        <default>         │
│ Second Arrow:       <default>         │
│ Tick Extension:     0"                │
└────────────────────────────────────────┘
  ( OK )   ( Cancel )   ( Help... )
```

Dimscale, Dimclrd, Dimasz, Dimtsz, Dimblk, Dimblk1, Dimblk2, Dimsah, Dimdle

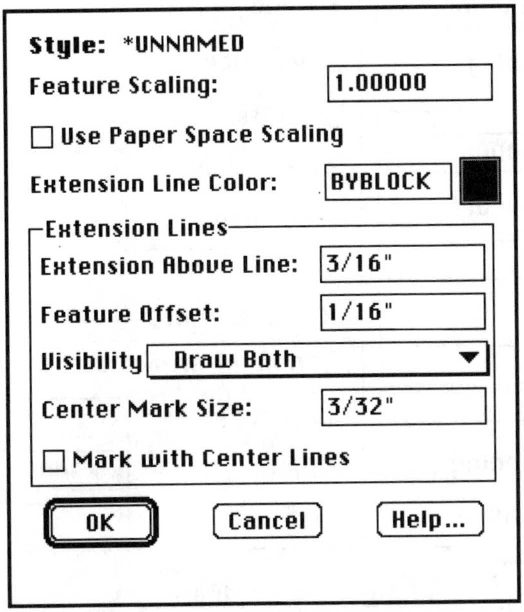

Style: *UNNAMED

Feature Scaling: `1.00000`

☐ Use Paper Space Scaling

Extension Line Color: `BYBLOCK` ▪

┌─Extension Lines─────────
Extension Above Line: `3/16"`

Feature Offset: `1/16"`

Visibility `Draw Both ▼`

Center Mark Size: `3/32"`

☐ Mark with Center Lines

[OK] [Cancel] [Help...]

Dimscale, Dimclrt, Dimtxt, Dimtfac, Dimtix, Dimsoxd, Dimtad, Dimtvp, Dimtih, Dimtoh

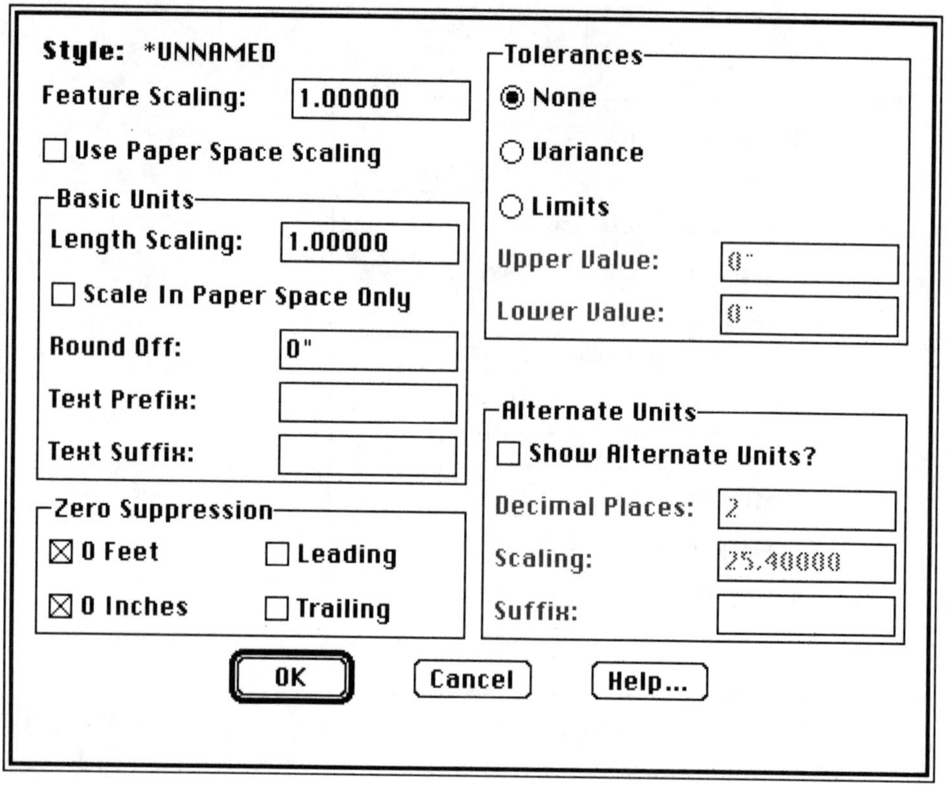

Style: *UNNAMED

Feature Scaling: `1.00000`

☐ **Use Paper Space Scaling**

┌Basic Units──────────────

Length Scaling: `1.00000`

☐ **Scale In Paper Space Only**

Round Off: `0"`

Text Prefix: `_____`

Text Suffix: `_____`

┌Zero Suppression────────

☒ **0 Feet**   ☐ **Leading**

☒ **0 Inches**   ☐ **Trailing**

┌Tolerances───────────────

◉ **None**

○ **Variance**

○ **Limits**

Upper Value: `0"`

Lower Value: `0"`

┌Alternate Units──────────

☐ **Show Alternate Units?**

Decimal Places: `2`

Scaling: `25.40000`

Suffix: `_____`

[**OK**]   [**Cancel**]   [**Help...**]

Dimscale, Dimlfac, Dimrnd, Dimpost, Dimzin, Dimtol, Dimlim, Dimtm, Dimtp, Dimalt, Dimaltf, Dimaltd, Dimapost

Style: *UNNAMED

Feature Scaling: 1.00000

☐ Use Paper Space Scaling

Dimension Line Color: BYBLOCK

Extension Line Color: BYBLOCK

Dimension Text Color: BYBLOCK

[OK]   (Cancel)   (Help...)

Dimscale, Dimclrd, Dimclre, Dimclrt

T I P

Take care when changing variables, since they automatically affect the style that is currently active. For new styles, the procedure to remember is: Name style, Make changes. If you wish to see the list of dimension variables, Type **Dim** ⏎ and then **Status**. Two variables, Dimaso, which activates associative dimensioning, and Dimsho, which drags dimension lines, are set to On in the prototype drawing. If you have to reset them, do so from the command line.

TUTORIAL

● Dimensioning the Office Plan

In this lesson you will dimension your PLAN drawing in the architectural format. You will have to change a number of dimension variables before you begin, because most of them are set for the mechanical style of dimensioning. You will create three different dimension styles: a base architectural one, one using dots for center line dimensioning, and one for interiors that eliminates extension lines for dimensioning between walls. You can modify these styles to make additional styles of your own.

To place your dimension points, make use of the various transparent Zoom options, and Dynamic in particular. Use Undo if you make a mistake.

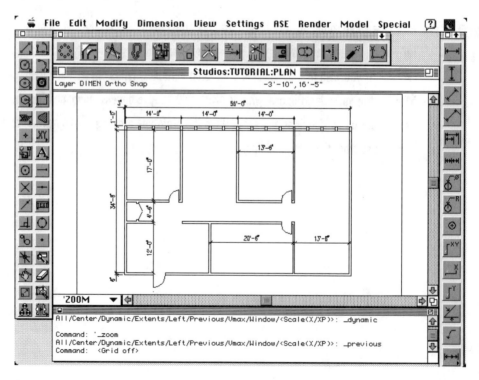

1. Open the PLAN drawing and, before you get into the dimensioning commands, go to the Settings menu and establish these settings:

Snap: **1"** *and set to* **On**
Grid: **1'** *and set to* **On**
Ortho: **On**
Units: Precision **1/64"** (This will enable you to see the values for the dimension variables)

2. Make a new text style to be used for dimensions. You will name a style, so the procedure for creating styles is slightly different from the standard method. Start by entering Style from the keyboard

Command: **STYLE**
Text style name: **DIMS**
Pick the **Fonts** *folder and click on* **Open**
Scroll down and pick ***romans.shx*** *and click on* **Open**
Ht: **0**
Width: **.75** (This compresses dimension text so it fits better)
⏎ *to all the other defaults*

3. You will be using a combination of NEA, MID, and END Osnaps to place dimension points. Set NEArest to On with the Osnap command and use the others in override mode.

4. You don't need furniture in the dimension plan, so freeze the FURN layer, and set the current layer to DIMEN.

5. Click on **Settings ➤ Dimension Style** to get the Dimension Styles dialog box. Enter the word **Standard** in the edit box and click in the edit box to save the current Unnamed AutoCAD dimension settings under the name STANDARD (in case you should want to restore it).

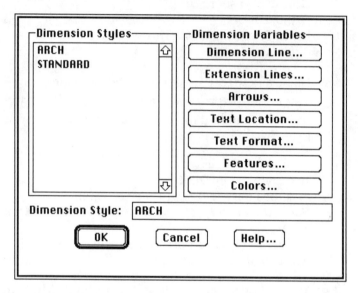

Setting Dimension Styles

6. Start a new style called ARCH by typing in the name in the edit box; click in the edit box and ARCH will be highlighted in the list box. All changes you now make to the dimension variables will create the ARCH style. Open the Features dialog box and make changes according to the example.

Style: ARCH

Feature Scaling: `96.00000`

☐ Use Paper Space Scaling

┌Dimension Line──────────────
☐ Force Interior Lines

☐ Basic Dimension

Text Gap: `0"`

Baseline Increment: `3/8"`

┌Arrows──────────────
○ Arrow ⦿ Tick ○ Dot ○ User

Arrow Size: `3/64"`

User Arrow: `<default>`

☐ Separate Arrows

First Arrow: `<default>`

Second Arrow: `<default>`

Tick Extension: `3/64"`

┌Extension Lines──────────────
Extension Above Line: `1/16"`

Feature Offset: `1/16"`

Visibility `Draw Both` ▼

Center Mark Size: `3/64`

☐ Mark with Center Lines

┌Text Position──────────────
Text Height: `1/8"`

Tolerance Height: `1/8"`

Horizontal `Default` ▼

Vertical `Above` ▼

Relative Position: `0"`

Alignment `Align With Dimension ...` ▼

[**OK**]   [Cancel]   [Help...]

You will set the variables that will make the style look like architectural dimensions: text height above the dimension line, aligning dimension text with the dimension line, and replacing arrows with ticks. The Features dialog box is a combination of four of the other dialog boxes so it is easier to make changes here.

7. Additional changes will be made in the Text Format dialog box. To make the dimension read in the architectural style of 7'-0" and not 0'-6" you have to uncheck 0 Inches and check the box marked 0 Feet. To eliminate fractions of inches, set the round off to 1".

Style: ARCH	**┌Tolerances────**
Feature Scaling: `96.00000`	⦿ None
☐ **Use Paper Space Scaling**	○ Variance
┌Basic Units────	○ Limits
Length Scaling: `1.00000`	**Upper Value:** `0"`
☐ **Scale In Paper Space Only**	**Lower Value:** `0"`
Round Off: `1"`	
Text Prefix:	**┌Alternate Units────**
Text Suffix:	☐ **Show Alternate Units?**
┌Zero Suppression────	**Decimal Places:** `2`
☒ **0 Feet** ☐ **Leading**	**Scaling:** `25.40000`
☐ **0 Inches** ☐ **Trailing**	**Suffix:**

[**OK**]   [Cancel]   [Help...]

8. Create a dimension style called INTERIOR, basing it on the ARCH style. In the Dimension Styles dialog box, type INTERIOR in the edit box, click in the edit box so INTERIOR will now be highlighted. For interior dimensions, extension lines between wall dimension are unnecessary. Click on the Features box and suppress the visibility of extension lines.

Style: INTERIOR

Feature Scaling: `96.00000`

☐ Use Paper Space Scaling

Dimension Line

☐ Force Interior Lines

☐ Basic Dimension

Text Gap: `0"`

Baseline Increment: `3/8"`

Arrows

○ Arrow ◉ Tick ○ Dot ○ User

Arrow Size: `3/64"`

User Arrow: `<default>`

☐ Separate Arrows

First Arrow: `<default>`

Second Arrow: `<default>`

Tick Extension: `3/64"`

Extension Lines

Extension Above Line: `1/16"`

Feature Offset: `1/16"`

Visibility `Suppress Both` ▼

Center Mark Size: `3/64"`

☐ Mark with Center Lines

Text Position

Text Height: `1/8"`

Tolerance Height: `1/8"`

Horizontal `Default` ▼

Vertical `Above` ▼

Relative Position: `0"`

Alignment `Align With Dimension ...` ▼

[OK] [Cancel] [Help...]

9. The last style, named DOT, uses dots to dimension to center lines. It will also be based on the ARCH style. Follow the same procedure as for the INTERIOR style: open the Dimension Styles dialog box; make the current style ARCH; name the new style Dot; select the Features box; and click on radio button for DOT.

Style: DOT

Feature Scaling: `96.00000`

☐ **Use Paper Space Scaling**

Dimension Line
☐ **Force Interior Lines**
☐ **Basic Dimension**
Text Gap: `0"`
Baseline Increment: `3/8"`

Arrows
○ Arrow ○ Tick ● Dot ○ User
Arrow Size: `3/64"`
User Arrow: `DOT`
☐ **Separate Arrows**
First Arrow: `<default>`
Second Arrow: `<default>`
Tick Extension: `3/64"`

Extension Lines
Extension Above Line: `1/16"`
Feature Offset: `1/16"`
Visibility `Draw Both` ▼
Center Mark Size: `3/64"`
☐ **Mark with Center Lines**

Text Position
Text Height: `1/8"`
Tolerance Height: `1/8"`
Horizontal `Default` ▼
Vertical `Above` ▼
Relative Position: `0"`
Alignment `Align With Dimension ...` ▼

[OK] [Cancel] [Help...]

Drawing Dimensions

10. You will first dimension the midpoints of columns. The DOT dimension style you have created is currently active. Dimension the first three column bays, the last one does not need to be dimensioned. Use a MIDpoint Osnap override.

Command: **DIM Horizontal**
First extension line origin or RETURN to select: *Pick midpoint of first column*
Second extension line origin: *Pick midpoint of second column bay*
Dimension line location <Text/Angle>: *Pick a point about 2' above building line*
Dimension text <14'-0">: ⏎ (Accepts dimension)

Command: **DIM Continue**
Second extension line origin or RETURN to select: *Pick midpoint of third column bay*
Dimension text <14'-0">: ⏎ (The dimension line is continued)

Command: **DIM Continue**
Second extension line origin or RETURN to select: *Pick midpoint of fourth column bay*
Dimension text <14'-0">: ⏎

11. You are now finished using the DOT dimension style. Return to the Dimension Styles dialog box and make ARCH the current style.

12. Now dimension the overall window line. First dimension the 56' length, then use Dim Continue for the 3" dimension on the left-hand side. When numbers don't fit between extension lines, they are placed next to the second extension line, so by dimensioning that section from right to left, the 3" comes out on the side you want. You could also have used the Change Text command to move the text. Use the MID and END Osnap overrides to place your dimensions.

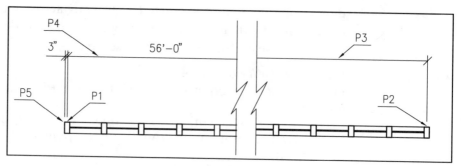

Command: **DIM Horizontal**
First extension line origin or RETURN to select: *Pick P1*
Second extension line origin: *Pick P2*
Dimension line location <Text/Angle>: *Pick P3* (About 4-1/2′ above the building line)
Dimension text <56′-0″>: ⏎

Command: **DIM Continue**
Second extension line origin or RETURN to select: ⏎
Select continued dimension: *Pick P4 to continue an existing dimension*
Second extension line origin or RETURN to select: *Pick P5*
Dimension text <3″>: ⏎

13. Use the same technique for the outside dimension on the left side of the drawing. Continue using Osnaps and Zooms as needed. Refer to the PLAN drawing for dimension locations.

Command: **DIM Vertical**
The dimension text should be: **34′-6″**

Command: **DIM Continue**
The dimension text should be: **1′-0″**

Command: **DIM Continue** *Continue from the 34′-6″ dimension line*
The dimension text should be: **6″**

14. Now dimension the interior spaces. Return to the Dimension Styles dialog box and make the INTERIOR style current. Your dimension placements can vary from those in the book, because you can place them at various points along the wall. The remaining dimensions are simple Horizontal or Vertical dimensions. The Nearest Osnap, which you have already set, will ensure that the dimension lines touch the walls. Your dimensions should match the ones shown on the plan at the beginning of the tutorial.

15. You have finished dimensioning your plan. Remove any Osnaps you have set, thaw the FURN layer, freeze the DIMEN layer, Quit AutoCAD and Save changes. AutoCAD offers numerous options for dimensioning, so you can develop a style for your specific needs. Take the time to set up dimensioning procedures and styles—it will enable you to quickly produce clear and un-ambiguous dimensions.

18

Working in 3-D

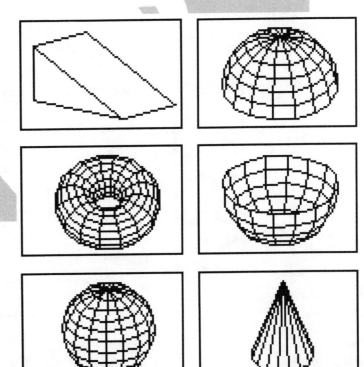

In this chapter you begin to explore some of AutoCAD's capabilities for working in three dimensions. The commands you'll learn will show you how to set up split-screen viewing, construct both simple extruded shapes and actual 3-D objects, create perspective views, and render.

- 3D Face
- 3D Objects
- Tiled Viewports
- Viewpoint
- Plan
- Mslide
- Vslide
- Dview
- Hide
- Shade
- Render

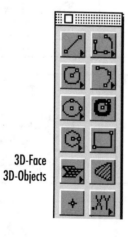

3D-Face
3D-Objects

Render	Model
Render	
Shade	
Hide	
Views...	
Lights...	
Scenes...	
Finishes...	
Preferences...	
Statistics...	
Files	▶
Unload Render	
RenderMan...	

View	Settings
Redraw	⌘R
Redraw All	
Zoom	▶
Pan	
Tilemode	▶
Toggle UP	
Model space	
Paper space	
Mview	▶
Dview	
Plan View	▶
Viewpoint	▶
Named view...	
Layout	▶

● 3D Face

Draws a surface that appears as a wire frame but will be opaque when the Hide command is used. The 3D Face command is similar to the Solid command, but the points are entered in a clockwise or counterclockwise order.

Using the 3D Face Command

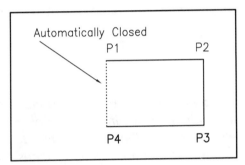

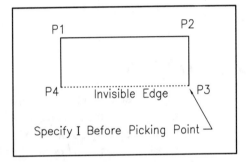

3D Faces are built of three or four points. After you draw four points, Auto-CAD closes the figure and prompts for additional third and fourth points. The Invisible (I) option makes an edge of a 3D Face invisible. This is used to hide the lines between faces when constructing shapes made up of more than one face. You must specify the I before beginning the first point of the edge you want to make invisible. It is much easier to draw all the edges as visible and make the edges you want to be invisible by using Ddmodify.

3D Face Notes

- When you make the edges of a 3D Face invisible, it can present a problem in editing. To make the edges visible, set the variable Splframe to 1.
- 3D Faces cannot be extruded.
- Points defining a 3D Face need not be in the same plane.

- Continuing a shape by drawing the third and fourth points can produce unexpected results. Sometimes it is easier to begin the command for each section.
- Lines that are extruded do not have "tops" on them (a table made from extruded lines appears to have a glass top). 3D Faces are useful for putting tops on things so they won't appear transparent. Solids can also be used for this purpose (see "Hide" in this chapter).
- 3D Faces are useful for placing "floors" on spaces to be rendered.
- Ddmodify can be used to change the visible/invisible state of 3D Faces.

● 3D Objects

3D Objects is not a command but a series of some basic forms made from polygon meshes. AutoCAD has set up the formulas in AutoLISP; all you have to do is supply some size parameters. Although the selection includes the sphere, torus, and cone, this book covers the construction of shapes more useful in architecture: the box, wedge, pyramid, and dome.

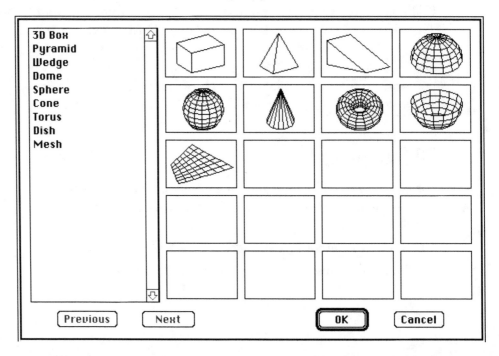

Using 3D Objects

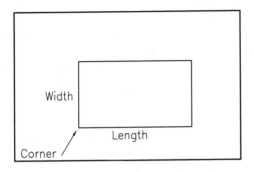
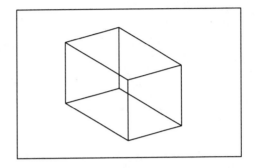

To form the box you are asked for the corner of the box, length, width, height, and the rotation angle about Z (you must specify 0 for no rotation). You can show the length and width on the screen; the dimensions start from the corner of the box. The height is easier to enter from the keyboard, but you can enter it on-screen if you are in a 3-D view. If you are drawing a cube, you only have to specify one side and then pick C for cube.

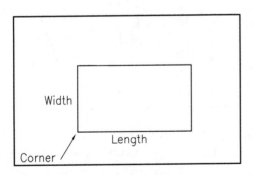
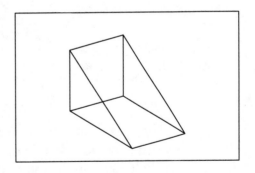

The prompts are the same for the wedge as for the box. The height for the wedge is always drawn from the corner originally specified.

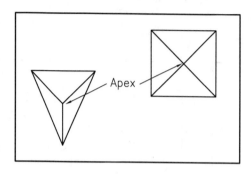
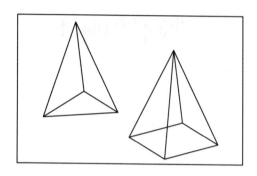

Pyramids can be constructed with three- or four-sided bases; you are prompted to specify lengths for the three or four (tetrahedron) sides. The sides of the base need not be equal. Specification for the apex must have x, y, and z coordinates. The easiest way to do this is to use filters and pick the x-y point from the screen and specify z from the keyboard.

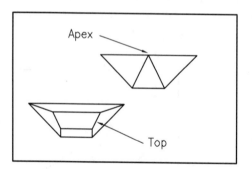
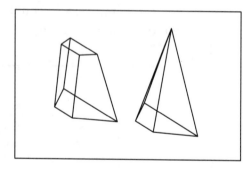

The apex of the pyramid can be placed off to one side. If you want a flat-topped pyramid, specify Top (T). The x, y, z coordinates must be specified for each point on the top face. (The Ridge option is not as useful, so it is not dealt with in this book).

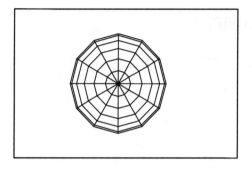 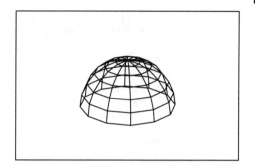

The dome is constructed by first specifying the center and then the radius. The number of segments determines how smooth the dome will be. Start by accepting the defaults and adjust them if necessary. You can modify these shapes, but first they have to be exploded. The dome can then be flattened by removing the bottom segments; or, an opening (like the oculus in the Pantheon) can be placed in the top by erasing the center section.

● Tiled Vport

It is sometimes helpful to see more than one view of your drawing. The Tiled Vports command allows you to divide your screen into different ports, each able to have a separate view. Although only one viewport can be active at a time, commands can be started in one viewport and carried over into another one, enabling you to work in multiple views.

Using the Tiled Vports Command

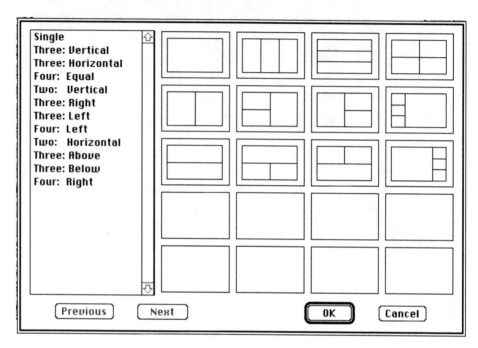

Multiple views of your drawing can be useful in a number of drawing operations. Views can be zoomed-in views of the drawing; different parts of the drawing; or 3-D views. Lines can be started in one viewport and continued into the next. While working in one viewport, the effects are visible in all of them, so you can place items in plan view and see the effects in your 3-D view. Though you can see your drawing in all the viewports, you can work in only one viewport at a time. You can distinguish this active port by the cross-hair cursor. In nonactive ports the cross hair changes to an arrow. Ports are activated by moving the cursor into the port and clicking the mouse. Active viewports have heavier borders around them.

There are certain advantages you get by typing the **Vports** command:

Save   Saves a configuration with a given name so you can retrieve it later. The view and the settings in each port are saved.

Restore   Brings back a previously saved viewport configuration.

Delete   Removes viewport configurations that you no longer need.

Join   Ports can be joined as long as they are adjacent and their joining forms a rectangle. With Join you can design other types of viewport configurations than those shown in the Tiled Viewports icon screen.

T I P

Each viewport can have its own settings, such as snap, grid, 3-D view, pan, and zoomed orientation. Layer settings must be the same in all viewports. You can set up your prototype drawing with a viewport configuration. Do not confuse this command, Tiled Vports, with the Viewport option in MView. The latter draws ports in paper space; these viewports can have different layer settings in different viewports.

● Viewpoint (Vpoint)

Lets you pick the orientation for viewing your drawing in 3-D. There are essentially three methods to help you orient your view:

- Presets
- Axes
- Rotate

Using the Viewpoint Command

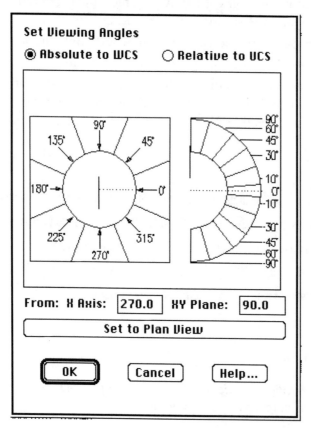

Presets is probably the easiest way of setting up a 3-D view. It is done by picking angles on the plan and height compass. Or, you can type in the angles in the *From: X Axis* and *XY Plane* edit boxes. The pointer may appear off-center on some machines, so check the edit boxes to make sure that the angles are those you want.

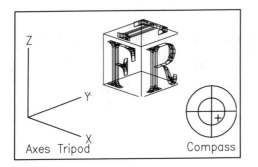

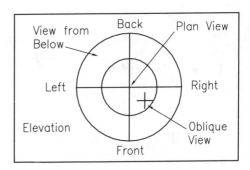

Axes will cause the compass and axes tripod to appear on your screen. As you move your cursor, the tripod moves to simulate the orientation of your drawing. Sometimes it is easier to get a feel of a 3-D view by working with this option.

You choose your view by moving your cursor within the small circle. The small circle represents the view of the top of the object; the larger circle is the view from below the object. For most purposes, you will only be working in the small circle. Where the cross hairs intersect is the plan view. The perimeter of the small circle represents elevations at ground level. As you move from the perimeter to the crosshairs, the viewing angle from ground to plan is increased to produce an oblique view.

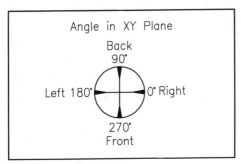

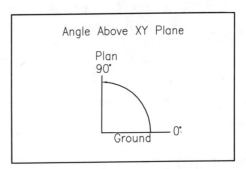

The Set Points ➤ Rotate option requires you to specify two angles: an angle *in* the x-y plane and an angle *above* the x-y plane. This is actually easier to set in the Presets dialog box.

After setting a few views, you will probably have some preferred ones. This is where specifying angles for views comes in handy. It's fast and accurate. Save 3-D views using Named View. This way they can always be retrieved.

Viewpoint Notes

- Viewpoint lets you specify a view direction but not distance. You can use Zoom to change the magnification.
- The views you get by using Viewpoint are parallel (axonometric) projections. To get a perspective view, use the Dview command.

● Plan View

Restores your 3-D image to a plan view.

Using the Plan View Command

The options are Current UCS, World, and Named UCS. World is the one you want, at least in the tutorials in this book.

UCS stands for *user coordinate system,* which is a reorientation of the x, y, and z coordinates by the user. (This book uses the *world coordinate system.*) Because some users work in more than one coordinate system, the Plan command provides the option of returning to the plan view of a specific coordinate system.

● Mslide

Makes a slide of your current screen. A file dialog box appears to allow you to enter the name of the slide file. The default is the name of the drawing. All slide files have an .sld extension. If you want more than one slide of a draw-ing, provide different names for each slide file. Slides cannot be modified or printed, and Print Window won't work. They are like a photo of your screen at a point in time. Slides are a useful way to view multiple drawing images. Mslide must be entered from the keyboard.

● Vslide

Views slides that you have made. The command is entered from the keyboard. To remove a slide from the monitor use the Redraw command. When you select the command, a file dialog box appears listing the available slide files. You can view slides made from any drawing.

TIP You can make a quick slide presentation by setting up multiple viewports and displaying different slides in each viewport.

● Dview

Stands for dynamic viewing. This is the command that makes perspective views. It also enables you to work interactively to get the views you want instead of using the static Viewpoint command.

Dview Options

POints	Hide
CAmera	PAn
TArget	Zoom
Distance	TWist
Off	Undo
CLip	eXit

Using the Dview Command

The first prompt, which you have to respond to before you can use any of the options, asks you to select the object. If it is a complicated drawing, limit the parts you choose to those that define the boundary edges or show the identifying features. The fewer entities you pick, the quicker your view will be displayed. You can consider placing objects on a layer and freezing them, and then thawing them when you have the view you want.

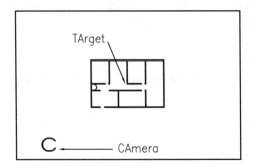

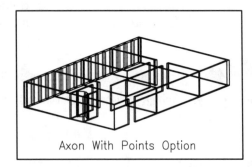

Axon With Points Option

The Points option is a good starting place for manipulating 3-D views. You are asked to enter the target point and then the camera point. The default starting point for the target is the center of the screen. A rubber-banding line extends from the target point and follows the movement of your cursor to help you visualize the sight line when you pick the camera location. The center of the screen often is not where your target is, so you generally have to specify target location.

Pick the points on the screen using .xy filters, and give the height when prompted for the z-coordinate. Alternatively, you can just pick points on the screen and set heights later with the Camera and Target options.

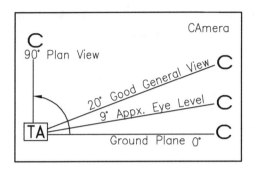

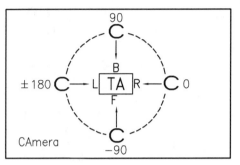

With Camera you can fine-tune your view. You are first prompted for the angle from the x-y plane. The simplest way to handle the camera is to ignore this prompt and use your mouse. This way you move naturally in both plan and elevation simultaneously. If you wish to enter angles, respond to the prompt for angles. You can toggle between the two choices, angle in the x-y plane and then the angle from the x-y plane by typing **t**. You can think of the angle *from* the x-y plane as height above the ground plane (excluding below for this example) and the angle *in* the x-y plane as rotation on the ground plane.

The effect of the Camera option is as though you were walking around the object. It seems to be more natural to move the camera rather than the target but you do have the option to move the target while the camera is stationary.

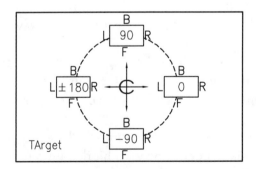

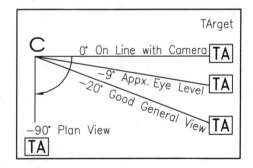

In the Target option, the target revolves around a center point. The numbers have the opposite sign from those for Camera: Plan view is −90 and front view is +90 degrees. Again, using the mouse is the most natural method to navigate this command, but entering coordinates is also an option.

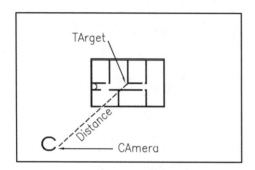
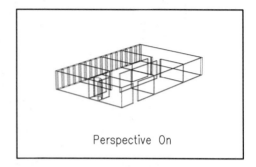

Perspective On

The Distance option turns on perspective, which is determined by the distance between the target and camera. Although you may have set the distance with the Points option, you will again be prompted for distance; the default is the original distance you specified. If you have not previously set the camera to target distance, the default is *1 inch*. The slider bar on the top of the screen is a multiplier of the default number in the prompt area.

The Off option turns perspective viewing off. You can use the regular Zoom command when perspective is off.

The Clip option removes portions of your drawing that are obscuring portions you want to show. The target is considered to be at 0. A negative distance places a clipping plane behind the target, and a positive distance places it in front. Using the slider and watching the effect is the easiest way to perform this function.

Clipping works best with straight-on views: left, right, front, and back. Oblique views result in walls with odd diagonal sections clipped out. You can achieve better results by placing unwanted walls on a separate layer and freezing that layer.

The Hide option in Dview provides only a temporary hide, useful in helping you set up your view. To actually get a view with hidden lines removed, you have to use the Hide command outside the Dview command.

The Pan option repositions the image on the screen. Once you exit Dview, the standard Pan command will not work on a perspective view.

The Zoom option operates as the standard zoom function when you are *not* in perspective. Once you turn on Distance and are working in perspective, Zoom changes to a camera-lens mode. The default is 50mm (a standard 35mm camera with a 50mm lens); the higher the number the closer the view (a telephoto lens) and the lower the number the further away the object appears (a wide angle lens) A wide-angle lens is a good choice for buildings.

N O T E

Zoom doesn't affect the perspective view, because the distance for perspective depends on the distance you set between the camera and the target point, not on AutoCAD's zoom function, which is based on the drawing extents. You cannot zoom or pick a point once you are in a perspective view.

The Twist option rotates the ground plane (this is more appropriate, for example, for views of planes taking off or landing). The Undo option reverses the effect of the last thing you did in Dview. You can step back and undo successive operations. The Exit option takes you out of Dview with the view you have made. An extra ⏎ does the same.

Dview Tips

- When you use the Distance option to get perspective and have not previously set the distance for the camera with the Points option, the default distance for the camera is 1″. This ant's-eye view of your space generally results in a blank screen. Depending upon the size of your building or space, this distance should range from 30 to 300 feet.

- Use the house icon to try out the different options. To avoid the common problem of being so close to your image that you can't see it, zoom out so the house is quite small.

- By setting your coordinate readout to On, you can use the numbers to provide information when placing camera and target points.

- If you get disoriented, exit Dview, get a plan view, and start again.

- If you press ⏎ after the options, the default settings are those of the existing view. You can use these numbers to make adjustments to your view.
- Distances can only be set with the Points and Distance options. Camera and Target change the orientation between Camera and Target only.
- Zoom affects the wide or narrow angle aspect of your perspective and should not be substituted for Distance.
- Use Undo a lot if what you get is not what you want.

● Hide

Obscures lines and planes that lie behind other objects. The Hide command has different effects on different entities. The time it takes to hide lines depends upon the size of your drawing. Recent versions of AutoCAD have greatly increased the speed of the hide, shade, and render functions.

Using the Hide Command

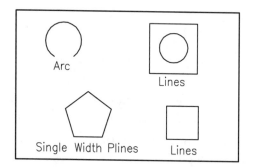
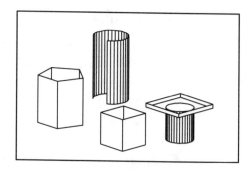

The Hide command works automatically to produce views with hidden lines removed. Vertical surfaces of extruded lines, single-width polylines, and arcs will be rendered opaque. However, these entities have no top or bottom and as a result, horizontal surfaces appear transparent. Hide used in the plan view with these entities has no effect.

All the surfaces of circles, 3-D solids, and wide polylines and those sur-

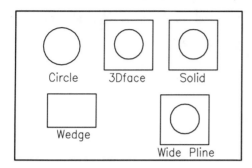

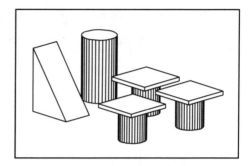

faces produced by 3D Face and Solid look opaque when hidden. These objects will appear to have closed tops and bottoms. Hide used in the plan view
obscures objects that lie under these entities.

Hide Notes

- Wide Plines and surfaces produced with the Solid command will hide
  objects even when Fill is off.
- The hidden-line effect is only temporary. Objects revert to wire-
  frame mode as soon as you use a command that requires a regeneration or when you use Zoom or Pan.
- A saved view will not save your drawing with the hidden lines removed, but you can make a slide showing the lines hidden.
- When you want to plot a drawing with the hidden lines removed, you
  have to use the Hide option of the Plot command—and yes, it takes a
  long time.
- Every so often, some lines that should be hidden won't be. This is
  caused by minute round-off errors in calculating the position of two
  objects that touch. It can generally be fixed by moving the objects
  slightly away from one another

You can shorten the time it takes to hide a view by zooming in to a smaller portion of the drawing. Hide works on the number of lines displayed on your screen—the fewer the lines, the shorter the time. Entities on layers that are off will still hide. Freeze layers with entities that you don't want to obscure other entities.

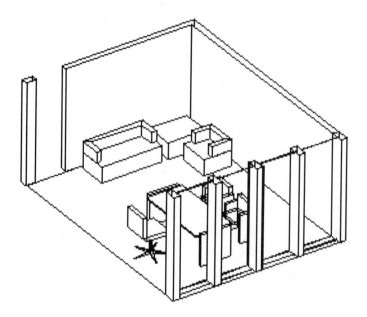

This is an example of Hide used on a room from the office plan. Examples of Shade and Render will follow for comparison.

● Shade

Produces shaded images of drawings. You can make slides of, but cannot plot, these images. You can however make a hard copy using File ➤ Print Window. The image is composed with a single light source in the viewing direction. You can make some modifications to the image by changing the variable Shadedif.

The default is 70, which means that 70 percent of the light is diffused and 30 percent is ambient. The range is from 0 to 100 and the higher the number, the more contrast the image will have. You can also modify the variable Shadedge, although the default <3> probably produces the best results.

0 = Faces shaded; effected by Shadedif; monitor must be capable of displaying 265 colors. Color assignment sometimes surprising.

1 = Same as above but edges are drawn in background color

2 = Effect is similar to Hide effect.

3 = Faces are drawn in the color associated with the entity

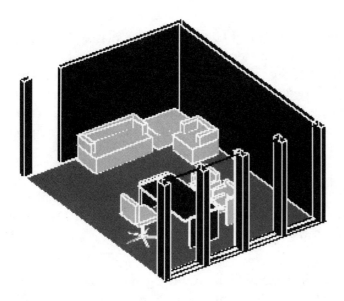

● Render

Rendering is the next step up from hide and shade. You can use different lighting effects, and place textures. While AutoCAD provides many options for manipulating lights, finishes are limited to surface characteristics—how shiny, dull, or rough the surface is. What follows is a brief entry into rendering. If you are serious about rendering, you will want to invest in an actual rendering program that will supply textures, a materials library and the ability to do ray tracing and radiosity. Meanwhile here is a start.

Using Render

Many of the effects in AutoCAD's Render are achieved through the placement and use of lights. There are numerous dialog boxes to effect various parameters, but here we will only deal with simply placing two different light sources—Point and Distant.

Point Light A single source, similar to a light bulb, radiating in all directions. Its property is that it gets dimmer the further away you are from it—the light intensity "falls off". You have choices as to how fast it falls off or whether it does not fall off at all. Generally, the *Inverse Linear* is a good middle-of-the-road choice. It means that it does not fall off too fast. These lights are placed as you would lamps and lighting. In a building type space; try numbers between 60 and 150.

Distance Light The light from this source is like the sun, it is parallel and does not fall off. These lights are placed with a source point and a target point. The light intensity can be a number from 0 to 1.

Ambient Background lighting, which provides general overall illumination. Values can be from 0 to 1. This light is not placed but you can vary its brightness.

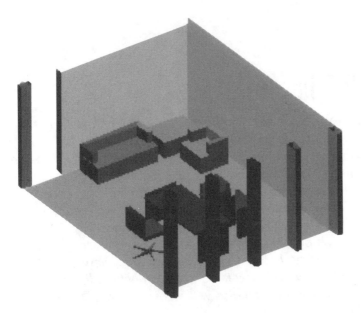

A brief tutorial to produce the rendering shown here occurs at the end of this chapter. Instead of showing the rendering dialog boxes here, they will be used in the tutorial to step you through the process of placing lights for rendering.

TUTORIAL

● Transforming 2-D into 3-D

In your use of AutoCAD so far, you have been drawing mostly in two dimensions. In this lesson you will complete the transition from 2-D to 3-D. Although working drawings are done in 2-D, the third dimension contributes greatly to the understanding of a space—both for the architect and designer, and even more so for their clients. New techniques using animation, rendering, sound, and video are all being explored as tools for producing more effective presentations. But it all begins with 3-D. Drawing an item in 3-D is similar to actually constructing it. Each part must be made, and the sequence of putting together all the parts is important. In this lesson, you will draw new 3-D furniture and replace 2-D furniture by updating the office plan with oldblock=new block, as you learned in Chapter 12. You also will modify some 2-D blocks directly by giving them thickness (height).

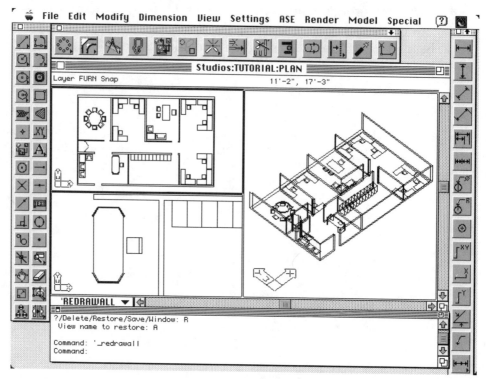

This lesson uses a variety of entities to make 3-D furniture; in this way you can see the effect the Hide command has on the various entities. Start by opening the PLAN drawing.

1. We can finally use the UCS icon. Click on Settings ➤ UCS ➤ Icon On.

2. Divide the screen into three viewports using the View ➤ Layout ➤ Tiled Vports.... Your screen will look like the one at the beginning of the tutorial, except that the plan view will be in all the viewports.

Command: **VIEW ➤ Layout ➤ Tiled Vports**...
Select: **Three: Right**

3. Leave the plan view in the upper-left port, but change the view in the large port to a 3-D view. Remember, to activate a port, you move your cursor into that port and click; the arrow will change to crosshairs, indicating that this is the active port. (On some computers, the images from the ports may overflow one into the other. If this happens, click on View ➤ Redraw All.)

Command: **VIEW ➤ Viewpoint ➤ Presets**...
From: X Axes: **225**
X-Y Plane: **45**

4. As you can see, only the doors and windows have vertical dimensions. Before you go on to the furniture, change the thickness (height) of all the walls except the window walls. (If you give the window wall thickness, it will be solid and obscure the windows when you use Hide. If 0 is not the current layer, make it so, and then turn off all the other layers. This way, it is easier to change only the walls. Pressing Shift lets you pick multiple layers.

Command: **CHANGE POINTS**
Select objects: **W** *Window the entire plan*
Select objects: **R** *Remove the window walls from the selection*
Properties/<Change point>: **P**

Change what property (Color/Elev/LAyer/LType/Thickness)?   **T**
New thickness: **8'**

5. When you are finished, turn the layers back on and make FURN the active layer. Change the elevation and thickness of the conference table. You must explode the block first to be able to change it. When the block is exploded, the table will revert to layer 0. It will have to be changed back to layer FURN.

6. Activate the lower left-hand port and use it to zoom in and get close-up views of the objects you are working on. You can observe the changes taking place in 3-D in the large viewport.

7. It is not necessary to draw a base, because the chairs around the table will hide it. Use the Change (instead of Ddmodify) command to give the top thickness, elevate it 27″ from the floor and change it back to the Furn layer. (Since you have to use Change Points to change the elevation, you might as well use it to change the other properties.)

Command: **CHANGE POINTS**
Select objects: *Select conference table edge*
Properties/<Change point>: **P**
Change what property (Color/Elev/LAyer/LType/Thickness)?   **E**
New elevation: **27**
Change what property (Color/Elev/LAyer/LType/Thickness)?   **T**
New thickness <0'-0″>: **1-1/2**
Change what property (Color/Elev/LAyer/LType/Thickness)?   **LA**
New layer: **FURN**

8. To make a 3-D file, you will modify the old block to give it height and then redefine the original file block. First, insert another file, explode it, and change the height to 3'. Then remake the block with the same name. Remember that the insertion point is the midpoint of the line at the back of the file.

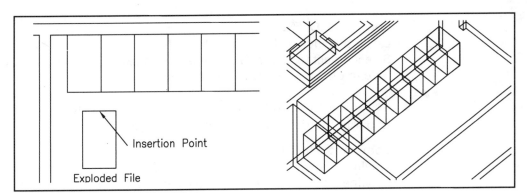

Insertion Point

Exploded File

Command: **INSERT**
Block: **B-FILE**
Select: **Explode**

Command: **BLOCK**
Select Name: **B-FILE**
Block FILE already exists.
Redefine it? <N>: **Y**
Insertion base point: MID of   *Pick back of file*
Select objects: *Window object*
Block FILE redefined.

9. The receptionist's desk is lying on the floor. Give it panel legs by using plines. You will need guidelines for the plines because they are drawn from the center of their width (it is difficult to line up the edges of wide plines). Offset the desk ends as guidelines. Make only one panel leg and mirror it to the other side of the desk. The desk top will be given thickness and raised from the floor—it's just like actually building it. Zoom as you need to.

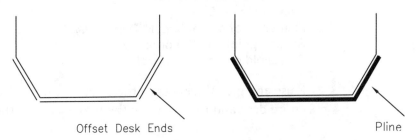

Offset Desk Ends   Pline

Command: **OFFSET**
Offset distance or Through <Through>: **1**
Select object to offset: *Pick one of the edges on the side of the desk*
Side to offset: *Pick away from the desk edge*

10. Repeat for the other two edges. Then, use Fillet with a radius of 0 to join the three sections into a continuous line.

Command: **FILLET**
Polyline/Radius/<Select two objects>: *Join first two sections*
Polyline/Radius/<Select two objects>: *Join remaining sections*

11. Draw a panel leg by using Pline with a width of 1″, and draw over the guidelines snapping to each vertex.

Command: **PLINE ➤ 2D Polyline**
From point: *Use END Osnap*
Arc/Close/Halfwidth/Length/Undo/Width/: **W**
Starting width <0′-0″>: **1** (Sets width to 1″)
Ending width <0′-1″>: ⏎

12. Give the panel leg thickness (height).

Command: **CHANGE POINTS**
Select objects: **L** (Last object drawn)
Properties/<Change point>: **P**
Change what property (Color/Elev/LAyer/LType/Thickness)?   **T**
New thickness <0′-0″>: **30**

13. Mirror the leg to the other side of the desk using the midpoint of the desk as the mirror line.

Command: **MIRROR ➤ 2D**
Select objects: **L**
First point of mirror line: **MID** of   *desk top*
Second point: <Ortho on>: ⏎
Delete old objects? <N>: ⏎

14. Raise and give thickness to the desk top. It is easier to select the entire desk and then remove the two legs from the selection.

Command: **CHANGE POINTS**
Select objects: *Window the whole desk*
Select objects: **R** *Remove the two panel legs*
Properties/<Change point>: **P**
Change what property (Color/Elev/LAyer/LType/Thickness)?   **E**
New elevation: **29**
Change what property (Color/Elev/LAyer/LType/Thickness)?   **T**
New thickness <0'-0">: **1-1/2**

15. You have finished changing 2-D objects into 3-D ones. The next step is to construct 3-D objects from scratch. Save the changes to this drawing and open a new one.

Making 3-D Furniture

Now, on to more serious 3-D drawing.

1. Open a new drawing, name it FURN3D. Establish the following settings:

Units: **Architectural**
Precision: **1/2"**
Snap: X and Y: **1"** *and* **On**
Grid: X and Y: **6"** *and* **On**
Ortho: **On**
Solid Fill: **On**
Quick Text: **Off**
Blips: **Off**
Highlight: **On**
Limits: **-1',-1'** *and* **21',17'**
Command: **ZOOM ➤ All** (To set the new limits)

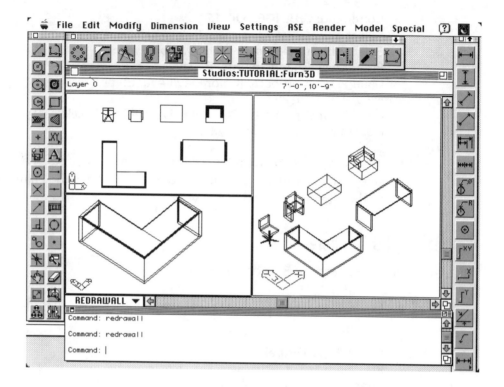

2. This drawing is used as a workspace to make blocks of 3-D furniture. Your drawing layout does not have to look exactly like the one in the book. You will first make the drawings of the furniture and then Wblock them. Divide the screen into three ports. Make one a plan view, one a 3-D view and use the other port to zoom in and work up close. The technique is to work in plan view and watch the results in 3-D view.

Command: **VIEW ➤ Layout ➤ Tiled Vports**…
Select: **Three: Right**

Command: **VIEW ➤ Viewpoint ➤ Presets**…
From: X Axes : **225**
X-Y Plane: **45**

3. Draw the side table using the 3D Object called Box.

> Command: **3D OBJECTS** *Select Box*
> Corner of box: *Place anywhere*
> Length: **3'2**
> Cube/<Width>: **2'4**
> Height: **15**
> Rotation angle about Z axis: **0** (You must specify something to get out of the command)

4. When drawing the three-dimensional side chair, using Pline makes it easier to select the different sections when you are changing elevation or thickness. The technique is to draw each part—seat, back, and arms—and to change their thickness and elevation immediately after you draw them. This allows you to select them as a unit instead of separate lines.

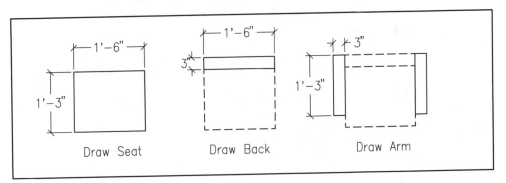

5. Draw the seat of the side chair.

> Command: **PLINE ➤ 2D Polyline**

6. Change the thickness of the seat to 2", and then move the seat up 15".

> Command: **CHANGE POINTS**
> Select objects: *Select seat*
> Properties/<Change point>: **P**
> Change what property (Color/Elev/LAyer/LType/Thickness)?   **T**

New thickness: **2**
Change what property (Color/Elev/LAyer/LType/Thickness)?   **E**
New elevation: **15**
Change what property (Color/Elev/LAyer/LType/Thickness)?   ⏎

7. Draw the back of the chair. Drawing in 3-D is different from drawing in two dimensions, because you have to draw all the planes.

Command: **PLINE ➤ 2D Polyline** *Draw all four sides*

8. Change the back thickness to 32". The back and arms of this chair have been designed as panels and go to the floor. Because you don't have to change the elevation, and there is only one object, use Ddmodify.

Command: **DDMODIFY**
Select object to modify: *Pick chair back*
Thickness: **32**

9. Draw one of the arms.

Command: **PLINE ➤ 2D Polyline** *Draw all four sides*

10. Change the arm thickness to 26".

Command: **DDMODIFY**
Select object to modify: *Pick chair arm*
Thickness: **26**

11. Mirror the other arm to the other side of the chair.

Command: **MIRROR ➤ 2D** (Use the midpoint of the chair seat as the mirror line)

12. Draw the lounge chair using a combination of 3D Objects and wide plines.

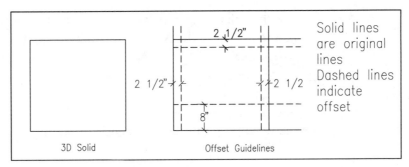

2 1/2"

2 1/2"   2 1/2

8"

Solid lines are original lines
Dashed lines indicate offset

3D Solid   Offset Guidelines

Command: **3D Objects** *Select Box*
Corner of box: *Place anywhere*
Length: **30**
Cube/<Width>: **28**
Height: **15**
Rotation angle about Z axis: **0**

13. Make guidelines for the centerlines of the plines. Draw lines over the box and then offset them.

Command: **LINE ➤ 1 Segment** *Draw four construction lines extending past the four sides*

Command: **OFFSET** (Offset the front side 8" inward)
Command: **OFFSET** (Offset the other three sides 2-1/2" inward)

14. Using the guidelines, draw the back and side of the lounge with a pline, with a width of 5". Turn on Fill if it is not already on.

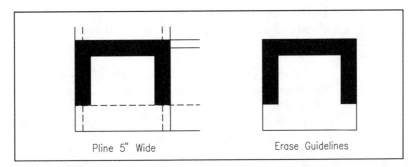

Pline 5" Wide   Erase Guidelines

Command: **PLINE ➤ 2D Polyline** (Use INT Osnap)
Command: **ERASE** *Turn Osnap off and erase the construction lines*

15. Change the thickness and elevation of the pline you just drew. To get a feel of how the Move command works to change elevation, use it in the next few steps requiring a change of elevation.

Command: **CHANGE POINTS**
Select objects: **L**
Properties/<Change point>: **P**
Change what property (Color/Elev/LAyer/LType/Thickness)?   **T**
New thickness: **10**

Command: **MOVE**
Select objects: **P** (Previous)
Displacement: **0,0,15**
Second point of displacement: ⏎

16. To make the executive desk, you will use plines for the legs and a 3D Face to make the top opaque.

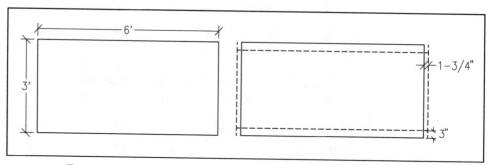

First, draw the outline of the desk top using the dimensions shown. Then, make guidelines for the panel leg by offsetting the lines from the desk.

Command: **OFFSET** *Offset the sides of the desk outward 1-3/4"*
Command: **OFFSET** *Offset the front and back edges of the desk inward 3'*
Command: **EXTEND** *Extend the lines to get intersections*

17. Draw the side panel legs with a Pline width of 3".

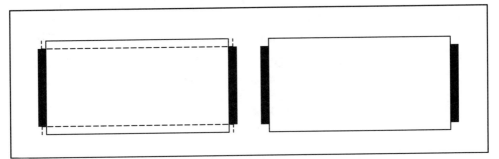

Command: **PLINE ➤ 2D Polyline** (Use INT Osnap)
Command: **ERASE** *Turn Osnap off and erase the guidelines*

18. Change the thickness (height) of the two legs.

Command: **CHANGE POINTS**
Select objects: *Pick both legs*
Properties/<Change point>: **P**
Change what property (Color/Elev/LAyer/LType/Thickness)? **T**
New thickness <0'-0">: **30**

19. Put a 3D Face on the desk top. Use an END Osnap to make sure
that the face edges match the top exactly. Remember to pick the
points by going sequentially around the perimeter (not like
Solid). It is hard to see 3D Faces when drawn over existing lines.
If you are having trouble, make a layer with a different color and
draw the faces on that layer. When you are ready to Wblock the
furniture remember to change everything to layer 0.

Command: **3D Face**
First point:
Second point:
Third point:
Fourth point: (Specify only four corners; do not duplicate first point)
Third point: ⏎

20. Window the desk top and move it to an elevation of 29″. It is easier to window the entire desk and remove the two side panels with the Remove (R) option than to try to pick only the desk top. This will move both the desk top and the 3D Face.

Command: **MOVE**
Select objects: **W** *Window whole desk*
Select objects: **R** *Remove legs*
Displacement: **0,0,29**
Second point of displacement: ⏎

21. To get a top with thickness, specify a thickness of −1- 1/2″. Because 3D Faces cannot have thickness, this gives the top an extrusion thickness while leaving the face on the desk top. 3D Faces are difficult to separate from the lines they are drawn upon, so workarounds like this one have been developed.

Command: **CHANGE POINTS**
Select objects: *Select the desk top*
Properties/<Change point>: **P**
Change what property (Color/Elev/LAyer/LType/Thickness)?   **T**
New thickness: **−1-1/2**
Change what property (Color/Elev/LAyer/LType/Thickness)?   ⏎
Cannot change thickness of 3D Faces (OK by us)

22. The process for the workstation is similar to the one used for the executive desk.

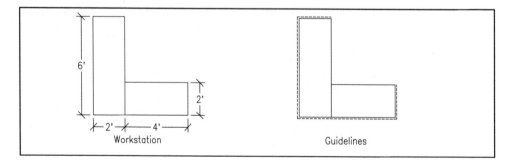

Workstation   Guidelines

Draw the workstation using the dimensions shown. Make guidelines for the panel by offsetting lines from the desk.

Command: **OFFSET** *Offset outside edges 1-1/4"*
Command: **FILLET** (Use 0 radius to make corners intersect)

23. Put a 3D Face on the desk top. Do each section separately.

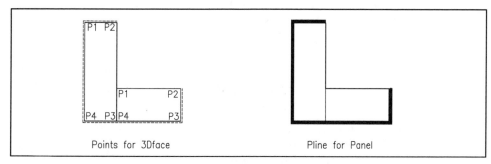

Points for 3Dface   Pline for Panel

Command: **3D Face**
First point: *Use End Osnap to place points at desk corners*
Second point:
Third point:
Fourth point: (When you specify this point, AutoCAD closes the polygon)
Third point: ⏎

Command: **3D Face** *Do the same for the other section*

24. Draw the panel around the desk with a 2" wide pline.

Command: **PLINE ➤ 2D Polyline** *Use End Osnap to draw pline*

25. Give the panel thickness (height).

Command: **CHANGE POINTS**
Select objects: **L**
Properties/<Change point>: **P**
Change what property (Color/Elev/LAyer/LType/Thickness)?   **T**
New thickness <0'-0">: **30**

26. Elevate the desk top and 3D Face. As in the executive desk, window the entire workstation and remove the panels from the selection.

Command: **MOVE**
Select objects: **W** *Window the whole workstation*
Select objects: **R** *Remove panels*
Displacement: **0,0,29**
Second point of displacement: ⏎

27. Once again you will fool AutoCAD, as you did when you made the executive desk and gave the top thickness while leaving the face on the desk top.

Command: **CHANGE POINTS**
Select objects: **P**
Properties/<Change point>: **P**
Change what property (Color/Elev/LAyer/LType/Thickness)?   **T**
New thickness <0'-0">: **–1-1/2** (Remember the minus sign)
Change what property (Color/Elev/LAyer/LType/Thickness)?   ⏎
Cannot change thickness of 3D Faces (AutoCAD fooled again)

28. The best is for last—the desk chair. Start by constructing the base, which is made up of a wedge that is one of the 3D Objects.

Command: **3D OBJECTS** *Select Wedge*
Corner of wedge: *Place anywhere*
Length: **12**
Width: **1**
Height: **2**
Rotation angle about Z axis: **90**

29. Draw a circle for the post and give it thickness (height). This time use Ddmodify.

Command: **CIRCLE ➤ Center, Diameter**
3P/2P/TTR/<Center point>: *Place circle below wedge as shown in figure below* (Use osnap overrides for exact placement)
Diameter: **1.5**

Command: **DDMODIFY**
Select object to modify: *Pick post*
Thickness: **16**

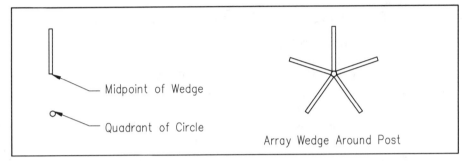

Midpoint of Wedge

Quadrant of Circle

Array Wedge Around Post

Command: **MOVE**
Select objects: *Pick the circle*
Base point: *Pick upper quadrant of circle* (Use QUA Osnap)
Second point: *Pick midpoint on width of wedge* (Use MID Osnap)

30. Array the wedge around the circle.

Command: **ARRAY**
Select objects: *Select the wedge*
Rectangular or Polar array (R/P): **P**
Center point of array: *Pick a point on the circle* (Use CEN Osnap)
Number of items: **5**
Angle to fill <360>: ⏎
Rotate objects as they are copied? <Y>: ⏎

31. Draw the chair seat and back with Pline. Draw all four sides of both parts.

Command: **PLINE ➤ 2D Polyline** (Draw a seat 18"×18")
Command: **PLINE ➤ 2D Polyline** (Draw a back 18"×3")

32. Change the thickness of the seat and its elevation. Go back to using Change Points for both operations.

Command: **CHANGE POINTS**
Select objects: *Select seat*
Properties/<Change point>: **P**
Change what property (Color/Elev/LAyer/LType/Thickness)?   **T**

New thickness: **3**
Change what property (Color/Elev/LAyer/LType/Thickness)?   **E**
New elevation: **16**

33. Change the thickness of the back and its elevation.

Command: **CHANGE POINTS**
Select objects: *Select back*
Properties/<Change point>: **P**
Change what property (Color/Elev/LAyer/LType/Thickness)?   **T**
New thickness: **15**
Change what property (Color/Elev/LAyer/LType/Thickness)?   **E**
New elevation: **19**

34. Move the seat and back onto the base. Use XY Filters to select the center of the seat. Moving between the viewports can make it easier to place the seat on the post.

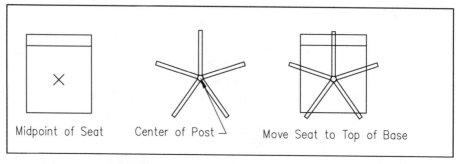

Midpoint of Seat   Center of Post   Move Seat to Top of Base

Command: **MOVE**
Select objects: *Select both seat and back*
Base point: **.X** *Pick the Midpoint of the seat front*
(need YZ): *Pick the Midpoint of the seat side*
Second point of displacement: *Select the top edge of the post in a 3-D view*

35. To make the seat and back of the chair appear opaque so that the base will not show through, put a 3D Face on them. Use the END Osnap to pick the points in one direction around the perimeter. Working in a 3-D view place the 3D Face on the top planes of the chair seat and back.

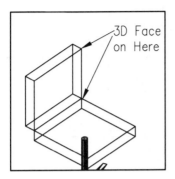

3D Face on Here

Command: **3DFACE** *Pick the four corners of the seat*
Command: **3DFACE** *Pick the four corners of the seat back*

Changing 2-D Block to 3-D

You have finished making all the furniture in 3-D. The next step is to Wblock these pieces and to replace the 2-D pieces in the PLAN drawing with the ones you just made. Keeping the correct names for the blocks is important and will make the instructions easier to follow.

1. Wblock the items you have drawn, giving them the insertion points and names shown in the drawing. Special handling is necessary for the chair blocks. When Wblocking the desk chair (B-3CHD) and the side chair (B-3CHS) you must use XY Filters to place the insertion point so you can specify that the Z elevation be 0. If you just pick the midpoints of the chairs the Z elevation will be at the top of the seat.

Command: **WBLOCK**
Filename: **B-3CHD**
Block name: ⏎
Insertion base point: > **.XY** *Pick the midpoint of chair seat*
<(needs Z)>: **0**
Select objects: *Window the chair*

2. Do the same for the side chair.

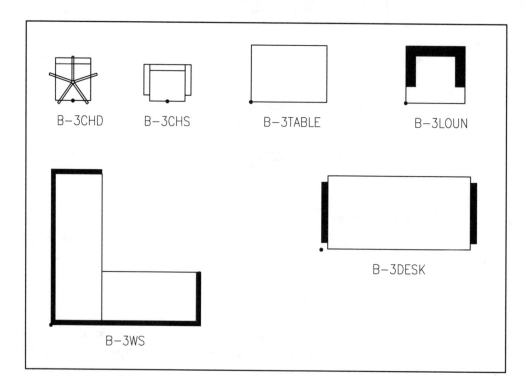

B—3CHD B—3CHS B—3TABLE B—3LOUN

B—3DESK

B—3WS

3. Open the PLAN drawing, get a 3-D view, and redefine the blocks. When asked for the insertion point, press ⌘-. or Ctrl-C. If you have Regenauto turned off, you must regenerate the drawing to see the change.

Command: **INSERT** (Type it)

4. Insert the following: (Type it)

B-CHD=B-3CHD
B-CHS=B-3CHS
B-TABLE=B-3TABLE

B-LOUN=B-3LOUN
B-WS=B-3WS
B-DESK=B-3DESK

5. You will notice that the sofa that you made by stretching the lounge chair was not updated. That is because you exploded it so you could stretch it. To make a new sofa, erase the old block and insert the new one, explode it, and stretch it (2'-6") again. You will have to change it back to the FURN layer. Notice that the block names have not changed even though their appearance has. The *name* of block is just a place holder—you can put anything in that place.

6. If you want the files to have a top so that you do not see through them, put a 3D Face on them. Use a height of 36-1/4". Adding the little extra ensures that there is no round-off error between the files and the top.

Getting a Perspective View

Now it's time to take a look at the plan in both axonometric and perspective views. You may find that you can work faster if you freeze all the layers but the one the walls are on (0 layer) and thaw them when you get the view you want. This is particularly true when working in perspective.

1. Return to a single view.

Command: **VIEW ➤ Layout ➤ Tiled V Ports**
Select: **Single**

2. To get a view of the reception area and the conference room, put the walls obscuring the view into the office on a separate layer. Call it *HIDE* and freeze it. In doing drawings for presentations, it is often necessary to hide walls and objects that obscure views.

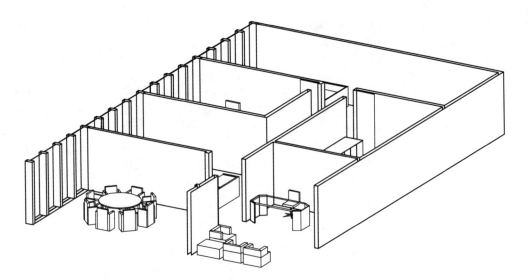

3. Although a 45 degree angle from the X-Y plane is good for working, for a presentation, 20 degrees is a more pleasing angle.

Command: **VIEW ➤ Viewpoint ➤ Presets**...
From: X Axes: **210**
X-Y Plane: **20**

4. It is a good idea to save the views you make so you can return to them.

Command: **VIEW ➤ Named Views ➤ New**
Name: **AXON**

5. To get a perspective of the office, return to the plan view and zoom out so that you have room to place the camera. If you haven't done so already, freeze all the layers except layer 0.

6. In Dview use the POints option to specify camera and target points. Use filters so you can pick the xy location and then specify the height. Once this is done use the Distance option to put the plan into perspective.

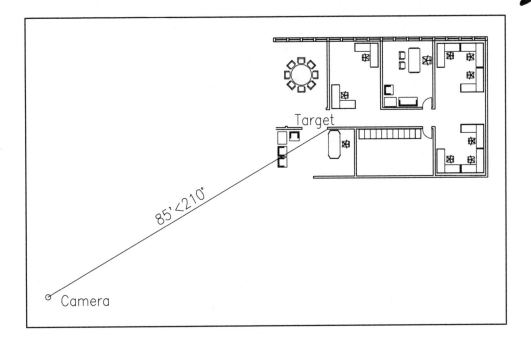

Command: **DVIEW** Select objects: *Select the plan*

CAmera/TArget/Distance/POints/PAn/Zoom/TWist
/CLip/Hide/Off/Undo/<eXit>: **PO**

Enter target point: **.XY** (Use filters and END Osnap to pick wall next to reception desk)

(need Z): **5'** (Target height)

Enter camera point: **.XY** (Use relative coordinates and filters to place the camera) **@85'< 210**

(need Z): **10'6** (Camera height)

CAmera/TArget/Distance/POints/PAn/Zoom/TWist
/CLip/Hide/Off/Undo/<eXit>: **D**

New camera/target distance <85'-2 9/64">: ⏎ (Distance already specified)

CAmera/TArget/Distance/POints/PAn/Zoom/TWist
/CLip/Hide/Off/Undo/<eXit>: **X**

7. Your plan is now in perspective and should look like this after the Furn and Window layers are thawed (Door can stay frozen) and the hidden lines have been removed:

Command: **RENDER ➤ Hide**

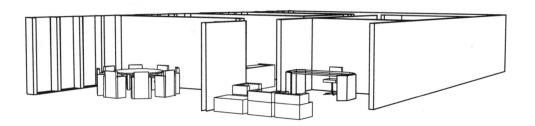

8. Before you end the session, save the perspective view, because you will need it in the next lesson.

Command: **VIEW ➤ Named Views ➤ New**
Name: **PERSP**

You have experimented with a number of different techniques to produce 3-D objects. Some are more successful than others, and some are easier to use. Extruded forms are the easiest to use, but as you can see from the receptionist's glass topped desk, although their vertical surfaces are opaque, their top surfaces are not. Circles are opaque on top. Plines are also opaque (as you can see from the lounge chair and the desk), but in plan view they are filled and can produce a heavy appearance on the plan if used excessively. 3D Faces are opaque but are trickier to use. 3D Objects are meshes and are opaque, but they increase the size of your drawing. Sometimes a simple extrusion will do; at other times, the presentation will require you to use all the 3-D tools available. Professional rendering makes use of 3D Faces and meshes so that textures can be placed on them.

Sampling Rendering

Rendering will provide many pleasurable hours of tinkering with color and lights. What follows is a brief entry into this world. Use the examples in the dialog shown here for your settings. First you will prepare a space for rendering.

1. First, you will need a sample space to work on. The full office plan is too large to allow for much experimenting so work on a single room. The executive office works well, or you could choose the conference room. The easiest way to do this is to make a copy of the PLAN drawing and trim out the room from the whole plan. Use the commands you are already familiar with, Trim and Erase. You will have to explode the window blocks to erase part of them. Wblock the room and then open the drawing you just Wblocked. You can discard the rest of the Plan drawing.

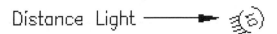

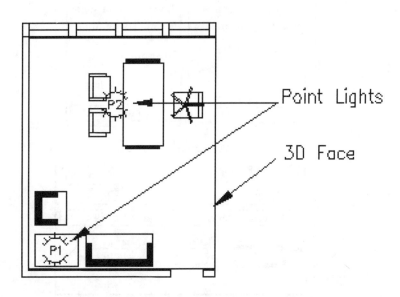

2. If you want the floor to be rendered you will need to put a face on the floor. Use 3D Face and outline the four corners of the room.

3. Set colors so that there is a range. For the book, only gray shades were used but you can experiment with many of the different shades available from the color palette.

4. Use Vpoint or Dview to get a view or views that you want to render and save them under Named Views. These will be available to you when you are in the rendering program. Save a plan view with enough room to place lights. Render will automatically initialize itself as soon as you select one of the Render related commands. For the arrangement in the book, two Point light sources and one Direct were used.

Placing Lights

```
┌─────────────────────────────────────────────┐
│  ┌─Rendering Type─────┐ ┌─Rendering Options─┐ │
│  │ ◉ Full Render      │ │ □ Smooth Shading  │ │
│  │                    │ │                   │ │
│  │ ○ Quick Render     │ │ □ Merge           │ │
│  │                    │ │                   │ │
│  │ ○ ACAD RenderMan   │ │ □ Apply Finishes  │ │
│  │  ┌─Select Query──┐ │ │                   │ │
│  │  │ Select All  ▼ │ │ │  More Options...  │ │
│  │  └───────────────┘ │ └───────────────────┘ │
│                                                │
│  ┌─Settings───────────────────────────────┐   │
│  │ □ RMan Prompting                        │   │
│  │ Icon Scale:                   │ 36 │    │   │
│  └─────────────────────────────────────────┘  │
│   │ Information... │        │ Reconfigure < │   │
│     ┌───────┐   ┌────────┐   ┌─────────┐       │
│     │  OK   │   │ Cancel │   │ Help... │       │
│     └───────┘   └────────┘   └─────────┘       │
└─────────────────────────────────────────────┘
```

1. Before you place the lights, go to Render ➤ Preference and set the scale for the icons to 36 so you can see them. Now place the first Point light.

```
┌─Select Light Type:─────────┐
│ ◉ Point Light              │
│ ○ Distant Light            │
│ ○ Spotlight                │
└────────────────────────────┘

[  OK  ]  [ Cancel ]  [ Help... ]
```

```
Light Name:              [P1    ]
Intensity:               [100   ]
◄ ▓▓▓▓▓▓▓▓▓▓▓▓▓▓▓▓░ ►
┌─Position─────────────────────┐
│ [   Modify <   ]  [ Show... ] │
│ [   Modify Light Color...   ] │
└───────────────────────────────┘
Depth Map Size:          [0]
◄                              ►

[   OK   ]  [ Cancel ]  [ Help... ]
```

Command: **RENDER ➤ Lights**
Lights: **New**
New Light Type: **Point Light**
Light Name: **P1**
Intensity: **100**
Modify: *Position the light using the .XY filters. Use **.XY** to pick a point over the corner table and for the Z height type in **5'***

2. Place the second Point light.

Command: **RENDER ➤ Lights**
Lights: **New**
New Light Type: **Point Light**
Light Name: **P2**
Intensity: **60**
Modify: *Position the light using the .XY filters. Use **.XY** to pick a point over the desk and for the Z height type in **5'***

3. Place a Distance light.

Command: **Render ➤ Lights**
Lights: **New**
New Light Type: **Distance Light**
Light Name: **D1**
Intensity: **14**
Modify: *First pick a point indicating the target—the outside of the first column on the right. Second, position the light off to the right of the columns. The light is at ground level so there is no Z component.*

4. For the Ambient light value enter .30.

5. You are finished placing the lights, now all you have to do is click on Render. The image should be similar to the render example shown earlier in the chapter.

Command: **RENDER**

6. If you like what you see, save the combination of lights and views as a scene. You can then go ahead and create more scenes by changing views and lights.

Command: **RENDER ➤ Scene**

```
┌─────────────────────────────────────┐
│        Scenes                        │
│  ┌──────────────┬─┐  ┌────────────┐  │
│  │*NONE*        │⇧│  │   New...    │  │
│  │243           │ │  └────────────┘  │
│  │BOOK252       │ │                  │
│  │GREY          │ │  ┌────────────┐  │
│  │              │ │  │  Modify...  │  │
│  │              │ │  └────────────┘  │
│  │              │ │                  │
│  │              │ │  ┌────────────┐  │
│  │              │⇩│  │  Delete     │  │
│  └──────────────┴─┘  └────────────┘  │
│  ┌──────┐ ┌────────┐ ┌──────────┐    │
│  │  OK  │ │ Cancel │ │  Help...  │    │
│  └──────┘ └────────┘ └──────────┘    │
└─────────────────────────────────────┘
```

7. Images can be saved in a variety of formats: TGA, TIFF, GIF, or RND.

Command: **RENDER ➤ File... ➤ Save**

Image Name: `EXEC`

Folder : `LIBRARY`

Format
- ○ TGA
- ◉ TIFF
- ○ GIF

Portion

[Options...]   [Reset]

Offset X: `0`   Y: `0`

Size X: `531`   Y: `278`

Default 531x278

[OK]   [Cancel]   [Help...]

8. Once saved you can replay the images.

Command: **RENDER ➤ File... ➤ Replay**

9. When you have finished, unload Render because it takes up a lot of memory.

Command: **RENDER ➤ Unload Render.**

10. You can print these images with File ➤ Print Window.

19

Plotting Drawings

-Plot Rotati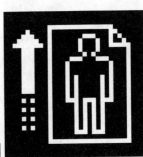

○ 0

-Plot Origin

X CAD doesn't seem real until you hold hard copy of your drawing in your hands. This chapter steps you through the plotting commands and introduces you to AutoCAD's boon to plotting—paper space.

In previous AutoCAD versions, if you wanted to plot a drawing that had various scales or had a 3-D view and a plan view on a single sheet, you had to go through complex gyrations. All this can now be done easily through paper space.

- Plot
- Print Window
- Tilemode
- Paper space
- Model space
- Mview
- Vplayer
- Zoom—XP

File Edit Modify Di	
New...	⌘N
Open...	⌘O
Save	⌘S
Save As...	
Recover...	
File Utilities	▶
Configure	
Page Setup...	
Plot...	⌘P
Print Window...	⌘D
Compile...	
Applications...	
Quit AutoCAD	⌘Q

View Settings	
Redraw	⌘R
Redraw All	
Zoom	▶
Pan	
Tilemode	▶
Toggle UP	
Model space	
Paper space	
Mview	▶
Dview	
Plan View	▶
Viewpoint	▶
Named view...	
Layout	▶

● Plot

Controls the process by which you transfer your drawings to paper. Specific sizes of plots and numbers of pens are governed by the type of plotter you have. The examples that follow are for printers. If you have a plotter, check for instructions in the plotter's manual.

Using the Plot Command

After you issue the Plot command the main plot dialog box appears. This dialog box has six sections, some of which access other dialog boxes. Generally, most of what you need to specify is on this main plot dialog box. Two others, which you will probably use often, are the ones for rotation and preview.

┌─ **Device and Default Information** ─┐
Chooser Printer
    [**Device and Default Selection...**]

┌─ **Pen Parameters** ─┐
[**Pen Assignments...**] [**Optimization...**]

┌─ **Additional Parameters** ─┐
○ **Display**   ☐ **Hide Lines**
◉ **Extents**
○ **Limits**   ☐ **Adjust Area Fill**
○ **View**
○ **Window**   ☐ **Plot To File**
[**View...**] [**Window...**] [**File Name...**]

┌─ **Paper Size and Orientation** ─┐
◉ **Inches**
    [**Size...**] **MAX**
○ **MM**
Plot Area 7.66 by 10.13.

┌─ **Scale, Rotation, and Origin** ─┐
[**Rotation and Origin...**]
Plotted Inches = Drawing Units
[0.125] = [1']
☐ **Scaled to Fit**

┌─ **Plot Preview** ─┐
[**Preview...**]   ◉ **Partial**   ○ **Full**

[**OK**]   [**Cancel**]   [**Help...**]

Scale, Rotation, and Origin This section on the main plot dialog box is where you specify the scale to plot your drawing and the rotation of the paper. You may specify scale as you would in a drawing $1/8'' = 1'$. AutoCAD will translate it to decimal. The Scaled to Fit option will plot the entire drawing area you specify on the size sheet you have selected.

```
┌─────────────────────────────────────────────────────────────┐
│  LaserWriter Page Setup                    7.1.2    ┌──────┐  │
│  Paper: ◉ US Letter  ○ A4 Letter                    │  OK  │  │
│         ○ US Legal   ○ B5 Letter  ○ │ Tabloid  ▼│  ┌────────┐│
│         Reduce or ┌───┐                            │ Cancel ││
│         Enlarge:  │100│ %   Printer Effects:        ┌────────┐│
│                   └───┘     ☒ Font Substitution?   │Options ││
│         Orientation         ☒ Text Smoothing?                │
│            ┌──┐┌──┐         ☒ Graphics Smoothing?            │
│            │↑👤││↑ │         ☒ Faster Bitmap Printing?        │
│            └──┘└──┘                                          │
└─────────────────────────────────────────────────────────────┘
```

Selecting Rotation and Orientation provides another dialog box. Vertical orientation is 0. Horizontal or landscape is 90. Print origin is lower left at 0,0. If you wish your plot to start somewhere else on the page, specify the offset in inches.

If you want hidden lines removed, specify it here. Images on your screen that have hidden lines removed will *not* plot with these lines removed unless you also specify it here.

Plot Preview This is a great addition. You can preview how your plot lays on the paper. Before you plot you can tell if you have specified the scale incorrectly. You have a choice of Partial or Full Preview. Generally Partial gives you sufficient feedback. Full takes longer but shows the entire drawing and does hidden line removal if that was specified.

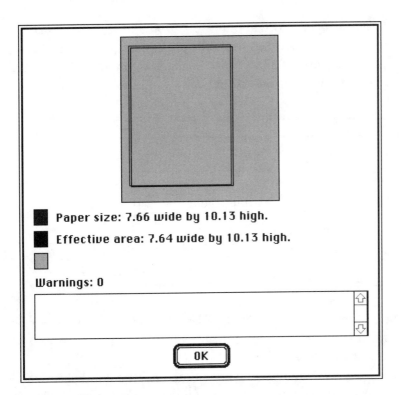

Paper size: 7.66 wide by 10.13 high.

Effective area: 7.64 wide by 10.13 high.

Warnings: 0

OK

Device and Default Selection The type of printer you are using is set during configuration but you can configure an additional 26 configurations. These configurations can include pen assignments and output configurations.

Pen Assignments On printers, numbers indicate the width of the lines. Generally .003″ is the thinnest.

Paper Size and Orientation Contains a list of paper sizes and options for specifying user sizes.

Optimization Controls pen motion. Not relevant for printers.

Macintosh Page Setup A word about orientation and scale that is specific to the Macintosh. Leave the settings in the Page Setup in their normal setup for general printing (vertical and 100%). Make your changes in orientation and scale for your drawings in AutoCAD.

```
┌─Plot Rotation──────────────────────────┐
│  ○ 0      ● 90      ○ 180      ○ 270     │
├─Plot Origin────────────────────────────┤
│  X Origin: [0.00]    Y Origin: [0.00]   │
└────────────────────────────────────────┘
        [  OK  ]      [ Cancel ]
```

One thing that you can do in the Mac Page Setup dialog box is to use the Option for Inverse printing to get white lines on a black background—a striking effect for presentations.

To plot drawings where the width of the lines are controlled by the pen specifications you will have to reconfigure your printer driver to something other than Chooser, such as the AutoCAD PostScript device ADI 4.2 driver.

Plotting Line Weights

To use pen assignments to control line weight, your Chooser device must be a PostScript device. You will then have to configure a second plotter using the ADI driver, set pen thickness linked to color, plot to a file, change the file type of the plot file, and use the Laser Writer Font Utility to send the file to the printer. It sounds more complicated than it really is and once you have done it a few times, it will go quite quickly.

Configure Plotter In AutoCAD:

- Go to **File ➤ Configure**.
- Select Configure Plotter.
- Select Add a plotter configuration.
- Select PostScript device ADI 4.2 - by Autodesk, Inc.
- Accept all defaults in the configuration.
- When asked for "Description for this Plotter" give it a name. I call mine *PenWidth* but you can call yours *George*. I find descriptive names easier to remember.
- Exit the configuration menu and keep the changes.

Set Pen Widths Pen widths are set in the Plot dialog box under **Pen Parameters ➤ Pen Assignments** and are keyed to color. Click OK when you are done. You can assign widths similar to the ones I have set or make assignments that more specifically suit your needs. Pen width .003 is the thinnest line you can get on a 300 dpi printer; .010 is the default line width; .36 is pretty wide.

Color	Pen No.	Linetype	Speed	Pen Width
1	1			0.003
2	2			0.006
3	3			0.009
4	4			0.009
5	5			0.018
6	6			0.036
7	7			0.010
8	8			0.010
9	1			0.010
10	1			0.010

Modify Values
Color: 1 (red)
Pen: 1
Ltype:
Speed:
Width: 0.003

Feature Legend...
Pen Width:

OK   Cancel

To save these defaults to a file, click on Device and Default Selection, highlight the new configuration, and save. For simplicity, give it the same name as the new plotter configuration. The file will automatically be given a .PCP extension.

Plotting the File All the above is the setup, which you will do only once. What follows is what you have to do each time you wish to plot:

- Click on the Plot command and select what you want to plot.
- Check Plot to File.
- Name the file and click on Save button.
- Click on OK in the Main Plot dialog box. This produces a file with the extension .PLT.

Changing the File Type Go to File ➤ File Utilities ➤ File Info. Open the .PLT file. In the Type box, change PLT to TEXT (all caps) and click OK.

Sending the File to the Printer Get out of AutoCAD (do not close) and open Laser Writer Font Utility (you can find this in Utilities folder on the Tidbit disk of your Apple System 7 disk set). Click on Utilities and select Download PostScript File. Open your .PLT file. Save PostScript output as: PostScript Log (the default). You will get the following prompt "Downloading the file," and then "No output was returned from the PostScript printer, so no output file was created." (This means that the file was successfully transferred.) Click OK to this message. This will print a file with the line widths you have assigned to the pens for the different colors.

● Print Window

The old familiar Print Window option under the File menu works here as you might expect it to. This option will print rendering images and views of the screen showing multiple ports. The resolution is poor but good enough for check plots.

● Tilemode

The variable that switches you from your actual drawing to paper space. When Tilemode is On, you are in your original full scale drawing space; when Tilemode is Off, you are in paper space. The term Tilemode comes from whether the viewports can overlap as they can in paper space or if they are constrained to be next to each other like tiles.

● Paper Space

Refers to the paper that you will be printing on. It allows you unlimited ways to design your drawing sheet. You can produce plots with different scales and views on the same sheet.

Using the Paper Space Command

In paper space you open up views of your actual drawing, now called *Model space*. You actually manipulate two separate spaces—model space and paper space—each with its own grid, scale limits, and layer settings.

When you are in paper space, a *P* appears on the status line, and the triangle icon appears in the lower-left part of your screen. You must set Tilemode to 0 before you can access paper space. Paper space has no options; it is just used to return you to paper space when you are in model space.

Vplayer and Mview work *only in paper space.* You can insert text in paper space and modify the size and location of the viewports with the standard editing commands. The commands: Copy, Scale, Move, Stretch, and Erase. Zoom XP and the standard Vports command do not work in paper space.

TIP

If you become confused in paper space, reset Tilemode to 1. You will find your old drawing just as you left it. If necessary, you can start constructing paper space again— it's only paper, it's not the drawing. When you plot your drawing, make sure that you issue the Plot command from paper space.

● Model Space

You can think of model space as a window into your actual drawing. You must have Tilemode Off to access model space. The standard AutoCAD commands work on your drawing when you are in model space. Zoom ZP (covered later in the chapter) works only in model space.

Using the Model Space Command

It is easier to work in model space, because you are switched to paper space automatically for those commands that work only in paper space. When fitting your drawing into a viewport you are in model space. Take care that you use Zoom and Pan to manipulate the view. The Move command actually *moves* things in your drawing. You can tell which viewport you are in because it is the one with the crosshairs and a heavier border. Click in the viewport to make it the active viewport.

To change views inside paper viewports, go into model space and activate the paper port you want to change, and use any of the AutoCAD commands, such as Pan, Zoom, View, Viewpoint, and Dview, to get the view you want.

TIP

In paper space you select the *frames* of the viewports, in model space you select the *contents* of the viewports. If you find working in the viewports too tight, work in your full scale drawing (turn Tilemode On, save the views in Named Views and restore them in paper space.

● Mview

The main command by which you manipulate paper space (Mview is the paper-space version of Tiled Vports). This command makes and controls paper viewports. Mview doesn't deal with the content of the ports, only the viewport frames. It will also remove hidden lines from selective viewports when you plot.

Mview Options

On/Off   Turns selected paper viewports on or off by picking edges of the frame. Turning ports off saves regeneration time.

Hideplot   Removes hidden lines from the selected paper ports when plotting; Tilemode must be 0. Selections are made while in paper space mode. The Plot command is issued from paper space. These settings will override the standard Plot command.

Fit   Produces a paper viewport that fills the zoomed area of your screen (the maximum size is the limits of your paper space).

2/3/4   Similar to the 2/3/4 option in the Vports command in model space. It divides your screen into the specified number of paper ports in the horizontal or the vertical orientation. The Fit suboption sizes the configuration and scales it to the window area you specify.

Restore   Copies a viewport configuration from actual full scale drawing space into paper space. The Fit suboption asks you the size of the screen area for the configuration. A useful option if you have been working in Tiled viewports and would like to plot them on one sheet. You must enter this option from the keyboard.

N O T E   All the paper viewports can be moved and sized independently of one another.

● Vplayer

Selectively controls layer visibility in paper viewports. This is an option that would be nice in Tiled Vports. Allows you to show drawings with selective layers frozen.

Vplayer Options

Freeze/Thaw Can be used by first making your choice to freeze or thaw, selecting the layers, and selecting whether this should apply to the current paper viewport (the default), all the paper viewports (A), or only those ports selected (S).

Vpvisdflt Sets the layer visibility defaults for *subsequent* paper viewports.

Reset Restores the Vpvisdflt settings in all (A) or only selected (S) paper viewports. You first specify the layers you want reset and then select the viewports that should be affected.

Newfrz Creates new layers that are frozen in all paper viewports; this makes it simpler to thaw those layers you want to appear in selective paper viewports. (Vplayer does not override the frozen conditions set by the standard Layer command.)

The current viewport is wherever your cursor appears full-screen. In paper space, it is the whole page; in model space, it extends across the port you have picked.

● Zoom—XP

Special option in the Zoom command that is specifically used to scale images from model space into paper space viewports. The option must be accessed from model space and entered from the keyboard.

Using the XP Option

Select the paper space viewport first, then use the Zoom command with the XP option to specify what scale the image should be zoomed to. This number is the reciprocal of the scale factor. For example:

$3' = 1'$	Zoom to $1/4$ XP
$1/2'' = 1'$	Zoom to $1/24$ XP
$1/4'' = 1'$	Zoom to $1/48$ XP
$1/8'' = 1'$	Zoom to $1/96$ XP

TUTORIAL

● Plotting Your Office Plan

In this lesson you will plot your drawing of the office using standard plotting and plotting with paper space. Using the standard techniques, you will plot a plan view with the title block you drew in Chapter 14. Using paper space, you will plot the office drawing, showing plan view, perspective view, and an axonometric view of the receptionist's desk.

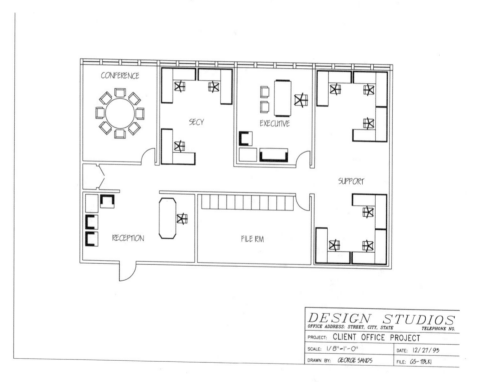

1. Open the PLAN drawing. Get a plan view of the drawing, thaw the HIDE layer you froze to get objects out of the way and thaw the layers necessary to get a complete plan. Make TEXT the current layer.

2. Now you are ready to label the spaces in the drawing. Remember that the size of text is dependent on the scale at which the drawing will be plotted. You will plot this drawing at $1/8'' = 1'$. For text to appear $1/8''$ high on the drawing, you will have to use a Dtext height of 12" ($96 \times 1/8$). However, CityBlueprint will be used for the labels and because it is a PostScript font the size will have to be increased to 16". Set Style as CityBlueprint and label the spaces on the plan according to the drawing.

3. Bring your title block into the drawing. Instead of inserting it as a block, bring it in as an Xref, because you will use the title block differently when you use paper space to plot a drawing.

Command: **SPECIAL ➤ Xref ➤ Attach**
Xref to Attach: **TBLOCK**
Attach Xref TBLOCK: TBLOCK.DWG
Insertion point: *Lower-right corner*
X scale factor<1>/Corner/XYZ: **96** (Scale factor for $1/8''$)
Y scale factor (default = X): ⏎
Rotation angle <0>: ⏎

4. Select the plan and border to be plotted. This plan and border have been sized to fit on an A size sheet. After you have set up the plot parameters but before you plot, check out the Plot Preview.

Command: **PLOT**
Paper Size: **A** (Size may vary depending upon printer but should be in the vicinity of 8×10″)
Rotation: **90**
Plotted Inches: **1/8**
Drawing Units: **1′**
Additional Parameters: **Extents**

5. Detach the Xref because you will be inserting it in paper space.

Command **SPECIAL ➤ Xref ➤ Detach**
Xref to Detach: **TBLOCK**

Paper Space

6. You will now set up and plot a drawing using paper space. With paper space, you can develop much more sophisticated plots. Arranging views on the final plot is more an art than a science. The plot you will do here only offers a hint of what you can do. Set up three viewports, the largest one on top and the two smaller ones on the bottom.

Command: **VIEW ➤ Layout ➤ Tiled VPorts**
Select: **Three: Above**

7. Restore the perspective view in the upper port. Keep the plan view in the lower-left viewport.

Command: **VIEW ➤ Named View**
Restore:
View name to restore: **PERSP**

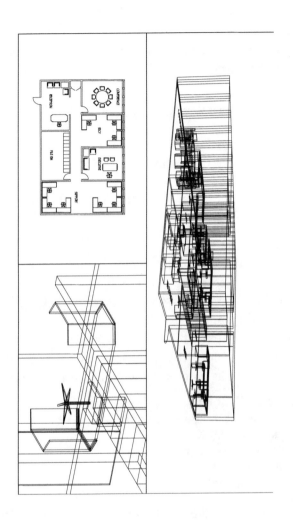

8. Use Viewpoint to get an axonometric view of the receptionist's desk in the lower-right viewport. Zoom the desk so it looks similar to the drawing.

Command: **VIEW** ➤ **Viewpoint** ➤ **Presets** …
From: X Axes : **210**
X-Y Plane: **20**

9. You are now ready to enter paper space, which you will do by setting the variable Tilemode. A triangle will appear in the lower left of a *blank screen*.

Command: **VIEW ➤ Tilemode ➤ Off**

10. Make three new layers for use in paper space *HIDE2*, *P-FRAME*, and *P-TB*. Make P-TB the current layer.

11. Draw a border for the paper space. Use a Polyline with a width of .01. The border should be less than A size. In this case, it is 10″×7-1/2″. (Your plotter limits may vary.)

12. Insert your title block in the lower-right corner. Notice that in paper space you insert it at a scale of 1, while in model space you had to insert it at a scale of 96. This is because you are not reducing the paper sheet, so your 3 1/2″ title block will be plotted at 3 1/2″. Text will also be inserted at the size you want it to appear on the plot. (If you want to change information in the title block such as date or name you will have to explode it first.)

Command: **INSERT**
Insertion point: *Lower-right corner*
File name: **TBLOCK**
X scale factor<1>/Corner/XYZ: ⏎
Y scale factor (default = X):
Rotation angle <0>: ⏎

13. Use Mview to make views of your model space. In this case you will restore the Vports configuration you set up in model space. When asked for the size, window the area above the title block. To get the Restore option of Mview, you must enter it from the keyboard. First, make P-FRAME the current layer.

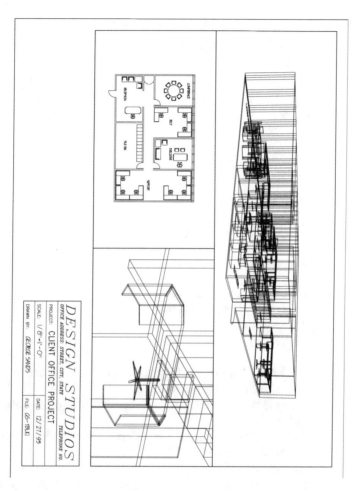

Command: **VIEW ➤ Mview**
ON/OFF/Hideplot/Fit/2/3/4/Restore/<First Point>: **R**
?/Name of window configuration to insert <*ACTIVE>: ⏎
(Inserts the tiled viewport configuration)
Fit/<First Point>: *Window the area above the title block*

14. Fix up the views by freezing various layers in the different view-ports. When asked to "Select objects" you must select the edge of the viewport frame. Continue in this command until all the desired layers are frozen. You will freeze the following layers: TEXT in the perspective view; HIDE2 in the desk view; BOR-DER in all views; HIDE and DOOR in perspective and desk views.

Command: **VIEW ➤ Mview ➤ Vplayer**
?/Freeze/Thaw/Reset/Newfrz/Vpvisdflt: **F**
Layer(s) to Freeze: **TEXT**
All/Select/<Current>: **S**
Switching to paper space. (Done automatically so you can select the paper port)
Select objects: *Pick the perspective frame*

?/Freeze/Thaw/Reset/Newfrz/Vpvisdflt: **F**
Layer(s) to Freeze: **HIDE2**
All/Select/<Current>: **S**
Select objects: *Pick the desk frame*

?/Freeze/Thaw/Reset/Newfrz/Vpvisdflt: **F** (More layers to freeze)
Layer(s) to Freeze: **BORDER**
All/Select/<Current>: **A** (Selects all three automatically)

?/Freeze/Thaw/Reset/Newfrz/Vpvisdflt: **F** (More layers to freeze)
Layer(s) to Freeze: **HIDE, DOOR**
All/Select/<Current>: **S**
Select objects: *Pick the perspective and desk views*

15. There are extraneous items in the paper ports showing the desk view. Select these items and put them on the HIDE2 layer; because HIDE is frozen, they will disappear. If you are not already in model space, get there now. You can continue to manipulate the desk with Zoom and Pan until you are satisfied with how it looks.

Command: **VIEW ➤ Model space** (Alternately, you can type **MS**)
Command: **CHANGE**
Select objects: *Select walls and files*
Properties/<Change point>: **P**
Change what property (Color/LAyer/LType/Thickness)? **LA**
New layer: **HIDE2**

16. To size the plan view to exactly $\frac{1}{16}'' = 1'$, use the XP option of the Zoom command. Click in the plan view first (you are still in model space).

Command: **ZOOM** All/Center/Dynamic/Extents/Left/Previous/Vmax/Window/<Scale (X/XP)>: **1/192XP**

17. Label the different views in paper space. Make P-TB the current layer and change to paper space.

Command: **VIEW ➤ Paper space** (Alternately, you can type **PS**)

Use the style CityBlueprint and a height of 0.166 (slightly larger than $\frac{1}{8}''$) to label the drawing. Labels can be placed inside or outside of the viewports.

Command: **DTEXT**
Style: City Blueprint
Height: .166

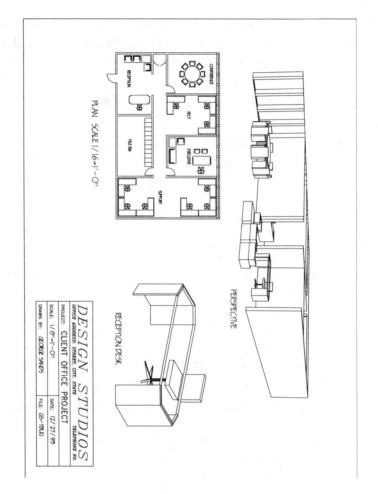

18. Use the Hideplot option of the Mview command to remove hidden lines from the perspective and desk views. The lines will not be hidden on your monitor but will be on the plot.

Command: **VIEW ➤ Mview**
ON/OFF/Hideplot/Fit/2/3/4/Restore/<First Point>: **H**
ON/OFF: **ON**
Select objects: *Pick the viewport frames of the desk and perspective views*

19. Remove the border frames on the paper viewports before plotting by freezing them. Make sure that you are in paper space, and issue the Plot command.

Command: **VIEW** ➤ **Mview** ➤ **Vplayer**
?/Freeze/Thaw/Reset/Newfrz/Vpvisdflt: **F**
Layer(s) to Freeze: **P-FRAME**
All/Select/<Current>: ⏎ (Turns off P-frame layer)

Command: **PLOT**
Paper Size: **A**
Rotation: **90**
Plotted Inches: **1″**
Drawing Units: **1″** (Paper space is always plotted full-scale)
Additional Parameters: **Extents** (Do not select Hide Lines. Hidden lines will be removed in selective viewports by the Hideplot option you have already activated).

20. Before you end this drawing, return the objects you moved to the Hide layer to their appropriate layers. You have come a long way since you first destroyed the globe. You have covered the commands and techniques that will allow you to produce drawings and even renderings. Your skill and speed will increase as you use the program. After a while AutoCAD will become automatic and almost invisible as you design and draw, your ideas translated quickly and intuitively from your mind to your computer screen. Eventually, you will find that using AutoCAD is much like driving a car. Develop your own ways; your preferred commands; your special tricks; make AutoCAD yours.

20

Goodies—
Beyond
AutoCAD

Now that you have AutoCAD under you belt, there are a number of third-party software packages that expand on the capabilities of AutoCAD and help you perform the task of getting the job out.

AutoCAD is often described as a "basic CAD engine." These third-party applications provide tools that are industry/profession specific, including architecture, engineering, mechanical design, landscaping, fashion, and many others.

You have just finished building some 3-D blocks, so you know how labor intensive it is. Imagine drawing people, trees, and cars. Many third-party programs have created libraries of blocks and routines to change back and forth from 2-D to 3-D.

These programs also make modifications and additions to the AutoCAD commands. You already know how often you use the change command to change the layer of an entity or how making a broken line whole requires the use of several commands. Developers of third-party applications are sensitive to these operations and create commands that will combine several commands into one such as Change Layer or Glue Line.

Software that is application specific will provide routines that make performing some function much easier to do. In the field of architecture, for example, these programs will:

- Automatically figure stair runs and draw them in 2- and 3-D.
- Draw complex roof shapes.
- Create walk-throughs and fly-bys of your building.

- Provide layering systems that will incorporate those of the AIA or CSI.
- Simplify the task of creating schedules and bill-of-materials lists.
- Use area takeoffs for space management and facilities tracking.

Third-Party Applications

I have selected a few third-party applications to demonstrate some of their special features. They are by no means the only ones that are out there.

Architectural Power Tools package provides essentially all the functions described above. The following series of images simulates the effect of an animated walk-through.

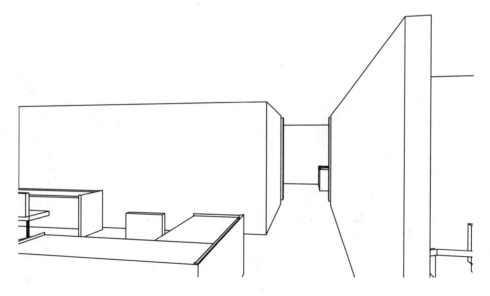

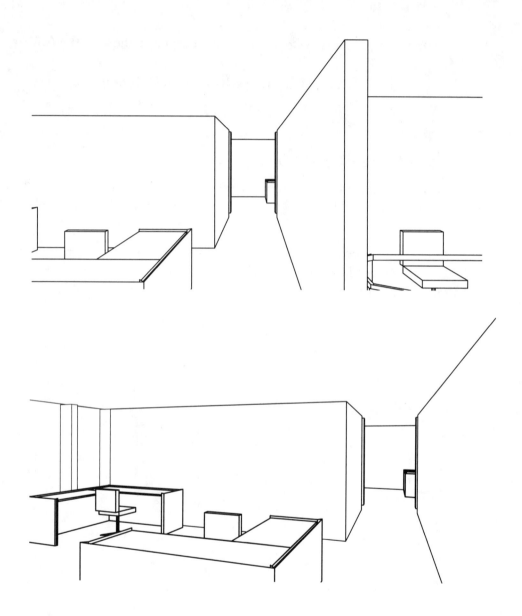

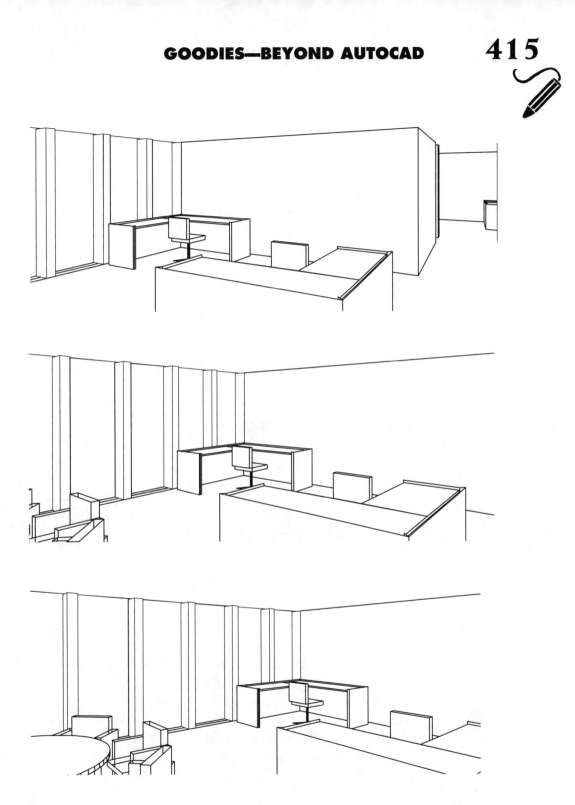

Total AE System is an architectural package that integrates the various disciplines architects interact with: mechanical engineering, structural engineering, plumbing, fire protection, electrical engineering, civil engineering, and facilities management. The software produces schedules easily, which can be placed on the drawing, issued separately, or integrated into a database. Here is an example of how Total AE System would create a schedule of the furniture in Plan drawings.

Furniture Report						
Description	Manufacturer	Model	LOCATION	COST	DATE_PUR	COUNT
Conference Chair	Herman Miller	Conf–23B		87	09–12–91	1
Corner Table	Herman Miller	W–782030		211	12–04–92	1
Loveseat Sofa	Statten	Plush 301		0	— —	1
Circular Conference Table	Steelcase	2901	Conference Room	1122	09–12–93	1
Conference Chair	Herman Miller	Conf–23B	Conference Room	87	09–12–91	7
Corner Table	Steelcase	W–783030	Executive Office	234	11–30–91	1
Executive Chair	Lane	E–7823	Executive Office	456	11–30–91	1
Executive desk	Steelcase	E–60–48	Executive Office	1344	11–30–91	1
Loveseat Sofa	Statten	Plush 301	Executive Office	343.99	09–01–92	1
Reception Chair	Statten	Plush 301	Executive Office	173	09–01–92	1
Visitor Chair	Steelcase	KK–789AB	Executive Office	87	09–12–91	2
Reception Chair	Statten	Plush 301	Reception	173	09–01–92	3
Reception Desk	Herman Miller	S786–SP5	Reception	173	09–01–92	1
Standard Chair	Herman Miller	2901–Std	Reception	123	09–12–92	1
Desk with Return	Steelcase	345Y	Secretarial	119	01–01–91	2
Standard Chair	Herman Miller	2901–Std	Secretarial	119	01–01–91	2
Desk with Return	Steelcase	345Y	Technical Support	119	01–01–91	6
Standard Chair	Herman Miller	2901–Std	Technical Support	119	01–01–91	5
Standard Chair	Herman Miller	3901–Std	Technical Support	119	01–01–91	1

Arch T on the other hand, is a different process for creating plans and presentations and allows you to start your drawings in 2- or 3-D. The program uses doors, windows, and walls instead of lines, arcs, and circles. The process starts with a rough sketch or single line schematic. These lines are indicated as representing walls, interior or exterior, and the program draws them in. Doors and windows are separate entities and inserted rather than "drawn in." Walls are constructed with 3-D faces, which allows for openings, doors, and windows to be inserted without the tell-tale vertical lines that appear when inserting openings into extruded walls. Because these architectural elements

are complete units, they can be easily modified or updated. The following
series of drawings show several stages in how one would develop the Plan
drawing using Arch T.

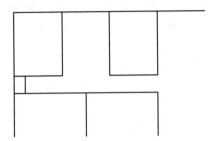

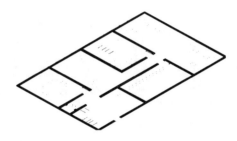

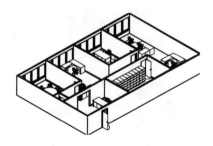

suitpeople—studentpeople are used to populate drawings. Block libraries of people dressed in various degrees of casualness, such as college students, offer you a selection appropriate to your design. The library comes with multiple views and layers for specific clothing. The people are fully three dimensional mesh drawings and can be imported into AutoCAD for rendering.

DOS Mounter Plus is one of the utility programs that lets you mount 3½″ DOS disks, cartridges, and magneto-optical drives on Macintosh computers and access them as if they were Macintosh volumes. This makes it easy to import AutoCAD drawings from DOS machines. Drawings made on a DOS version of AutoCAD can be opened directly (without translation) and edited on the Macintosh, and then returned to the DOS machine for further editing.

Capture was used to capture the Macintosh screens for illustrations in this book. A useful program that produces raster files in TIFF and PICT format.

Information Sources

When should you start looking around for third-party applications? When you find yourself thinking "This is too hard to do" or "This is taking too long."

An excellent listing of third-party applications is *The AutoCAD Resource Guide*. It lists applications, books, AutoCAD user groups, and training centers. The Guide is free and available from your AutoCAD dealer, or you can call Autodesk in Sausalito California at (415) 332-2344 or (800) 964-6432.

The Apple A/E/C Solutions Guide from Apple Computer, Inc. in Cupertino is another useful source. It is available at trade shows and exhibitions where Apple products appear.

User groups are useful sources for information about new applications, tips, and tricks. For Apple user group information, call (800) 446-3000.

Product Information

Arch T ($895)

KETIV Technologies, Inc., 6601 NE 78th Court, A-8, Portland, OR 97218; (800) 458-0690.

Architectural Power Tools ($800)

Eclipse Software. Inc., 301 West Holly, Bellingham, WA 98225; (206) 676-6175.

Total AE System ($1195)

CadPLUS Products Company, PO Box 30167, Albuquerque, NM 87190; (800) 423-8127.

suitpeople ($95—$145)

people for people, $1337\frac{1}{2}$ Cliff Drive, Laguna Beach, CA 92651; (714) 497-9610.

DOS Mounter Plus ($99.95)

Dayna Communications, Inc., Sorenson Research Park, 849 Levoy Drive, Salt Lake City, UT 84123; (801) 269-7200.

Capture ($129.95)

Mainstay, 591-A Constitution Ave., Camarillo, CA 93010; (818) 991-6540.

Appendix

A

Installing
AutoCAD

Files and Folders

☐ Warn before....

☐ Beep on Error...

Environment .1...

☐ Full-time AutoC...

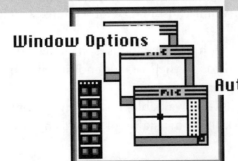

Window Options

Automatic Saves

Hardware and Software Requirements

Before you start installing AutoCAD, check to see that you have the appropriate software and hardware configurations.

- System 7.1 or higher and 32-bit addressing.
- AutoCAD Release 12 will run on the Quadra series 610, 650, 660 AV, 700, 800, 840 AV, 900, and 950; the Centris 650; the IIci, IIcx, IIvx, IIfx, IIsi, IIx, and the PowerBook 170, 180. In the Quadra and Centris, AutoCAD 12 takes advantage of the '040 cache Switch to increase its speed.
- Macintosh Floating Point Unit (FPU) 68881 coprocessor or higher.
- Minimum of 8 Mb internal RAM, but up it to 16 Mb RAM if you are using AME (AutoCAD Modeling Extension) for solid modeling, AVE (AutoCAD Visualization Extension) for rendering, or ASE (AutoCAD SQL Extension) to link with databases.
- Color monitor supporting a minimum of 256 colors, with a minimum display size of 640×480.
- You will need about 30 Mb of hard disk space for AutoCAD, AME (2 Mb) support files, and your drawings.

Installation

Installing AutoCAD Release 12 is quite straightforward, as Autodesk has provided you with an automated procedure. Just answer the questions as they appear on your screen, and the task will be done for you. The following describes the "plain-vanilla" installation procedure, which will quickly get you up and running.

Release 12 comes with six 1.4 Mb disks, plus one additional disk for AME. Installation is done through the Installer and simply requires inserting the correct disks when prompted.

Your AutoCAD disks are valuable; make backup copies of your original disks. Lock your disks before installing them as an extra precaution.

Installation Procedure

- Start your Macintosh and hold the Shift key down until you get the message that the Extensions are off.
- Insert the Install disk, and double-click to open it.
- Double-click on the Installer file icon
- If you have more than one drive, select the drive where you want AutoCAD to be installed.
- Click on the Install button, not the Customize button. This will install basic AutoCAD but not AME. AME can be installed at a later time if you wish. This book does not cover AME.
- Insert the disks as prompted.
- When the installation is completed you must fill out the Personal Information dialog box before you can continue: Your Name, Company, Dealer, Dealer's Phone Number. While it may be tempting to be humorous, be advised that this information will appear on your opening screen each time you start AutoCAD. As a minimum, you must enter at least four characters in each field.
- Quit the AutoCAD Installer and eject the disk.
- Insert the Extensions disk and double-click to open it.
- Double-click on the Installer file and click to install the Thread Manager and Apple Shared Library Manager (ASLM).
- When the Installer prompts you to restart the machine, do so.

Configuring AutoCAD

AutoCAD comes pre-configured for an Apple-compatible monitor and printer. The standard default settings are a good beginning; however, you may want to check out some of the features in the Preferences dialog box (choose Edit ➤ Preferences).

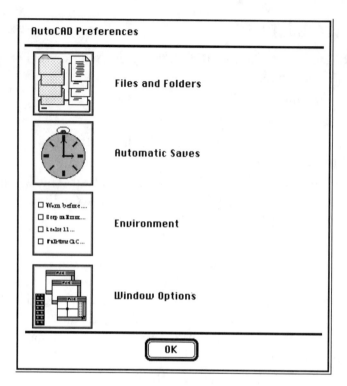

Click on the icons with the following headings.

Automatic Saves

The default for Automatic Saves is 120 minutes—20 minutes is more appropriate when working. These automatic saves create drawing files with a .SV$ extension and are saved in the AutoCAD folder. If a disaster occurs and you lose your drawing, you can open this file by changing the extension to .DWG.

```
┌──────────────────────────────────────────┐
│  Automatic Saves                          │
│  ──────────────────────────────────────── │
│  Interval :   [20]   minutes              │
│                                           │
│  Filename :   [auto.sv$          ]        │
│  ──────────────────────────────────────── │
│           ( Cancel )  [[ OK ]]            │
└──────────────────────────────────────────┘
```

Environment

Click to activate the Warn Before Regens and Beep on Error option boxes.

```
┌──────────────────────────────────────────┐
│  Environment                              │
│  ──────────────────────────────────────── │
│  ⊠ Warn Before Regens                     │
│                                           │
│  ⊠ Beep on Error                          │
│                                           │
│  ☐ Release 11 "HIDE" Command              │
│                                           │
│  ☐ Full-time CRC Validation               │
│                                           │
│  ☐ Auto Audit Imported files              │
│                                           │
│  ⊠ File Dialogs                           │
│  ──────────────────────────────────────── │
│  AutoLISP Stack : [32]    Kbytes          │
│  ──────────────────────────────────────── │
│           ( Cancel )  [[ OK ]]            │
└──────────────────────────────────────────┘
```

Window Options

These features are covered in Chapter 8.

Placing AutoCAD on the Apple Menu

Once you have installed AutoCAD you may want to have an alias of its icon conveniently located in the Apple menu. To do so, follow these steps:

- Open the System Folder and find the Apple Menu Items folder.
- Drag the AutoCAD alias, into the Apple Menu Items folder.

AutoCAD alias

The AutoCAD icon will immediately appear in the Apple menu.

Another way to have AutoCAD at your fingertips is to make an *alias* of its icon and store the alias on your desktop. An alias is a pointer to a program. You can have as many AutoCAD aliases as you wish and store them wherever you want. The alias name will always appear in italics. To make an alias of AutoCAD:

- Click on the AutoCAD icon.
- In the Finder, choose File ➤ Make Alias.
- Move the alias to your desktop.

Appendix

B

Styles, Patterns, and Linetypes

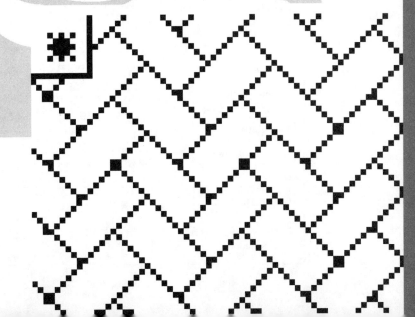

Text Styles

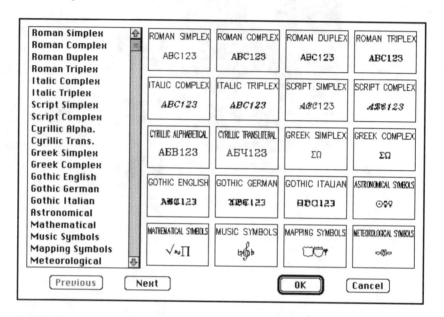

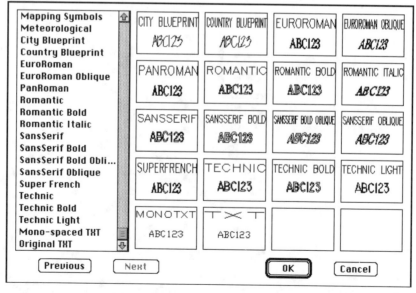

Hatch Patterns

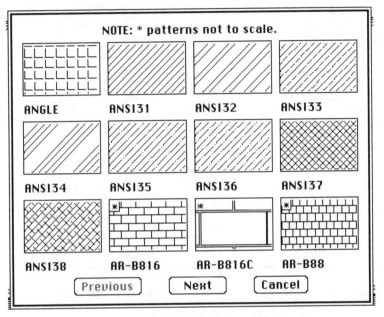

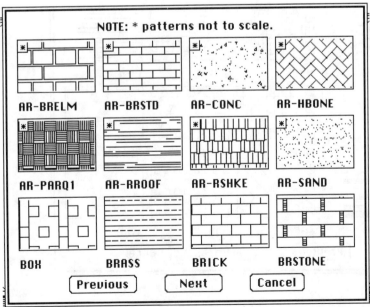

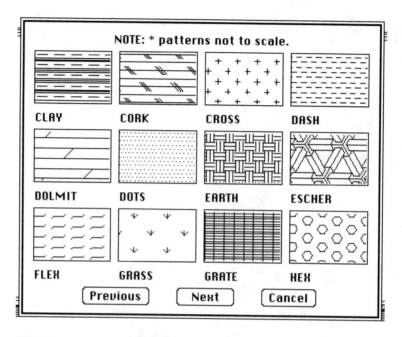

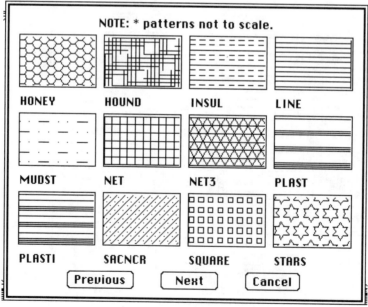

NOTE: * patterns not to scale.

STEEL   SWAMP   TRANS   TRIANG

ZIGZAG

Previous   Next   Cancel

Linetypes

— — — — — —	**BORDER**
·— ·— ·— ·— ·—	**BORDER2**
—— — ·—— — ·—— —	**BORDERX2**
—— — · —— — · ——	**CENTER**
— · — · — · — ·	**CENTER2**
—— — — —— — —	**CENTERX2**
	CONTINUOUS
· — · — · — · — ·	**DASHDOT**
·—·—·—·—·—·	**DASHDOT2**
—— · —— · —— ·	**DASHDOTX2**

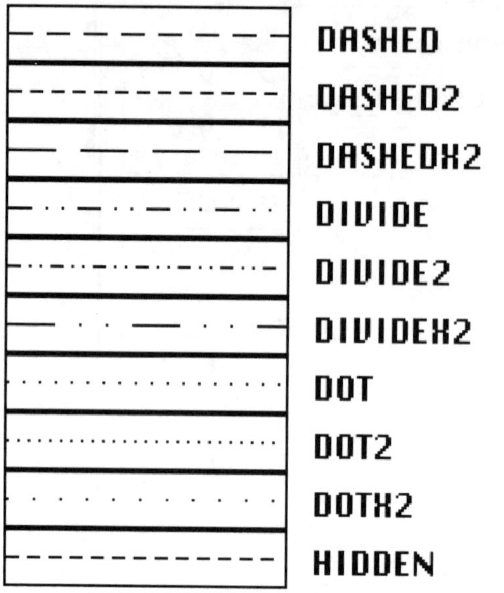

DASHED

DASHED2

DASHEDX2

DIVIDE

DIVIDE2

DIVIDEX2

DOT

DOT2

DOTX2

HIDDEN

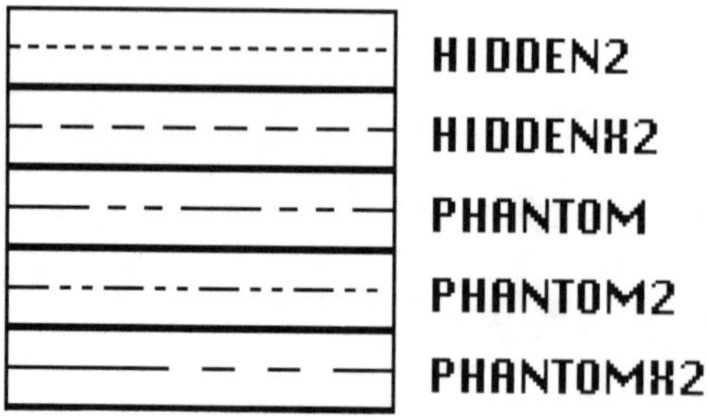

HIDDEN2

HIDDENX2

PHANTOM

PHANTOM2

PHANTOMX2

Appendix

C

Default Settings

Main Defaults

These are the settings that you get when you use the ACAD drawing as a prototype or specify no prototype drawing.

ATTRIBUTES	Visibility controlled individually; entry of values during Insert permitted (using prompts rather than a dialog box)
BASE	Insertion base point (0.0, 0.0, 0.0)
BLIPMODE	On
CHAMFER	Distance 0.0
COLOR	Current entity color Bylayer
DRAGMODE	Auto
ELEVATION	Elevation 0.0, thickness 0.0
FILL	On
FILLET	Radius 0.0
GRID	Off, spacing (0.0, 0.0)
HANDLES	Off
HIGHLIGHTING	Enabled
ISOPLANE	Left
LAYER	Current/only layer is 0, On, with color 7 (white) and linetype Continuous
LIMITS	Off, drawing limits (0.0, 0.0) to (12.0, 9.0)
LINETYPE	Current entity linetype Bylayer; no loaded linetypes other than Continuous
LTSCALE	1.0
MENU	acad
MIRROR	Text mirrored same as other entities
ORTHO	Off
OSNAP	None

PLINE	Line width 0.0
POINT	Display mode 0, size 0.0
QTEXT	Off
REGENAUTO	On
SHADE	Rendering type 3, percent ambient 70
SKETCH	Record increment 0.10, producing lines
SNAP	Off, spacing (1.0, 1.0)
SNAP/GRID	Standard style, base point (0.0, 0.0), rotation 0.0 degrees
SPACE	Model
SPLINE CURVES	Frame off, segments 8, spline type=cubic
STYLE	Only defined text style is Standard, using font Txt with variable height, width factor 1.0, and no special orientation or modes
SURFACES	6 tabulations in M and N directions, 6 segments for smoothing in U and V directions, smooth surface type=cubic B-spline
TABLET	Off
TEXT	Style STANDARD, height 0.20, rotation 0.0 degrees
TILEMODE	On
TIME	User elapsed timer on
TRACE	Width 0.05
UCS	Current UCS same as World, origin at World (0.0.0), Auto plan view off, coordinate-system icon on (at origin)
UNITS (linear)	Decimal, 4 decimal places

UNITS (angular)	Decimal degrees, 0 decimal places; angle 0 direction is to the right; angles increase counterclockwise
VIEWING MODES	One active viewport, plan view, perspective off, target point (0,0,0), front and back clipping off, lens length 50mm, twist angle 0.0, fast zoom on, circle zoom percent 100, Worldview 1
ZOOM	To drawing limits

Configuration File Defaults

These settings are set in a drawing and remain set for subsequent drawings. The initial defaults are:

Auditctl	Creates audit control file (file type .ADT) disabled
Dragging control	Dragp1 10, Dragp2 25
Entity selection	Pickadd 1, Pickbox 3 pixels, Pickfirst 1
Grips	On, one grip for Blocks, height 3 pixels, color blue, selected color red
Menuclt	Enables page switching of the screen menu
Object selection	Pick-box size 3 pixels, Pickauto 1, Pickdrag 0
Object snap	Aperture size 10 pixels
Plot dialog boxes	Cmddia On (1)
PostScript	Psquality 75, no name assigned to the prologue section of ACAD.PSF
Savefile	As configured
Savetime	Automatic save every 2 hours

Sortents	Entity sort operations disabled except for plotting and PostScript output
Sorting	On, 200 symbols maximum
Standard file dialog boxes	Fildia on (1)
Treedepth	Database spatial index setting 3020
Xrefclt	No external reference log file (file TYPE.LOG) written

Dimension Variable Defaults

The dimension variables have been organized in groups roughly relating to what type of dimensioning component they affect. The values given are those that come with the prototype drawing.

Numerical Modifications

DIMALT	Off	On enables alternate units
DIMALTD	2	Alternate unit decimal places
DIMALTF	25.4	Alternate unit scale factor (mm/inch factor)
DIMLFAC	1.0	Global multiplier for linear dimensions
DIMRND	0	Rounding value (not unit places)

Graphic Elements: Markers

DIMASZ	0.1800	Arrow size
DIMBLK		Arrow block name
DIMBLK1		First arrow block name
DIMBLK2		Second arrow block name

DIMCEN	0.0900	Center mark size
DIMSAH	Off	Separate arrow blocks
DIMTSZ	0.0000	Tick size

Graphic Elements: Color

DIMCLRD	BYBLOCK	Dimension line and arrow color
DIMCLRE	BYBLOCK	Extension line and leader color
DIMCLRT	BYBLOCK	Dimension text color

Graphic Elements: Dimension Line

DIMDLE	0.0000	Dimension line extension
DIMDLI	0.3800	Dimension line increment for continuation
DIMGAP	0.0900	Gap from dimension line to text
DIMTOFL	Off	Forces line inside extension lines
DIMSOXD	Off	Suppresses outside extension dimension line

Graphic Elements: Extension Lines

DIMEXE	0.1800	Extension above dimension line
DIMEXO	0.0625	Extension-line origin offset
DIMSE1	Off	Suppresses first extension line
DIMSE2	Off	Suppresses second extension line

Text Placement

DIMTAD	Off	Places text above dimension line
DIMTIH	On	Horizontal text inside extensions
DIMTIX	Off	Places text inside extensions
DIMTOH	On	Horizontal text outside extensions
DIMTVP	0.0000	Vertical text position
DIMTXT	0.1800	Text height

Text Modifications

DIMAPOST		Suffix for alternate text
DIMPOST		Default suffix for dimension text
DIMZIN	0	Zero suppression

These are examples of measurements, given different values for zero suppression for Dimzin:

0	1/2″	6″	1′
1	0′-0 1/2″	0′-6″	1′-0″
2	0′-0 1/2″	0′-6″	1′
3	1/2″	6″	1′ 0″

Associative Dimensions

DIMASO	On	Creates associative dimensions
DIMSHO	On	Updates dimensions while dragging

Tolerance

DIMLIM	Off	On generates limits from TM and TP values
DIMTFAC	1.0000	Tolerance text-height scaling factor
DIMTM	0.0000	Minus tolerance
DIMTOL	Off	Generates dimension tolerances
DIMTP	0.0000	Plus tolerance

Informational/General

| DIMSCALE | 1.0000 | Overall scale factor |
| DIMSTYLE | *UNNAMED | Current dimension style (read-only) |

Index

Note to the Reader

Boldfaced numbers indicate pages where you will find the principal discussion of a topic or the definition of a term. *Italic* numbers indicate pages where a topic is illustrated in a figure.

Numbers and Symbols

U

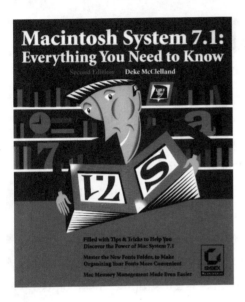

SYSTEM 7.1 IN THE PALM OF YOUR HAND.

300 pp. ISBN: 1277-3

*M*acintosh System 7.1 at Your Fingertips is a no-nonsense guide to every feature and function of System 7.1 for the Mac. Even if you've never used a Mac before, you'll find the answers you need in this palm-sized book.

This handy guide gives you a concise description of new System 7.1 features and capabilities and a comprehensive overview of the operating system. What's more, this book is organized by important features and cross-referenced for ease of use.

Whether you're a Mac maven or mortal, you'll get everything you need in this book—at you fingertips. Make sure this book is at your side every time you sit down at your Macintosh.

SYBEX. Help Yourself.

2021 Challenger Drive
Alameda, CA 94501
1-510-523-8233
1-800-227-2346

SYBEX

MAKE THE MOST OF YOUR MAC.

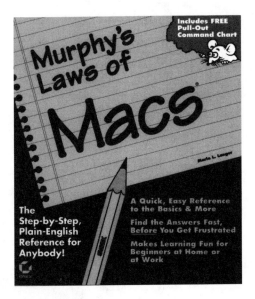

300 pp. ISBN: 1318-4.

The Macintosh is supposed to be one of the easiest computers to use. But even the Mac has its problems. That's when it's time to reach for *Murphy's Laws of Macs*. This simple, plain-English, problem-solving book gives you the answers you need and lets you have fun in the bargain.

Whether you're new to computers or just new to the Mac, you'll find a gold mine of useful information in this book. Learn how to buy a Macintosh computer, find the best programs for your Mac, get tips for avoiding Mac pitfalls and more.

You'll get all of this and more in an entertaining and easy-to-reference format. The Mac is a fun machine to use. *Murphy's Laws of Macs* helps you get more from your Macintosh.

SYBEX. Help Yourself.

2021 Challenger Drive
Alameda, CA 94501
1-510-523-8233
1-800- 227-2346

SYBEX

AutoCAD for the Mac Visual Guide—On Disk

In keeping with the visual approach of *AutoCAD for the Mac Visual Guide*, I have made the command drawings from the book available on disk. You can use them in going through the steps in the exercises. Students have found these exercises very useful in helping them get up to speed quickly with AutoCAD. The drawings come with layers and colors already set up, so you can actually experience the correct way to use each command by tracing over or duplicating the steps in the drawings. These exercises are useful both as a teaching and a learning tool.

To introduce beginners to 3-D drawing, I have also included a prototype 3-D drawing on the disk. This drawing is set up with the viewports and cube 3-D icon used in the book.

To order, please fill out the form below. Make check or money order payable to **Metron Computerware, Ltd.** and send to:

Metron Computerware, Ltd.
3317 Brunell Drive
Oakland, CA 94602

	Price	Quantity	Subtotal
AutoCAD for the Mac Visual Guide—On Disk	$13.00	_____	_____
California residents add 8.5% sales tax ($1.10)			_____
Shipping			_____
Foreign orders add $12.00 for postage and handling			_____
Total			_____

Name: _____

Address:_____

City/State/Zip: _____

Country: _____

Phone Number: _____

Sorry, no credit-card orders. Please allow three weeks for stateside delivery. A quantity discount is available to schools and AutoCAD training centers.

GET A FREE CATALOG JUST FOR EXPRESSING YOUR OPINION.

Help us improve our books and get a *FREE* full-color catalog in the bargain. Please complete this form, pull out this page and send it in today. The address is on the reverse side.

Name _____   Company _____

Address _____   City _____ State ____ Zip _____

Phone (___) _____

1. How would you rate the overall quality of this book?

❑ Excellent
❑ Very Good
❑ Good
❑ Fair
❑ Below Average
❑ Poor

2. What were the things you liked most about the book? (Check all that apply)

❑ Pace
❑ Format
❑ Writing Style
❑ Examples
❑ Table of Contents
❑ Index
❑ Price
❑ Illustrations
❑ Type Style
❑ Cover
❑ Depth of Coverage
❑ Fast Track Notes

3. What were the things you liked *least* about the book? (Check all that apply)

❑ Pace
❑ Format
❑ Writing Style
❑ Examples
❑ Table of Contents
❑ Index
❑ Price
❑ Illustrations
❑ Type Style
❑ Cover
❑ Depth of Coverage
❑ Fast Track Notes

4. Where did you buy this book?

❑ Bookstore chain
❑ Small independent bookstore
❑ Computer store
❑ Wholesale club
❑ College bookstore
❑ Technical bookstore
❑ Other _____

5. How did you decide to buy this particular book?

❑ Recommended by friend
❑ Recommended by store personnel
❑ Author's reputation
❑ Sybex's reputation
❑ Read book review in _____
❑ Other _____

6. How did you pay for this book?

❑ Used own funds
❑ Reimbursed by company
❑ Received book as a gift

7. What is your level of experience with the subject covered in this book?

❑ Beginner
❑ Intermediate
❑ Advanced

8. How long have you been using a computer?

years _____
months _____

9. Where do you most often use your computer?

❑ Home
❑ Work

❑ Both
❑ Other _____

10. What kind of computer equipment do you have? (Check all that apply)

❑ PC Compatible Desktop Computer
❑ PC Compatible Laptop Computer
❑ Apple/Mac Computer
❑ Apple/Mac Laptop Computer
❑ CD ROM
❑ Fax Modem
❑ Data Modem
❑ Scanner
❑ Sound Card
❑ Other _____

11. What other kinds of software packages do you ordinarily use?

❑ Accounting
❑ Databases
❑ Networks
❑ Apple/Mac
❑ Desktop Publishing
❑ Spreadsheets
❑ CAD
❑ Games
❑ Word Processing
❑ Communications
❑ Money Management
❑ Other _____

12. What operating systems do you ordinarily use?

❑ DOS
❑ OS/2
❑ Windows
❑ Apple/Mac
❑ Windows NT
❑ Other _____

13. On what computer-related subject(s) would you like to see more books?

_____

_____

_____

14. Do you have any other comments about this book? (Please feel free to use a separate piece of paper if you need more room)

_____

_____

_____

_____

- - - - - - - - - - - - PLEASE FOLD, SEAL, AND MAIL TO SYBEX - - - - - - - - - -

SYBEX INC.
Department M
2021 Challenger Drive
Alameda, CA
94501

AutoCAD's Menus

File Edit Modify D

New...	⌘N
Open...	⌘O
Save	⌘S
Save As...	
Recover...	
File Utilities	▶
Configure	
Page Setup...	
Plot...	⌘P
Print Window...	⌘D
Compile...	
Applications...	
Quit AutoCAD	⌘Q

Edit Modify Dimension

Undo	⌘Z
Redo	
Cut	⌘X
Copy	⌘C
Paste	⌘V
Clear	
Command Window	▶
Show Tools	
Preferences...	

Modify Dime

Array	▶
Chamfer	
Fillet	
Divide	
Measure	
Offset	
Block	
Entity...	
Break	▶
Extend	
Trim	
Align	
Stretch	
Change	▶
Explode	
PolyEdit	

Dimension Vie

Linear	▶
Radial	▶
Ordinate	▶
Angular	
Leader	
Edit Dim	▶

View Settings

Redraw	⌘R
Redraw All	
Zoom	▶
Pan	
Tilemode	▶
Toggle UP	
Model space	
Paper space	
Mview	▶
Dview	
Plan View	▶
Viewpoint	▶
Named view...	
Layout	▶

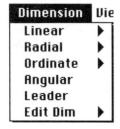

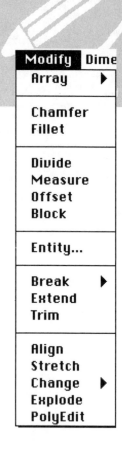